Democratic Spain

Spain has emerged from relative political isolation with the transition from authoritarian to democratic government. Its membership of both NATO and the EU have been crucial vehicles for Spain's reappearance on the world stage, though the traditional 'special relationships' with Latin America and the Arab world have also been of great importance.

By focusing on the relationship between external relations and domestic policy, *Democratic Spain* makes an important contribution to the literature on democratization, as well as showing how Spanish foreign policy evolved between the mid-1970s and mid-1990s. While the book is focused on Spain, its revisionist view of democratic transitions is of more general relevance. Democratization is seen as an integral process involving related though not simultaneous changes in domestic policy and external relations. Only with the transformation of its external relations did Spain's new democracy finally become consolidated.

This book will be required reading for students of Spanish politics and will also be useful to those interested in the process of democratization.

Richard Gillespie is Professor of Iberian and Latin American Studies at the University of Portsmouth. **Fernando Rodrigo** is Professor of International Relations at the Autonomous University of Madrid and Deputy Director of the Spanish Centre for International Relations (CERI), Madrid. **Jonathan Story** is Professor of International Relations at the Institut Européen d'Administration des Affaires (INSEAD), Fontainebleau.

European Public Policy Series

Edited by Jeremy Richardson
European Public Policy Institute, University of Warwick

Forthcoming titles

Policy-making, European Integration and the Role of Interest Groups
Jeremy Richardson and Sonia Mazey

The European Commission
Policy styles and policy instruments
Jeremy Richardson and Laura Cram

Making Europe Green
Environmental policy-making in the European Community
David Judge, David Earnshaw and Ken Collins

Democratic Spain

Reshaping external relations in a changing world

Edited by Richard Gillespie,
Fernando Rodrigo
and Jonathan Story

ROUTLEDGE

London and New York

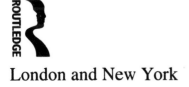

First published 1995
by Routledge
11 New Fetter Lane, London EC4P 4EE

Simultaneously published in the USA and Canada
by Routledge
29 West 35th Street, New York, NY 10001

Typeset in Times by
Ponting–Green Publishing Services, Chesham, Bucks

Printed and bound in Great Britain by
Mackays of Chatham PLC, Chatham, Kent

British Library Cataloguing in Publication Data
A catalogue record for this book is available from the British Library.

Library of Congress Cataloguing in Publication Data
Democratic Spain: reshaping external relations in a changing world / edited by Richard Gillespie, Fernando Rodrigo, and Jonathan Story.
p. cm. – (European public policy)
Includes bibliographical references (p.) and index.
ISBN 0–415–11325–3. – ISBN 0–415–11326–1 (pbk.)
1. Spain–Foreign relations–1975– I. Gillespie, Richard, 1952–. II. Rodrigo, Fernando. III. Story, Jonathan. IV. Series.
DP272.D46 1995
327.46–dc20 95–5717
CIP

ISBN 0–415–11325–3 (hbk)
ISBN 0–415–11326–1 (pbk)

Contents

Figures and tables

FIGURES

TABLES

Contributors

Esther Barbé is Professor of International Relations and Director of the Centre d'Estudis sobre la Pau i el Desarmament at the Autonomous University of Barcelona. She is the author of a forthcoming book entitled *España y la Comunidad Europea*.

Caterina García is Professor of International Relations at the Papeu Fabra University of Barcelona. She has published articles in journals such as the *Autonomies* and in the yearbook *Anuario Internacional CIDOB*, published in Barcelona.

Richard Gillespie is Professor of Iberian and Latin American Studies at the University of Portsmouth and author of *The Spanish Socialist Party* (Oxford University Press, 1989). He is also editor of the yearbook *Mediterranean Politics* (Pinter).

Jean Grugel is Lecturer in Politics at Sheffield University. She has written articles on Spanish foreign policy and European–Latin American relations and is the author of *Politics and Development in the Caribbean Basin* (Macmillan, 1994).

Andrés Ortega is a political scientist and journalist, the author of *El purgatorio de la OTAN* (*El País*, 1986) and *La razón de Europa* (*El País*/Aguilar, 1994). He heads the Policy Planning Department of the Prime Minister's Office in Madrid.

Charles T. Powell is Research Fellow at St Antony's College, Oxford, and also teaches at the Instituto Universitario Ortega y Gasset, Madrid. His works include an article on the international dimension of the Spanish transition (*Afers Internacionals*, 1993).

Fernando Rodrigo is Professor of International Relations at the Autonomous University of Madrid and Deputy Director of the

Spanish Centre for International Relations. He has written several articles on Spain's defence and security policy.

Keith Salmon is Senior Lecturer at the University of Luton. He is the author of *The Modern Spanish Economy* (Pinter, 1991) and *Andalucía: An Emerging Region in Europe* (Junta de Andalucía, 1992).

Jonathan Story is Professor of International Business and Politics at the European Institute of Business Administration (INSEAD). He has edited *The New Europe: Politics, Government and Economy since 1945* (Blackwell, 1993).

Alfred Tovias is Associate Professor of International Relations at the Hebrew University, Jerusalem and author of *Foreign Economic Relations of the European Community: The Impact of Spain and Portugal* (Lynne Rienner, 1990).

Series editor's preface

One of the most important trends in political science over the past two decades has been the increasing attention paid to the public policy process. There has been a recognition that the formation and implementation of public policies is one of the key functions of political systems, alongside the maintenance of public support and the defence of territorial boundaries. The gradual emergence of 'big government' has itself caused a prolification of policy studies, as intellectual endeavour has tried to keep pace with changing realities. This trend has been intensified by more recent debates about the processes by which most European governments have been attempting to roll back the state, irrespective of whether they are governments of the left or right. This 'mood change' in Western democracies has highlighted the complexities of the policy process and the difficulties which governments face when they try to change radically the public policy framework governing society.

Two further important trands have developed in Europe. There has been an intensification of the 'Europeanization' of public policy-making for those European states who are members of the European Union. This has caused an erosion of a central feature of national sovereignty – the power to decide the nature of public policy for the nation state. In essence, the power to decide a whole range of public policies has shifted from national capitals to Brussels, with possibly even a globalization of agenda setting and problem solving in which even the European Union is but one actor amongst many. A second trend has been democratization, broadly defined – first in countries such as Greece, Portugal and Spain and, more recently, in the former Eastern bloc countries.

The purpose of this series on European public policy is to review some of these trends via a combination of national and European level studies. Clearly, there is an ongoing dynamic to the processes of

Europeanization, globalization, and democratization, and the objective of the series is to further our understanding of these 'mega trends' in European society, via studies of the policy process.

This first contribution to the series focuses on the impact of democratization on a state's external relations. Spain's experience of democratization is remarkable. From General Franco's death in November 1975, it was less than a decade and a half before Spain took its first spell in the Presidency of the European Community. Thus, not only has Spain achieved the status of a recognized liberal democracy in an incredibly short period of time, it has also adjusted to the trend towards interdependence which has accelerated alongside internal democratization. As Jonathan Story notes in his introduction to this volume, Spain's deepening insertion into the Euro-Atlantic system provides an example of the more general phenomenon of the increased interrelatedness of domestic policies and the international context. Yet, as he notes, democratization and incorporation into the Euro-Atlantic system also presented a dichotomy which was at the heart of the struggles to reshape Spain's external relations post-Franco. Inevitably, incorporation into the wider international system forced Spain to confront one of the general phenomena outlined above – the constraints that internationalization places upon domestic policy-making as nations calculate the costs and benefits of reduced national autonomy. The main body of this volume, therefore, examines this problem in a number of contexts – for example, the redefinition of Spain's security policy, Spain's entry to the European Community, and the complexities of Spain's internal constitutional structures in the form of autonomous regions such as Catalonia. As with all states' external relations, history determines some special transnational linkages – in Spain's case with Latin America and the Maghreb. These two are analysed as a key element in viewing Spain as an international actor.

A central theme of the volume is, therefore, that it is essential to examine domestic and international factors together, and to emphasize the importance of recognizing that the redefinition of a country's external relations is a key aspect of democratization. Although, as Richard Gillespie suggests, one of the keys to Spain's successful transition can be found in the 'opening' of the country to the Western world over the last two decades of the Franco regime, the introduction of the new constitution facilitated the reshaping of Spain's external relations in the 1980s. Moreover, as he suggests, Spain was not merely reactive in the face of internationalization. It has been a proactive participant, bringing to international relations its own particular perspectives and interests. The volume demonstrates that European states can succeed in adjusting to Europeanization whilst retaining a significant degree of national autonomy. Taken together with its success in the process of democratization, Spain stands out as one of the success stories of post-war Europe. It is, therefore, a very fitting study to launch this series.

Jeremy Richardson

Acknowledgements

This project initially took shape in the course of 1991 and 1992, and a first meeting of the editors was held in May 1993 with the kind support of Warwick University. Contents and timetable were agreed upon for a meeting in Madrid the following September, when first drafts of the chapters were discussed. This workshop would not have been possible without the generous assistance and hospitality of the British Council and the venue provided by the Spanish Centre for International Relations (CERI). We benefited in particular from the comments of Joaquim Llimona, head of the Department of Foreign Initiatives in the Generalitat of Catalonia; Carlos Alonso Zaldívar from the Prime Minister's Policy Planning Department in Madrid; Alejandro Lorca Corons from the Autonomous University of Madrid; and Benny Pollack from the University of Liverpool. Our final meeting was held at the European Institute of Business Administration (INSEAD), Fontainebleau, in May 1994. We wish to thank the INSEAD research committee for its generous support, which enabled us to hold a series of lively meetings and bring the project to fruition.

Abbreviations

ACP	African, Caribbean and Pacific
CAP	Common Agricultural Policy
CCAA	Autonomous Communities
CCT	Common Customs Tariff
CFSP	Common Foreign and Security Policy
CIDE	Business Development and Information Centre (Catalonia)
COPCA	Commercial Promotion Consortium of Catalonia
COREU	Direct communication line between EU foreign ministries
CSCE	Conference on Security and Cooperation in Europe
CSCM	Conference on Security and Cooperation in the Mediterranean
ECSC	European Coal and Steel Community
ECU	European Currency Unit
EFTA	European Free Trade Association
EMS	European Monetary System
EPC	European Political Cooperation
ERM	Exchange Rate Mechanism
ETA	Euskadi Ta Askatasuna (Basque homeland and liberty)
FI	foreign investment
GATT	General Agreement on Tariffs and Trade
GDP	Gross Domestic Product
GNP	Gross National Product
GSP	Generalized System of Preferences
ICGI	Spanish tax on imports
ICI	Institute for Iberoamerican Cooperation
ITE	Spanish sales tax
MNC	multinational company
NGO	non-governmental organization

NIC	newly industrializing country
OECD	Organization for Economic Cooperation and Development
PCE	Spanish Communist party
PSOE	Spanish Socialist party
SI	Socialist International
UCD	Union of the Democratic Centre
UGT	General Workers Union
VAT	Value Added Tax
WEU	Western European Union

1 Introduction

Definitions and perspectives

Jonathan Story

Much has been written about Spain's political transition from a personal dictatorship to a parliamentary monarchy as an exemplary achievement with significant lessons on how to 'craft' emergent democracies in Europe and other parts of the world (Di Palma 1990). A central theme in this literature has held that the prime source of regime change is to be 'found predominantly in internal factors' (O'Donnell and Schmitter 1986: 18). More recently, the theme of regime change has been extended to the study of the international context of democratic transitions (Pridham 1991). The boundaries between external and domestic factors are characterized as increasingly 'blurred' as the incipient democratic state is incorporated into 'the wider and more secure democratic polity' of western Europe (Whitehead 1991: 52). Yet there have been fewer comprehensive studies, and a range of specific studies, on democratic Spain's external policies. One thoroughly argued work has weighed the changes in the process and content of Spain's external relations in the light of the move to a parliamentary democracy (Niehus 1989). The present book examines the reshaping of democratic Spain's external relations as both cause and consequence of the whole transition process from the pre-transition phase through to consolidation. The quality of Spain's external relations has been fashioned in the context of a dialectical relation between the timing of the tasks and stages in the domestic dimensions of Spain's transition, and the shifts in structure, processes and rhythms of the international context.

SOME INITIAL DEFINITIONS

The external relations of a state refer to all cross-border transactions by public officials or private persons. External policies may be more narrowly characterized as describing cross-border transactions by public or private organizations. Foreign policy refers more specifically to the action of the Ministry of External Affairs, as the specialized agency of the state. External relations always have an internal dimension, even when government policy is to restrict transactions across borders to a minimum. As controls over external relations are relaxed, transactions multiply at all levels. It follows that political transitions are always bound into and their paths shaped by wider conditions beyond the territorial boundaries of the state. They are always only 'domestic' in degree.

Political transitions have been defined as the interval between one regime and another (O'Donnell and Schmitter 1986: 6). Yet only after the fact is it possible to look back, and segment the past from the fleeting standpoint of the present. The familiar sequence is of a pre-transition or preparatory phase, a decision phase and a phase of habituation or consolidation (Rustow 1970). Whatever the terminology used, the content of the phases, themselves of sometimes greatly varied length in time, are comparable. The pre-revolutionary or pre-transition phase is characterized by such factors as class struggle, incomplete centralization of state power, a subversive role of intellectuals, and a gathering incapacity to withstand an external challenge. A decision phase is shaped by the actions of leaders, tending to accommodate differences. This phase is characterized by a struggle between contending parties over the rules and norms which are to prevail in the new regime. The moderates offer one set of proposals, which are not a priori doomed to failure. If they fail, the reign of the radicals is initiated, and the transition moves away from regime change to revolution (Brinton 1965). The third phase of consolidation, or habituation, involves a 'joint learning process' about the procedures of the new regime, where politics move into more pragmatic channels, and the procedures of the new regime gradually acquire the features of an old regime. This phase may last for an indefinite period of time, depending on whether the regime's norms, procedures or performance are compatible with the ever-changing conditions of its context. If they are compatible, consolidation continues to occur, but if they are not compatible, either consolidation is accelerated to confront a common challenge, or the regime moves towards breakdown in a hostile international context.

In our case, the sequence starts with an analysis of the legacy of General Franco's regime, and of the broad canvas of Spain's history. The decision phase may be dated from General Franco's death in November 1975 to December 1978, with the ratification by referendum of the constitution. Arguably, the phase may be extended through to 1982, when the Socialist government was elected by overwhelming majority. The intense phase of consolidation spans the decade from

1979 to 1989 when the parliamentary monarchy developed a complete panoply of external relations, while continuing to adapt policy to the programmatic injunctions of the constitution and to Spain's full entry to Europe's society. This was marked by Spain's first EC presidency in 1989, just prior to the collapse of the Soviet empire in central and southern-eastern Europe. That historic event in turn launched the world itself into transition from the international system created after 1945 (Story 1993).

Many factors contribute to the pattern of external relations. In a static presentation, the central feature is Spain's geopolitical position and value in the state system, and its relations within the European society of states. Spain is bound into complex interdependence with other states and markets, making it permeable to all manner of traffic and exchanges. The internal domain refers to aspects conditioning government policy which are specific to Spain, such as the electorate, the political parties and interests, the representative institutions at the level of the state or regions, as well as the cultures and histories of Spain, the nationalities within the state, the media and their selection of 'news', or firms, with their strengths and weaknesses. At the centre are the major institutions of the State, which has – according to the constitution – sole responsibility for the conduct of external and foreign affairs (see the appendix).

FOUR PERSPECTIVES

These definitions may serve to introduce four perspectives on external relations. The four perspectives are: the state system; Europe as a society of states and peoples; complex interdependencies; and the domestic factors which condition the external relations of a state. This introduction concludes with a brief overview of the subsequent chapters.

The state system

A neo-classical perspective on state relations would hold that political transitions are invariably played out in the state as a unit in a system. A primary factor conditioning the external relations of any state is the structure of the international system (Waltz 1979). States are the units of the international system, whose structure is defined by the distribution of capabilities between them. The states form part of a system to the extent that they interact with sufficient regularity to behave as parts of the whole.

Membership in the system is inescapable; all are affected differentially by events in any part of it. The units are bound to the precept of self-help, to tend to their own survival and prosperity. Great powers are distinguished from the rest by the resources at their command, their relative self-sufficiency, and the respect paid to them. No conflict of significance in the system may be settled without them. The actual configuration of the system's structure is conditioned by their number.

A bipolar system, such as existed in Europe between 1945 and 1989, is characterized by two alliances of states under the dominance of two powers, with a propensity to compete for the favours of states not incorporated in one of the two camps. Competitition in this case was inspired by an incompatible view of political community, and moderated by the operation of nuclear deterrence. Spain was incorporated into western defence through a bilateral relation with the USA, and thereby became one element in the US policy of containment, circling the Soviet Union with a ring of bases and alliances. In Spain's own geographic area, the USA came to dominate the Mediterranean, the Straits of Gibraltar, the eastern Atlantic, and the Bay of Biscay, leading into the English Channel and Rotterdam. There were a number of longer-term consequences for Spain's transition, which may be enumerated in the following way:

- The benefits to successive US administrations of the bases in Spain shifted along with the development of military technologies and the growing importance in US external policies of the eastern Mediterranean and the Gulf.
- In the regime, an influential strand of thinking developed in the 1960s that the government should establish more control over its own geographic space, rather than leave its value to be set by US preferences.
- Successive US administrations were ready to make Spain an ally of the West against communism (Whitaker 1961). A broad assumption in the State Department was that Spain after Franco would democratize and enter the Atlantic Alliance and the EC (Cortada 1980).
- Opponents of Franco accused the US of helping to perpetuate the regime. Franco had used external alliances to preserve and consolidate his position in Spain, both in the aid that his forces received from the Axis powers during the civil war of 1936–39 (Viñas 1984), and that the United States provided as a consequence of the secret pacts with Franco in 1953 (Viñas 1981).
- Given this inheritance, renewal of the US base accords and Spain's entry to NATO were a central theme running through all the phases of the transition. They formed the great rift in public opinion, with

both advocates and opponents debating in effect about the optimum place and role for Spain in the interstate system, and in Europe's society.

Europe as a society of states and peoples

A perspective incorporating international law and organisation would argue that Europe since 1945 has developed as a society of states, complementing traditional bilateral relations with multilateral fora. The concept of a society of states stands in contrast to a system of states in which fragmentation breeds competition. A society is defined as forming a subset within the system that is described by a sharing among the units of common interests and values (Bull 1980: 13). Membership implies the pursuit of joint goals according to general rules that sustain the autonomy of each, and reduce or channel the incidence of frictions in their mutual relations. A society also presupposes that the principles of domestic political and market structures are similar. The organizing principles of western Europe are constitutional democracy, human rights, individual freedoms laced with social duties, and moderation in applying the collective right of national self-determination.

A major cause of rupture within the regime in the pre-transition phase was thus the incompatibility between its normative basis and that of the post-1945 European society (Areilza 1984; López Rodó 1987). The 'Spain is different' of Franco's regime stated a claim to particularity, rooted in a specific view of Spain's demise as Europe's hegemonial power. Admiral Carrero Blanco, Franco's alter ego, made the point clearly enough in 1970 in response to German Foreign Minister Scheel's statement to leaders of the Spanish opposition, that Spain's entry to the EC was not possible on account of its political structure. Spain's reduction, wrote the admiral, to an impoverished backwater of Europe, rent by periodic civil wars, was due to the corrosive influence of liberal ideas on Spain's true, Catholic traditions. To propose that Spain adopt, in Carrero Blanco's words, 'the demoliberal system of inorganic democracy' as the price for joining NATO and the EC was a prescription for decline (*ABC*, 2 April 1970). Not surprisingly, aspirations to rejoin European society ran like a leitmotiv through Spain's transition from dictatorship to constitutional monarchy. The intellectuals (Frey 1988), and all main party political formations, were agreed on the desirability of entry to 'Europe'. Significant consequences for the content and timing of the transitional process ensued:

- Spain's democratic transition and its insertion in NATO and the EC made it possible to argue that external and domestic politics formed an indissoluble whole (Armero 1989). The protagonists of the transition from Franco's rule to the constitutional monarchy placed the constitution of 1978 in the lineage of its liberal predecessor of 1812. Its enactment meant the fulfilment of a long-deferred promise of modernization, as well as the recovery of rank and status lost in Europe at the Treaty of Vienna in 1815.

- In the decision phase of 1975–78, the domestic dimension of politics played a primordial role, as 'the forces of freedom in Spain' (Eaton 1981) negotiated the new constitutional compromise. Both foreign policy and the external relations of the new political parties with their European counterparts (Kohler 1982) were supportive of this central objective.
- Spain's external relations were essentially reshaped during the early years of consolidation from 1979 to 1986. Entry to the EC (Alonso 1985) prompted much less anguish than was the case for entry to NATO in 1982, confirmed by referendum in 1986 (Ortega 1986). But both required lengthy negotiations to accommodate conflicting interests between other states, as well as entailing difficult choices internally.
- Spain's full entry to the European society of states expanded NATO and EC territory, population and economic area. Spain entered Europe's society of states with the declared intent to represent its special relations with North Africa, the Muslim world and Latin America in the inner councils of Europe. Not least, Spain's entry negotiations to the EC culminated in 1985, enabling Spain to sign the Single European Act (SEA) which marked a new dynamic in European integration. This dynamic led to the Maastricht Treaty, signed by all member states in February 1992. Spain's proclaimed ambition was to join the 'lead group' of states in 'Europe', hinged on the Franco-German axis.

Complex interdependencies

A third perspective on the external relations of a state is their enmeshment in a web of political and market interdependence. The conditions for complex interdependence are provided with the growth in the number of international organizations, complemented by extensive consultative networks between government bureaucracies, and paralleled by the expansion of transnational exchanges of all types (Nye and Keohane 1977). States remain the pillars of the system, but their ability to formulate and implement policies alone has been modified as exchanges across frontiers have multiplied with the development of communications. This has enlarged the discretion of individuals, corporations or organizations to pursue their interests over a geographic scope which is far beyond that provided by the territorial boundaries of the state (Merle 1984). It has made for permeable frontiers, and is driven by the permanent revolution in technologies, understood as the organization of human capital in the pursuit of discrete purposes. As interdependence is extended across the world, established practices and institutions are summoned to adapt or to perish in the competition of ideas, products or life-styles. Public policies of governments are brought into competition one with another, leading in some cases to prime challenges to specific regimes or political systems.

The trend to interdependence resumed after 1945, and gathered pace throughout all periods of Spain's transition. Spain's deepening insertion in the Euro-Atlantic system provided an example of the more general phenomenon of the quickened interrelatedness between domestic politics and the international context (Gourevitch 1978). This was already abundantly visible before the dictator's death, with Franco presiding over a Nationalist regime which was open to the accusation of subordinating the country to US cultural and economic imperialism (Vásquez Montalbán 1974). Foreign policy, centralized in Franco's ageing hands, became increasingly fragmented as ministries followed their functional specialization into the international arena (Viñas 1980).

Inevitably, Spain's development has been affected by both flows and structures in the world political economy. The flows include variations in the prevailing climate in diplomatic or military relations between the major powers; in international trade and the operations of major corporations; in relations between the key currency countries, and developments on financial markets; or in the content of communications on a world basis. They may also be conditioned by the structure of the global political economy, whose four components – security, production, finance, knowledge – fashion the constraints within which organizations may exert discretion. 'Structural power', in Susan Strange's words, 'is the power to shape and determine the structures of the global political economy within which other states, their political institutions, their economic enterprises and (not least) their scientists and other professional people have to operate' (Strange 1988: 24–5).

Both flows and structures have significant explanatory power in tracing the course of developments over the periods of the Spanish transition:

- The prevailing climate in international relations was far from stable, providing different opportunities for policy inputs by participants in

Spain's transition process. The politics of nuclear weapons ran like a silver thread throughout the various periods, but public perceptions and policy styles varied in part as a function of the regular shifts in East–West relations between cold war and 'hot peace' (Hassner 1971).

- With the globalization of production and markets, the power to decide what shall be produced by whom, how and in what conditions exerts influence transnationally on employment, expectations or ideology. Spain was incorporated into this world system under Franco in the 1960s – the years of the regime's first two development plans under the aegis of the World Bank. The result was the greatest economic and social transformation in the history of Spain (Gilmour 1985; Ben-Ami 1980).
- The international financial markets, in permanent evolution, dictate the cost of credit, or the relative prices world-wide between commodities. Spain's transition was conditioned by the floating of the dollar and the efforts to stabilize intra-European exchange rates, as well as by the two oil price rises of 1973 and 1979, and the oil price fall of 1986.
- Control over knowledge and the channels through which it is communicated provides the means to create news, develop markets, and fashion perceptions of events. The Franco regime lost its near monopoly over information well before its demise; the collapse of the Communist party-states in 1989–91 was preceded by a similar loss of control.

Domestic factors

The central argument on which the case hangs for the primacy of domestic policy in originating a transition is the assertion that there is none that occurs without important divisions within the regime between hardliners and softliners. The struggle may take many forms, such as over the criteria governing access to office; the appropriate response to the use of political violence against the regime; the choice between timely reforms involving incorporation of the disloyal opposition (Linz 1978) and repression, or the domestic reforms required to operate effectively in a competitive interstate system (Skocpol 1979). It may also occur in conditions where the transformation of society and economy generated by the regime's own policies erodes traditional solidarities, widens wealth gaps across classes and regions, and multiplies sources of dissatisfaction (Huntingdon 1968). But for rebellion to succeed from mass pressures, discontent must be organized such that the resources at the disposal of the discontented outweigh those at the disposal of the incumbents (Tilly 1975). The hinge on which a revolutionary situation may turn into a revolutionary outcome is the organization of military force (Tilly 1993). An alternative reform path is provided in the example of Spain, where workers exercised a moderating influence upon labour leaders and the political parties of the left (Fishman 1990), opening the way to a negotiated transition with the dominant softliners in the regime.

Two variants of the domestic perspective are on offer. One contends that reform originated within the regime, where softliners sided with moderate opponents to the continuation of the dictatorship. Their main point of accord against hardliners was over the normative basis of the regime. 'Joining Europe' was another way of saying transforming the regime – a key point made by King Juan Carlos in his inaugural statement as head of state (*ABC*, 23 November 1975). The King used his inherited powers to set the broad guidelines for policy to be followed by his ministers, and at the same time successfully supervised the inclusion of opponents to the negotiations on the new constituent rules. The other variant holds that reform came 'from below', and through mass pressures. Why reform from below should have followed a moderate course is more disputed. One observation ascribes moderation to that fact that Franco's successor inherited a Spain that bore little resemblance, political, economic or cultural, to the impoverished country of 1936 (Carr and Fusi 1979). A complementary interpretation attributes the smoothness of transition to the rise of liberal democratic traditions in civil society prior to the dictator's death. The élites negotiating the transition were rule followers rather than choice makers (Pérez-Díaz 1993). Yet a more reserved conclusion on the years 1975–82 suggests that Francoism endured beyond the dictator's death, yielding a fragile democracy (Maravall 1982); it was only in 1982, with the Socialist government's election, that the transition could be counted as over (Preston 1986: 226).

The domestic perspective gains when set in a broader context. Incorporation in the Euro-Atlantic system has meant that the external relations of the parliamentary monarchy acquired a greater density at all levels, altering the balance of options between domestic players or public policies. Yet, at the same time, the political transition meant that Spain occupied the high moral ground in its prolonged negotiations to recover voice and vote in Europe's higher councils in the years 1979–89. Membership of Europe's society provided public officials with a host of opportunities to sustain the autonomy of the state against domestic societal groups, or to seek to export domestic preferences into the international arena. It enabled Spain to join the EC's practice of 'cooperative federalism' (Bulmer and Wessels 1987), associating intergovernmentalism with federalist practices of the EC, such as majority voting in certain domains among member states; the jurisprudence of the Court of Justice and direct elections to the European parliament. As was predictable, incorporation acted as a restrictive factor on democratic choice (Kaiser 1971:340–58). This dichotomy of democratization within and incorporation in the Euro-Atlantic system lies at the heart of the struggles to reshape parliamentary Spain's external relations.

The point of departure for *Democratic Spain: Reshaping External Relations in a Changing World* is an analysis of the roots of Spain's external relations from the vantage point of 1975. This provided the starting point for a process of reshaping apparently completed by 1989, although further adaptation became necessary in the following years in response to the end of the cold war. One chapter traces Spain's full entry to the Euro-Atlantic system, while another focuses specifically on the redefinition of Spanish security policy. The next chapters deal with Spain's interdependencies with the world economy, and entry to the European Community. A third set of chapters analyses the transformation of external policies at two levels of the state: through Spain's participation in the diplomatic process of European Political Cooperation (EPC), and through the development of external policies of Spain's autonomous regions, with specific emphasis on Catalonia. The fourth set of chapters deals with Spain's special relations with Latin America, and with the Maghreb. One chapter then analyses Spain in the post-cold war world. The conclusion assesses the varied dimensions of the reshaping of Spain's external relations in the light of the four perspectives.

2 Spain's external relations 1898–1975

Charles T. Powell

Spain's international standing at the time of Franco's death in 1975 has often been interpreted almost exclusively in terms of the constraints imposed on his regime by a hostile external environment. This chapter will seek to describe Spain's external relations during the first three-quarters of the twentieth century, with a view to underlining long-term trends and themes, many of which were common to other relatively peripheral, economically dependent, medium-sized powers during this period.

INTRODUCTION: THE LEGACY OF 1898

The Spanish–American War of 1898 and the resulting loss of Spain's remaining colonial possessions in the Americas and the Far East (Cuba, Puerto Rico and the Philippines) is traditionally regarded as the point at which the country's long-term economic and military decline was widely acknowledged both at home and abroad. In many ways, however, it could be said that Spain had formally surrendered its status as a great power at the Congress of Vienna (1815). Throughout the rest of the nineteenth century, domestic political strife and economic backwardness combined to keep it out of continental European affairs. Thus Spain played no part in the Crimean war (from which even a newly emerging power such as Piedmont sought to profit), and remained aloof from the Franco-Prussian war, even though it was the choice of a candidate to the Spanish throne which served as the excuse to unleash the conflict.

The 'disaster' of 1898 was not a uniquely Spanish experience, however. Indeed this event should be seen in the context of a decisive decade (1895–1905), which saw the transition from a European state system to a new, global system, symbolized by the defeat of two peripheral European powers, Spain and Russia, at the hands of two emergent non-European powers, the USA and Japan. Neighbouring Portugal suffered her own 'disaster', in the form of a British ultimatum (1890) which put an end to her dreams of colonial expansion in Africa (Jover 1986).

The impact of the 'disaster' was to have far-reaching consequences for Spanish foreign policy. Many informed observers attributed the magnitude of the defeat to the policy of *retraimiento* (withdrawal) followed since 1875 by successive Restoration governments, which had left Spain without significant allies. Partly as a result of this, the new monarch, Alfonso XIII, actively sought a rapprochement with France and Britain, the great Atlantic and Mediterranean powers of the day. Given that Spain's industrialization was largely being financed with British and French capital, this also made sound economic sense.

Deprived of its American and Far East colonies, Spain concentrated its efforts on the western Mediterranean and North Africa. Anxious to safeguard Gibraltar and prevent Germany from gaining a foothold in the area, in 1904 Britain agreed to French ambitions in Morocco on condition that the territory opposite the colony remain in weaker, Spanish hands. Later that year, France ceded the least fertile, northern portion of Morocco, which was inhabited by notoriously warlike tribes. In 1912, Paris finally granted Madrid its own protectorate over the northern 5 per cent of Morocco, the native population of which was only subdued after a fifteen-year-long struggle.

Spain's foreign policy was essentially dictated by the belief that it would not be taken seriously as a European power unless it had an active presence in Africa (Sueiro 1993: 12–13). In economic terms, this policy merely represented yet another drain on already limited resources, which Spain could ill afford. Largely instigated by a glory-starved monarch, by army officers anxious for promotion, and by a handful of civilian africanistas, the political price paid was often high as well. In 1909, for example, the success of Riff tribesmen in repelling Spanish advances resulted in a call-up of reservists which in turn triggered the rioting and repression of Barcelona's 'Tragic Week'.

It is in any case doubtful whether Spain's African policy contributed to improve her standing amongst the great European powers. In 1911, for example, the Agadir crisis with Germany was resolved when France compensated the latter with fresh territorial concessions at Spain's expense. Similarly, in 1912 the port of Tangier, which lay within the boundaries of the Spanish zone, was given a special international status, thereby undermining Spain's position. Ultimately, Madrid was only able to have an African policy because Britain favoured nominal Spanish control over the Mediterranean coast of Morocco as a way of checking France, which Paris tolerated because it did not represent a significant hindrance (Morales Lezcano 1984: 28ff.).

Madrid's reluctance to accept the international consequences of the 'disaster' was also evident in its efforts to redefine a new relationship with the former American colonies. Paradoxically, the 'disaster' opened the door to a long-overdue reconciliation, which had been hampered by Spain's continued physical – and often military – presence in the continent. Thus both liberal 'regenerationists' and conservative nationalists called for closer ties between the hispanic peoples, a policy generally referred to as *hispanoamericanismo*. This policy lacked a solid economic base, however, as Spain was unable to compete with British and North American penetration of Latin American markets (Pike 1971: *passim*).

The outbreak of war in Europe in 1914 exposed deep domestic cleavages which were to influence the formulation of Spanish foreign policy for decades to come. Liberal *aliadófilos* clashed in the streets with conservative *germanófilos*, in the knowledge that the outcome of the war would have a direct bearing on the future of the restoration monarchy. Those in power nevertheless decided to keep Spain neutral, largely out of fear of coming under even greater pressure from the political forces – socialism, anarchism and peripheral nationalism – which the restoration system had failed to accommodate. (Indeed Spain experienced a proto-revolutionary situation in 1917, partly as a result of the high inflation which resulted from the war.) Additionally, and in spite of the naval build-up initiated in 1908, Spain's armed forces were not ready for war (Pereira 1983: 154–7).

Spain is generally thought to have done well out of the war, exploiting its neutrality to good effect. In economic terms, Spanish industry benefited greatly from a temporary lack of competition and access to new markets. Little was done, however, to consolidate newly won markets in the USA and Latin America, nor were the windfall gains invested in re-equipping traditional industries to meet the threat of renewed competition once the war was over.

SPAIN IN THE INTER-WAR YEARS

As a result of its war-time neutrality, Spain was not present at Versailles, and had no say in the reordering of post-war Europe. Together with other neutral nations, Madrid was nevertheless invited to join the League of Nations, and subsequently occupied one of the non-permanent seats on the Council. At home, membership of the League was opposed by the Monarchy's critics, on the grounds that Spain was not sufficiently democratic, an attitude strongly reminiscent of anti-Francoist opposition to Spanish membership of the United Nations in the 1950s, and of the European Community in the the 1960s–70s.

Anxious to compensate for its secondary role in European affairs, the Spanish government sought to make its protectorate in Africa effective. These efforts suffered a major blow in 1921, when Spanish positions in the eastern zone of the protectorate collapsed under attack from Abd el Krim's Riff tribesmen, leading to a major defeat at Annual. This military disaster, for which the king was held responsible, paved the way for General Primo de Rivera's bloodless coup in 1923, undertaken with the monarch's consent.

Earlier in his career, Primo had been regarded as an *abandonista*, and had even advocated exchanging Gibraltar for the enclave of Ceuta. On coming to power, however, and after duly obtaining permission from the French, he embarked on a full-scale occupation of the Protectorate, which was successfully completed by 1927. Determined to raise Spain's profile in the world, Primo adopted an ultranationalist, paternalistic variety of *hispanoamericanismo*. A special Latin American department was created at the Foreign Ministry, new financial institutions were set up to encourage trade, and vast sums were spent on a grand Exposición Iberoamericana, held at Seville in 1929. The Latin American republics were assiduously courted at the League of Nations, a policy which resulted in the adoption of Spanish as one of its official languages. Predictably, Spanish efforts to create a 'Hispanic bloc' in the League led to renewed diplomatic friction with the USA.

On entering the League, Spain had embarked on a fierce diplomatic struggle for a permanent seat on the Council, which was seen as synonymous with recognition of great power status. The battle for *permanencia* was stepped up under Primo, who threatened to incorporate the international city of Tangier into the Spanish protectorate unless Madrid was invited to join the Council. The League was unmoved, however, and Spain obtained neither a seat on the Council nor Tangier. This crisis illustrated both a determination to keep up with the major powers and an inability to act without their consent (Bledsoe 1975).

Overall, Primo de Rivera's coup had less long-term impact on Spanish foreign policy than might have been expected, though the dictator did deprive Alfonso XIII of his virtual decision-making monopoly (Palomares Lerma 1994: 47–9). Their joint visit to Rome in 1923 was the first major foreign visit by a Spanish head of state in the twentieth century, and although both were attracted to Mussolini's Italy, largely because it was the only other non-democracy in western

Europe (until Portugal joined the club in 1926), they were careful not to antagonize Britain and France.

The fall of the monarchy in April 1931 and the subsequent proclamation of the Second Republic was initially expected to result in significant changes in Spain's foreign policy. The democratic idealism of the founding fathers of the Republic certainly coloured their attitudes to Spain's role in the concert of nations, to the extent that the constitution of 1931 explicitly rejected war as an instrument of foreign policy. However, this idealism was difficult to uphold in a Europe which had plunged into economic recession in the wake of the Wall Street crash and had largely turned its back on liberal democracy.

Throughout the Republic's brief existence (1931–36), domestic priorities – and a succession of acute crises – left governments little or no time for foreign-policy formulation, something they would later greatly regret. Britain and France greeted the Republic with apprehension, which grew into alarm as the socio-economic reforms introduced by the centre-left Republican governments of 1931–33 began to threaten their investments. The Vatican, on the other hand, resented the separation of Church and State sanctioned by the 1931 constitution, as well as legislation passed in 1933 declaring the former an administrative department of the latter. Finally, Nazi Germany and Fascist Italy were alarmed by the emergence of a 'socialist' republic, and Mussolini no doubt hoped it would weaken Spain's standing in Africa. Indeed the new regime was only greeted with enthusiasm by a number of Latin American states, notably Mexico, which was to become one of its staunchest supporters. Partly in response to this, the governments of 1931–33 adopted a liberal-democratic variety of *hispanoamericanismo*, but this was deprived of substantial economic backing by the Depression.

The Republic's early internationalist enthusiasm was of course partly motivated by self-interest, as the nascent democracy required peace and collective security in order to carry out its domestic programme. This manifested itself in a blind faith in the pacifying role of the League of Nations, leading Spain to play a prominent part in numerous disputes. Madrid's high profile in the League is generally associated with the efforts of its representative, Salvador de Madariaga, notably in the field of disarmament, the subject of a major international conference in 1932.

Republicans were somewhat embarrassed by Spain's role in Morocco, and sought to compensate for this by placing more emphasis on the 'civilizing' mission of the colonial adminstration, while simultaneously seeking to reduce its cost. The centre-left governments also sought to bring the Protectorate under greater civilian control, though with little success, a failure which was to prove extremely costly after 1936. When it came to dealing with renewed pressure from Moroccan nationalists, however, republican governments proved just as brutal as their predecessors.

The change of regime was not without its consequences for Spanish foreign policy, however. The decision-making process remained highly personalized under the new democracy, with almost negligible parliamentary control. In 1934 a permanent Committee on Foreign Affairs was established in the Cortes, but premier Manuel Azaña refused to attend its meetings. Ideological differences were most in evidence in Spain's activity in the League of Nations. In Primo's hands, Spain's membership became an instrument with which to extract recognition of nationalist aspirations to great power status; for the Republicans, it represented a major weapon in their struggle for domestic survival, as well as a means of contributing to world peace.

Overall, however, there was considerable continuity during the interwar years. Spain remained militarily weak, diplomatically isolated, and economically dependent. Furthermore, the (not unjustified) obsession of successive governments with domestic issues bred a lack of awareness of the connections between internal and external conditions, as republicans would learn at their own expense. Overall, however, Spain's behaviour was not unlike that of other small, neutral powers which placed their faith in the promise of collective security embodied by the League of Nations, reverting to isolationism after its failure (Quintana Navarro 1993: 365ff.).

FROM CIVIL WAR TO WORLD WAR, 1936–45

In July 1936 sectors of the Spanish armed forces, seconded by numerous civilians, rose in arms against the recently elected Popular Front government of the Second Republic. The outcome of the ensuing three-year civil war was to be greatly influenced by the response of the major European powers, as would the nature and fortunes of the resulting regime. During this period, there were effectively two Spanish foreign policies, that of the Republican government and that of the insurgents, or Nationalists.

It should be noted that it was the Nationalists who first internationalized the conflict by requesting German and Italian aid in airlifting the African army to the peninsula in the summer of 1936. Hitler and Mussolini came to Franco's assistance for reasons of both ideology and self-interest. Germany was happy to discomfort France by meddling in her neighbour's affairs, and looked forward to privileged access to vital Spanish raw materials for her war industry, as well as other economic advantages. Furthermore, Hitler wished to distract international attention from his own actions in central Europe. Similarly, Mussolini provided aid in the hope of enhancing Italy's presence in the western Mediterranean at Britain's expense, and in Morocco at France's. Franco's cause also received backing from Salazar in Portugal, who believed the future of his own regime to be at stake.

Significantly, it was the decision to intervene militarily in Spain, taken in August 1936, which paved the way for the Rome–Berlin Axis in October. A month later, the Axis powers officially recognized Franco, who quickly signed a secret treaty of mutual friendship and assistance with Italy, providing for Spain's benevolent neutrality in the event of war with France. In early 1937, Madrid signed a similar agreement with Berlin.

As was to be expected, the Republic reacted to Axis involvement in Spain by requesting the support of the leading western democracies, France and Britain. The French Popular Front government (established in May 1936) was keen to assist its sister republic, but premier Blum knew Britain would not defend him from German retaliation in the event of French involvement. The Conservative government in London was determined to avoid war with Germany at all costs, and was in any case lukewarm about a republic widely perceived as a threat to British economic interests. Largely at Britain's instigation, in August 1936 the major European powers and the USA officially adopted a policy of non-intervention, subsequently monitored by an ineffective Non-Intervention Committee established in London.

Frustrated in its efforts to obtain assistance from Britain or France, the Republic later turned to the Soviet Union, which it had only recognized in 1933. Stalin was theoretically committed to the Popular Front cause, but his first prority was to achieve a collective security agreement with the western democracies in anticipation of war with Germany. The Republic also sought the mediation of the League of Nations (1936–38), but to no effect. By 1937 the League officially acknowledged that the policy of non-intervention had not prevented the Nationalists from openly receiving men and military equipment from Portugal, Germany and Italy, while the Republicans took delivery of weapons and advisers from the Soviet Union, and welcomed the International Brigades to their side.

Throughout the war, Franco faced the challenge of resisting German and Italian attempts to raise the price of their contribution to his cause while simultaneously seeking not to alienate France and Britain altogether. German appetite lay in the field of mining concessions, while the Italians were more interested in territorial ones, including the possibility of a permanent naval base in Mallorca. After the fall of Vizcaya in mid-1937, Franco sold substantial amounts of iron ore to Britain so as to obtain the foreign currency with which to purchase imports Germany could not provide, such as oil from the US.

Both Republicans and Nationalists knew that the outbreak of war in Europe would have a decisive impact on the situation in Spain. Following Germany's invasion of Austria in March 1938, both sides assumed war was imminent, but the Munich Pact of September 1938 effectively sealed the fate of the Second Republic, though it did not succumb finally until April 1939.

It has become something of a cliché to describe the Spanish civil war as the first round of the second world war. In many ways, however, it is more helpful to see it as the last, most radical round of the first world war. The revolutionary/counter-revolutionary process experienced in Spain in the 1930s was not unlike the conflicts witnessed elsewhere in Europe in 1917–20 (in Russia, Hungary, the Baltic states, and to some extent, Germany). If radicalization and 'the breakdown of democracy' came later to Spain it was at least partly due to its neutrality in the first world war (Payne 1987: 87).

It is also important to note that although the civil war played a major role as a focus of international attention and intervention, it was not of truly crucial concern to any of the great powers, except perhaps to the least important of them, namely Italy. Furthermore, contrary to popular belief, the civil war did not pave the way for the second world war; indeed the latter could only begin once the alliances of the civil war had been fundamentally reversed by the Nazi–Soviet Pact of 1939.

Franco greatly regretted the outbreak of war in Europe, for it threatened to delay Spain's internal post-war recovery. The signing of the Nazi–Soviet pact came as a great shock, as did the invasion of Poland, a country with a Catholic–authoritarian regime not unlike his own. When France and Britain declared war on Germany in September 1939, his first reaction was to call on all parties to reconsider a negotiated solution to their differences. Having failed to make an impact, he immediately announced Spain's neutrality, a decision which proved popular with a war-weary population.

Franco's foreign policy during the second world war has been the object of heated academic and political debate. Given the circumstances, it was no mean achievement to survive the war with Spain's territorial integrity intact. Strictly speaking, Spain was only neutral during the opening (1939–40) and closing (1944–45) phases of the war, when German victory seemed uncertain, and later virtually impossible. Franco had been ready to enter the war in July–October 1940 and even at several later stages, notably the spring of 1942, something the Allies would never forgive. A more genuinely neutral position, however, could have resulted in a German occupation in 1940–41. The General's greatest mistake was probably not to have returned to genuine neutrality after US entry into the war in 1942, which might have enabled him to reap short-term economic advantages and long-term political ones.

FROM OSTRACISM TO REALIGNMENT, 1945–57

The victorious powers subjected the Franco regime to an unprecedented amount of international pressure on account of its former association with the Axis (Portero 1989: Introduction). In March 1946 France closed her border, and joined Britain and the USA in issuing a communiqué expressing the hope that Spaniards would find a way of achieving Franco's peaceful removal and a peaceful transition to democracy. At Poland's instigation, in December 1946 the UN General Assembly passed a motion condemning the regime and recommending the severance of diplomatic relations. Only Portugal, Ireland, Switzerland and the Vatican refused to comply, while Perón's Argentina defiantly appointed an ambassador to Madrid.

The regime's post-war ostracism was generally justified on account of its 'original sin': Franco had been imposed on Spain with the aid of the Axis powers, and later assisted them against the Allies. Even though it had supported Franco actively during the civil war, Salazar's regime in Portugal met a very different fate, largely because its origins were remote and obscure, and because it had remained more genuinely neutral during the war.

Allied hostility to the regime partly explains Franco's efforts to institutionalize the regime by creating the Cortes (1943) and adopting a charter of the Spanish people (1945), the first of the so-called fundamental laws. Most importantly, in 1947 Spain was declared a monarchy without a king, a decision which was particulary well received in Britain and the USA. Abroad, Franco ordered the evacuation of Tangier, thereby reversing his only wartime conquest.

It was developments well beyond Franco's control, and in particular the outbreak of the cold war, that gradually allowed Spain to overcome its post-war ostracism. Fully in keeping with the 'Truman doctrine' of assisting Greece and Turkey against communist pressure, Franco began to be considered a potential ally. Indeed Spain was initially included amongst the recipients of Marshall aid (1948), though the US administration later bowed to international censure. By 1949–50, however, the US government was authorising major public and private loans, and in 1950 Washington sent its first ambassador to Madrid.

As anti-communism took precedence over anti-Fascism, Spain's standing with the European democracies also improved. In early 1948, France reopened its border, and two years later it expelled the exiled Spanish Communist party leadership, which had been mounting guerrilla attacks on Spain. Additionally, Franco's government signed major commercial agreements with Britain and France in 1948. Nevertheless, Spain was excluded from NATO in 1949 (largely at the insistence of Norway and the Benelux nations), and from the Council of Europe.

In order to mitigate its isolation, the Franco regime actively wooed its former American colonies. Argentine economic aid was to prove decisive in 1946–48, and Eva Perón's visit to Madrid in 1947 was a major morale-booster. In 1948–49 a number of Latin American countries became the first to seek a reversal of Spain's condemnation by the UN, and in 1950 a handful of them defied the latter by appointing ambassadors to Madrid.

Franco also sought new allies in more unexpected quarters, namely the Arab world. This was somewhat paradoxical, given the prominence traditionally ascribed to the Reconquest in conservative Spanish mythology. Furthermore, the modern Spanish army, and Franco himself, had been forged in a war against Muslim insurgents in Morocco. A pro-Arab policy made sound ideological sense, however, since at this stage most Arab nations were conservative monarchies which shared Franco's anti-communism. Additionally, Israel had refused to establish relations with the regime on account of its former association with the Axis powers.

Franco's Spain thus recognized the Arab League in 1946, and supported the Arab cause in the ensuing Middle East war. In September 1949 King Abdullah of Jordan became the first foreign head of state to visit Spain since 1939, and in 1952 the Spanish foreign minister toured the Middle East. Franco also cultivated the Sultan of Morocco, who succeeded in obtaining Spain's return to the international administration of Tangier in 1952. Surprisingly, Spain's role as a colonial ruler of Muslims in Africa never appeared to trouble Franco's Arab allies.

The above diplomatic activity partly explains the UN General Assembly's decison to revoke the 1946 condemnation of Spain in November 1950. Votes were cast in Spain's favour by most Latin American members, the Arab countries, and the USA, amongst others, while Britain and France abstained. This paved the way for the return of ambassadors in 1950, and Spanish membership of the UN's dependent organizations. Full membership of the UN was finally achieved in 1955, as a result of a deal reached by Washington and Moscow, whereby each agreed to accept new members belonging to their respective spheres of influence.

In the immediate post-war period, Franco sought to gain respectability in the eyes of the West by emphasizing the dictatorship's Catholic component (Tusell 1984: 115ff.). This policy, enthusiastically supported by the Spanish church, gradually eroded the Vatican's initial reluctance to recognize a regime which had identified itself so closely with the Axis powers. Unhappy with the partial accord signed with the Vatican in 1941, Franco pressed hard for a full Concordat which would replace that of 1851. The cold war and Pope Pius XII's conservatism came to his aid, and after protracted negotiations a new Concordat was signed in August 1953. This granted the fullest possible recognition of the regime by the Vatican, and reaffirmed the confessionality of the Francoist state, thereby reaffirming its legitimacy in the eyes of Spanish Catholics.

The outbreak of the Korean war in June 1950 increased the USA's already considerable interest in incorporating Spain into the Western security system, an interest soon borne out by the exchange of ambassadors later that year. Spain was perceived as an important element in the control of the western Mediterranean and as a useful fall-back area in the event of a Soviet attack on western Europe. The USA would have liked to bring Spain into the recently formed NATO, but met the firm opposition of a number of her European allies, in view of which the Eisenhower administration opted for a bilateral agreement.

In December 1953 lengthy negotiations with Washington finally led to the signing of the Pact of Madrid. This threefold agreement, which fell short of a treaty or alliance, comprised a defence pact, a commitment to mutal defence and a convention on economic aid. Subject to renewal, it provided the USA with access to three airbases and one naval base on Spanish territory. As well as direct military and economic assistance (amounting to $1,183 million over 1953–63), Spain received significant credit, and was able to purchase American goods at reduced prices.

The 1953 agreement represented a major departure from Spain's tradition of neutrality, tying the country firmly into the defence of the West. At the same time, it made Spain strongly dependent on the world's most powerful nation, to the extent that many Spaniards feared their sovereignty had been jeopardized (Viñas 1981: Conclusions). This, however, was a price Franco was willing to pay in return for assuring his regime's survival. Thereafter, the general could be confident that domestic challenges to his authority would not enjoy substantial Western support.

By 1953 Franco had not only abandoned Spain's 'right to territorial renewal' – the wild scheme for constructing a North African empire mooted in 1940 – but was rapidly losing interest in Spain's remaining possessions. This partly explains the short-sighted policies followed in the Protectorate, where Moroccan nationalism was encouraged at France's expense. Predictably, by late 1955 nationalist activity had begun to manifest itself in the Spanish zone as well. When France finally granted Morocco its independence in 1956, Spain had no option but to follow suit, a decision facilitated by the relatively small size of the settler population. Spain did not obtain formal recognition of its remaining possessions from the Moroccans, however, and in 1957 the latter launched attacks on both Sidi Ifni and the Spanish Sahara, which were repelled with French assistance. Under mounting Moroccan pressure, in early 1958 Spain ceded the district of Cape Juby.

CONSOLIDATION AND GROWTH, 1957–69

During the first two decades of its existence, the regime followed an autarkic strategy of inward-looking development and import-substitution, an economic policy strongly favoured by the army and much of the Falange. By the mid-1950s, however, these policies were resulting in severe domestic economic difficulties and widespread social unrest. Largely in response to this, in 1957 Franco appointed a new government dominated by neo-liberal technocrats, who set out to implement the most important economic policy change in the regime's history, embodied in the Stabilization Plan of 1959. The plan, which entailed a substantial liberalization of foreign trade and investment, aimed to align Spain with the major Western economies, a goal which resulted in membership of the OEEC (later OECD), the International Monetary Fund and the World Bank by 1958–59.

The 1959 plan should be seen against the background of the broader process of European economic integration, and in particular the signing of the Treaty of Rome (1957). The Spanish government could not remain indifferent to subsequent applications by EFTA members (1961), to requests for association by several Mediterranean countries, or to the signing of an association agreement with Greece (1962). Furthermore, the authorities had reason to fear that the recently formulated Common Agricultural Policy (CAP) would affect Spanish agricultural exports. Closer integration with the major European economies clearly necessitated far-reaching economic reforms at home, and vice versa.

Spanish experts had begun to study the implications of the emergence of the EEC in 1957, and in 1960 Madrid appointed its first ambassador to Brussels. Franco and his closest adviser, Admiral Carrero Blanco, regarded the EEC with deep suspicion, but their fears were largely allayed with the argument that if De Gaulle's vision of a *Europe des patries* prevailed, Spain would not be required to pay a political price for closer integration.

These hopes were soon dashed, however. In February 1962, Spain's carefully worded application for association with the EEC came up against the concerted opposition of Franco's European enemies. Earlier, at the suggestion of the German Social Democrat Willy Birkelbach, the European Parliament had adopted a resolution which effectively barred non-democratic states from EEC membership. In June the regime made matters worse for itself by reacting hysterically to a gathering of anti-Franco opposition leaders at Munich, who demanded that the EEC observe the Birkelbach resolution when dealing with Spain. In view of the subsequent stalemate, in 1964 Madrid requested talks on some form of economic relationship. In the event, Brussels agreed to open talks while insisting that major constitutional changes would be necessary before any form of political link could be contemplated.

In the 1960s EEC membership became increasingly important to Spain owing to the European dimension of the three factors which most affected its economy, namely foreign investment, tourism and emigration. In the wake of stabilization, European capital gradually began to perform the role previously reserved to US investments. Similarly, by 1967 over 80 per cent of tourists visiting Spain originated in the Six. Finally, most of Spain's emigrant workers, whose remittances increased sharply in value, chose EEC countries as their destination. Spain was paying a high economic price for its exclusion, importing from the EEC twice what it exported (by value). Understandably, Madrid hoped closer relations with Brussels would grant it a greater say in decisions which affected its economy.

European political hostility to the Franco regime – which did not prevent the larger European powers from making a decisive contribution to Spain's 'economic miracle' in the 1960s – merely confirmed the importance of Franco's 'special relationship' with the USA. Even this, however, was to experience new strains, partly as a result of the more openly nationalistic and independent approach of Foreign Minister Castiella (1957–69). The launching of Sputnik in 1957, which was seen as evidence of a major Soviet breakthrough in missile technology, raised fresh doubts about the US's military bases, and in 1958–59 Spain unsuccesfully requested that nuclear weapons be withdrawn from Torrejón air base near Madrid. However, Eisenhower's visit to Spain in 1959, undoubtedly the high-point of Franco's international career, did much to restore Spanish confidence in the 'special relationship'.

Castiella's brinkmanship was intended largely as a means of extracting a higher price in subsequent negotiations with the US. On the eve of the renewal of the base agreement in 1963, Spain restricted NATO overflights to Portugal, and established closer military relations with France. Earlier, Germany had expressed interest in using Spanish airfields, but domestic political pressure forced it to reconsider. In the event, however, the renewal was signed largely on US terms.

The run-up to the second renewal (due in 1970) was to witness even greater tension. In early 1966, an American B-52 carrying four unarmed hydrogen bombs crashed in the Mediterranean off the Spanish coast, forcing the US to ban nuclear flights over Spain.

Two years later, Castiella's only visit to Washington proved an unmitigated disaster. Franco had hoped to extract significant new economic and military concessions, but the interim agreement signed in 1969 failed to achieve them. Nevertheless, throughout the 1960s Spain was among the top ten countries receiving US military aid, and the sixth largest purchaser of US military hardware.

Spain's foreign policy during this period was largely dictated by the struggle for power between rival factions within the regime. The technocrats were primarily interested in obtaining external support for their new economic policy. In this they were backed by Castiella, who sought their support in winning greater religious freedom at home. The minister's major foreign policy objective was the restoration of Gibraltar to Spanish sovereignty, a goal which largely dictated his enthusiastic endorsement of the UN's programme of decolonization, which won him Latin American, African and Arab support for his favourite cause. This policy brought him into direct conflict with Carrero Blanco – deputy prime minister after 1967 – who wished Spain to keep its remaining African possessions. Similarly, while Carrero was determined to consolidate Spain's 'special relationship' with the US, Castiella was openly critical of Washington's lack of support over Gibraltar. Thus when it came to the base agreements, Carrero allowed the military to bypass the foreign minister, dealing directly with their US counterparts. Finally, since the technocrats had risen to power in Carrero's shadow, they were generally hostile to most of Castiella's non-European policies.

Partly to compensate for its limited success in Europe, Spain attempted to raise its economic and political profile in Latin America. By 1966 Latin American countries were buying 17 per cent of Spanish exports, a figure which reflects both Spain's new-found prosperity and the adverse effects of EEC tariffs on its foreign trade. (By 1975, this had fallen to 10 per cent.) The nature of Madrid's interest in Latin America is also evident in its efforts to obtain membership of organizations such as the Latin American Free Trade Association (CEPAL) and the Organization of American States (OEA). Ultimately, the goal was to create an Iberoamerican common market, which would make Spain more attractive as a prospective EEC member. (Indeed the concept of Spain as a 'bridge' between Europe and Latin America was already present in Castiella's application for associate status in 1962.)

Madrid also sought to strengthen its ties with the Arab world, sometimes with surprising results. In countries such as Egypt, Syria, Iraq and Algeria, many of the reactionary Arab rulers initially courted by Franco in the post-war years had been replaced by populist, Soviet-backed regimes, rendering Spanish friendship with them somewhat awkward. This contradiction – heightened by Castiella's systematic opposition to Israeli policies in the Middle East and his outspoken support for the Palestinian cause – never caused major problems for the Franco regime, however, because of the relative modesty of its role in the area and its ultimate subservience to US interests. Thus, in 1967 Spain's pro-Arab policy did not prevent the USA from making use of the Spanish bases in Israel's favour.

Spanish policy towards its African possessions continued to suffer from a lack of direction. In 1958, at Carrero's instigation, Spain elevated Sidi Ifni and the Sahara to the status of provinces, thereby reaffirming its commitment to two territories which could serve to defend the Canary Islands. Complete military withdrawal from the former Protectorate was achieved by 1961, opening the door to renewed military and diplomatic pressure on Spain's remaining North African possessions. A year later, Morocco unilaterally extended her territorial waters to a distance of 12 miles off the coast, thereby hindering Spanish fishing interests. Spain refused to accept this act, and the question of fishing rights was to remain a major source of contention until well after Franco's death. Overall, Spain failed to develop a coherent policy towards independent Morocco, wrongly assuming that Algeria and Mauritania would take her side in the event of blatant Moroccan aggression.

Under mounting pressure from the UN, in 1962 Madrid announced that Spanish Guinea could have its independence in the near future if it so wished. In the light of growing tribal rivalry, in 1967–68 Spain called a conference to draw up a constitution which was subsequently ratified by referendum, leading to full independence in October 1968. A year later, Spain peacefully relinquished Sidi Ifni.

Spain's continued presence in Africa had major implications for the issue which absorbed most of Castiella's attention, namely that of Gibraltar. Franco had intentionally down-played Spain's long-standing dispute with Britain over Gibraltar in the 1940s-50s so as not to jeopardize his rapprochement with the Western powers. In 1954 a visit to the colony by Queen Elizabeth II briefly disturbed the peace, prompting Spanish reprisals. In 1963 Castiella took the Gibraltar issue to the UN, which subsequently urged the opening of bilateral talks leading to the restoration of Spanish sovereignty. Spanish diplomats showed considerable skill in forging a coalition of mainly Latin American and Arab allies committed to decolonization, while defending both their claim to Ceuta and Melilla in North Africa and their rejection of the Gibraltarians' right to national self-determination.

When talks finally began in 1966, Britain offered minor concessions, and relations deteriorated further. The UN repeatedly urged Britain to withdraw, and rejected the plebiscite held in 1967, in which Gibraltarians voted unanimously to retain their colonial status. In late 1968 the UN instructed Britain to withdraw by October 1969, and when Britain refused Spain cut off all communications with the colony. Castiella's lack of progress in this matter was partly responsible for his dismissal in 1969; his successors refused to let Gibraltar stand in the way of improved relations with Britain.

The one issue over which Carrero, the technocrats and Castiella were fully in agreement was the appointment of Juan Carlos de Borbón as Franco's successor in July 1969. This measure enjoyed the explicit support of the USA and the Vatican, and the tacit support of the major European democracies, all of which looked forward to some degree of democratization under the future King.

THE REGIME IN CRISIS, 1969–75

In late 1969 Franco appointed a new, blatantly 'technocratic' government from which Castiella was removed on account of his reluctance to renew the 1953 agreement on Washington's terms and his differences with Carrero over decolonization. The final phase of the regime's foreign policy was characterized by attempts to maintain an overall continuity with earlier policies in the face of growing western apprehension at the prospect of Franco's demise (Pollack 1987: 47ff.).

Under Foreign Minister López Bravo (1969–73), a neo-liberal, modernizing technocrat, relations with the EEC remained of paramount importance. In August 1970 the negotiations initiated in the mid-1960s finally culminated in a preferential agreement which opened EEC markets to Spanish imports without substantially disturbing Spanish protective tariffs. The agreement resulted in a rapid increase in Spanish exports to the EEC, while imports remained stable; more importantly, and contrary to what had been expected, industrial products accounted for much of this increase. Overall, the 1970 agreement proved highly favourable to Spain, providing a new outlet for Spanish goods without subjecting the domestic economy to greatly increased competition.

Spain's satisfaction with the agreement was short-lived, however. The EEC's first enlargement in 1973, and particularly British membership, posed a threat to Spanish agricultural exports, but Madrid was forced to accept that the terms of the 1970 agreement would not apply to exchanges with the three new members for the time being.

In spite of Spain's efforts to integrate in Europe, the regime's non-democratic nature could still be invoked to prevent the sale of Leopard tanks and Harrier jump-jets by Bonn and London respectively. Nevertheless, France succeeded in selling Madrid its Mirage fighters, and signed a military agreement in 1970 envisaging joint manoeuvres and arms production. Given this climate of opinion, it is not surprising that US efforts to win European support for Spanish membership of NATO – particularly after the Portuguese revolution of 1974 – proved unsuccessful.

Given Spain's limited success in Europe, relations with the USA remained the key pillar of its foreign policy, and López Bravo proved considerably more accommodating than his predecessor. In the run-up to the renewal of the bases agreement in August 1970, he was forced to drop earlier demands for increased military aid, but obtained new scientific, cultural, educational and economic aid. Spain also failed both to obtain an explicit security guarantee from the USA, and to raise the status of what remained an executive agreement to that of a treaty, which would have required Senate approval. The USA nevertheless officially acknowledged the bases as Spanish property.

Franco actively sought Western support for his succession plans, and tried to allay rapidly growing fears that the USA's 'special relationship' with Spain would come under threat after his death, given Washington's role in propping up his regime. Anxious to contribute to a peaceful succession, Nixon travelled to Madrid in late 1970, and later played host to Juan Carlos and Sofia in Washington in early 1971. Nixon had hoped that Franco would stand down and supervise the early stages of his successor's rule to ensure a measure of continuity, but Franco reassured him that this would not be necessary. However, the assassination of Carrero Blanco in late 1973, only six months after his appointment as prime minister, raised fresh fears about the succession.

Fully in keeping with the spirit of détente fostered by the USA, López

Bravo launched his own version of Ostpolitik. In 1970 he visited Moscow unofficially, and in 1972 signed a commercial agreement with the USSR. A year later, Spain established diplomatic relations with China and East Germany, and reached consular agreements with Hungary, Poland, Bulgaria, Romania and Czechoslovakia.

US interest in the Spanish bases had been in decline at the time of the signing of the 1970 agreement, but events in 1973–75 soon reawakened it. The international oil crisis of mid-1973 and the outbreak of the Yom Kippur war later that year transformed the eastern Mediterranean into the world's most volatile area. Subsequently, Portugal and Greece witnessed the establishment of governments which associated the USA and NATO with their recently defeated dictatorships. Finally, this period saw a marked increase in the electoral strength of the Italian and French Communist parties, which the USA interpreted as an additional threat to NATO's southern flank.

These developments encouraged Washington to consolidate its relationship with Spain at all costs, and in July 1974 it signed a joint declaration aimed at paving the way for a fresh renewal of the 1953 agreement. In May 1975 President Ford visited Madrid against the advice of his ambassador and in the face of mounting domestic opposition to US support for the regime. In October 1975, in the midst of a major international scandal prompted by the execution of five anti-Francoists, and only a month before the general's death, the USA signed a pre-agreement with Spain. This eagerness to reach a final accord with a regime which was patently moribund was condemned as short-sighted by many in Europe, who anticipated substantial political changes which would finally allow Spain into the Western fold.

The final months of the regime's existence witnessed a partial unravelling of the bonds it had so patiently established with the major international actors in the post-war years. The domestic political situation led to a major clash with the Vatican in March 1974 which upset negotiations for a new Concordat, persistently demanded by Rome and the Spanish Church since the second Vatican Council. Soon afterwards, the Portuguese revolution effectively deprived the regime of its staunchest political ally, and when General Spinola requested Spanish assistance in March 1975, Franco turned him down on the grounds that the Iberian Pact (which he and Caetano had renewed in 1970) was dead. Finally, the September 1975 executions mentioned earlier triggered an international wave of hostility such as the regime had not seen since the post-war period. Negotiations with the EEC were frozen and most European governments withdrew their ambassadors.

Possibly so as to underline the parallels with the 1940s, Mexico promptly requested Spain's expulsion from the UN.

Spain's growing isolation was nowhere more apparent than in its final colonial conflict in North Africa, which had its roots in Carrero's refusal to allow Castiella to initiate the decolonization of the Spanish Sahara in the late 1960s. Alarmed by the Portuguese example and the emergence of anti-regime elements within the Spanish armed forces – the Unión Militar Democrática – the government of Arias Navarro, appointed in early 1974, sought to disentangle itself from the Sahara by any means available, abandoning earlier attempts to guarantee the native population's right to self-determination. Determined to prevent the USSR from benefiting from the collapse of another Iberian dictatorship, the USA (and France) tacitly supported King Hassan II's long-standing claim, leaving Spain with no option but to accept the territory's virtual annexation by Morocco.

CONCLUSION

Spain's international standing in 1975 should be seen in terms not only of the non-democratic nature of the Franco regime, but also of longer-term trends in the country's external relations. In the wake of the 'disaster', Spain was allowed to play a subordinate role both in Europe and North Africa under Anglo-French influence. The second world war briefly raised the possibility of replacing this tutelage with an Italo-German one, and of benefiting from the ensuing Anglo-French decline. After the war, Spain readily abandoned its traditional neutrality in return for membership of the US sphere of military and economic influence. This was fully compatible with closer integration with Europe, which underpinned the dramatic socio-economic changes of the 1960s-70s. In North Africa, Spain's behaviour was largely dictated by French policy, as in the past. Finally, relations with the former Latin American colonies and the Arab world were largely fostered to compensate for Spain's relatively minor role in Europe and its dependence on the USA. As we shall see, there was to be considerable continuity between these policies and those pursued after Franco's death.

3 Spain's external relations redefined: 1975–89

Jonathan Story

The redefinition of Spain's external relations between Franco's death in November 1975 and the Madrid European Council of June 1989 entailed first the ratification of the constitution of 1978 and then the prolonged negotiations for full membership in all major Euro-Atlantic institutions. Domestic debates on external entanglements and commitments were woven into the politics of the domestic transition, while the timing and content of policies were set by the interactions between internal conditions and the evolution in world markets and politics.The principal agent in the initial years of 1975–76 was King Juan Carlos, whose use of the prerogatives inherited from Franco launched the country on the simultaneous process of domestic transition and redefinition of external relations; it was only after ratification of the constitution by referendum in December 1978 that the Union of the Democratic Centre (UCD) and the Socialist party (PSOE) governments of 1979–86 could start the task of fully reshaping Spain's external relations. Only the Socialist government of 1982–86 possessed the stable parliamentary majority and international prestige, augmented by the King's receipt of the Charlemagne prize following his crucial role in thwarting the coup d'état of 23 February 1981, to negotiate Spain's insertion in the Western community of states. The years 1986–89 rounded off unfinished business, culminating in Spain taking over the EC presidency in the early months of 1989.

Redefinition was fashioned in the shifting international climates of East–West relations, characterized by détente between the United States and the Soviet Union in the 1970s, followed by a return to the verbal ferocity of cold war in the years 1979–84, and a swing back to greater civility in the latter part of the 1980s. As Spain's economy opened, a close correlation developed between the cycles of the world economy and Spain's political calendar. Over the period, the Federal Republic emerged as Europe's prime political and industrial power, while the dynamic of Franco-German relations prompted significant modifications in the EC's functioning. The Paris summit of 1974 set up the European Council composed of the heads of state or government, as the supreme political authority covering both the Community and European Political Cooperation (EPC). The decision was then taken in 1976 to hold direct elections to the European Parliament, further reducing the distinction between domestic and foreign policies in European countries, while stimulating the development of trans-European party groupings.

THE DEATH OF THE OLD REGIME, AND THE REBIRTH OF THE POLITICAL PARTIES

Spain's domestic politics began their fusion with European politics in the last two years of Franco's reign, when European governments and political parties turned to play a more active role in Spain. The alarm was raised by the collapse of the Caetano regime in Portugal in April 1974, leading to the inclusion of the pro-Moscow Communists in General Spinola's interim governments. Spain's Communists – considered by far the most formidable anti-regime force – called for an 'offensive against the cost of living' (Carrillo 1974: 15). Inflation had been edging upwards, with wage pressures promoted by tight labour markets and by workers' dissatisfaction with the state-controlled syndicates. The rise in oil prices in 1973–74 faced the weakening regime with a dilemma of whether to move to economic stabilization and risk confrontation with militant workers; or to try to continue to expand, at the risk of having to finance the external deficit on the international financial markets. In July, an ailing Franco momentarily handed the reins of government to Juan Carlos. Ecclesiastical, military and business voices multiplied, calling for change. Franco's return to power was followed in September by an outbreak of strikes. Secretary-General Carrillo had announced in Paris the formation of a Democratic Junta, calling for constitutional rights and government. The kernel was formed by the Communist party (PCE), flanked by former regime personalities, left socialists, regional parties and others. Spanish Socialists and Christian Democrats sought to organize, with firm encouragement from the Federal Republic.

The Communist bid in Portugal in April 1975 to create a party-state in the manner of the eastern European regimes was promptly condemned by the PCE, and in July the party signed a statement with the Italian Communists (PCI) at Leghorn, emphasizing the abandonment of the dictatorship of the proletariat, rejecting Moscow's leadership in the

Communist movement, and in favour of political pluralism (Bourgois 1977: 27–31). That month, the Platform of Democratic Convergence was set up, by the PSOE, some Christian Democrats, Social Democrats and some anti-PCE Marxist groups. The move to 'Euro-communism' by the Communist parties, the PSOE's emergence, and the convergence of the two umbrella organizations – Junta and Platform – hastened the regime's end. On 30 October 1975 both issued a statement rejecting the regime's continuity, demanding liberties and the 'full and effective exercise of political liberties of the distinct nationalities' (Calvo Hernando 1976: 38). At the end of January 1976, Junta and Platform formed the Democratic Coordination, or Platajunta. It urged a 'period of constitutional reform that ends in a popular consultation to determine the form of state and government' (*Cambio 16*, 29 March 1976).

Juan Carlos took over as temporary head of state on 30 October, and ascended the throne on 22 November. Immediately, the King made clear his intent to introduce domestic reforms in order for Spain to participate fully in the concert of nations. Spanish troops were repatriated from the Sahara in order to avoid entanglement in a divisive conflict over decolonization. One of the monarch's first acts was to surrender the power to have a final say in the nomination of bishops, on which Franco had insisted to the Vatican's displeasure. Church support for separation from the state was affirmed by the Archbishop of Madrid, Cardinal Tarancón in his November 1975 sermon – previously cleared by the royal household – in favour of human rights, wider participation in decision-making, and more distributive justice. The monarch pledged in his inaugural speech to create 'a real consensus of national concord' and to prepare Spain for full membership in Europe, 'with all that this implies' (*ABC*, 23 November 1975).

The King struck a delicate balance between continuity and change: Arias Navarro was confirmed in his post as President of the government. Arias accorded a limited amnesty to political prisoners, and appointed three partisans of overture to the non-Communist opposition to the Ministries of Justice, Interior and External Affairs. Their programme was for national elections by 1977, so that Spain could lodge its candidacy for the EC and NATO. Foreign Minister Areilza visited European capitals to explain the new government's intentions (Menéndez del Valle 1993: 718–42) but his main achievement was to have the United States upgrade the military base agreements to the status of a treaty, to be ratified by the Senate. The Hispano-American security treaty, signed in January 1976, strengthened Spain's institutional links with NATO and its military–industrial ties to the USA. In June 1976 Juan Carlos visited the United States, paving the way for a $1 billion jumbo Kingdom of Spain loan. The loan served as a signal to financial markets that the US government backed Spain's transition, in that it acted as lender of last resort for the economic costs incurred. In his first major speech abroad, the King addressed the combined houses of the US Congress, presenting the monarchy as 'inspired by the principles of democracy' (*El País*, 4 June 1976). On his return, the King dismissed Arias and appointed Adolfo Suárez as his Prime Minister for reform. Political parties were legalized on 9 June, except for the Communist party, which regime diehards considered to be still subject to the discipline of Moscow.

Suárez then had proposals submitted to the Francoist Cortes to institute a senate and a lower house, both elected on universal suffrage. The government threatened dissolution in the case of a negative vote. Suárez's reform, submitted to referendum in December, was approved by 94 per cent of the voters. Seventeen million of the 23 million electorate voted. The parties began to mobilize in preparation for the elections in June. A crucial matter was the legalization of the PCE, finally accomplished by Suárez in April 1977. It had been preceded by a 'Eurocommunist' summit at Madrid, between Carrillo and the French and Italian communist leaders – Marchais and Berlinguer – as a demonstration of solidarity in favour of the PCE's legalization. Suárez's decision to legalize the PCE led the Supreme Council of the Army to state that the government 'had blackened the image of the King'. There were rumours of a coup. Suárez henceforth lost the confidence of the hardliners, who accused him of 'treachery' (Preston 1986: 114–16).

Meanwhile, the Popular Alliance was created in October 1976 out of a collection of regime dignitaries and conservative Christian Democrats. The new party – reportedly backed by the Banesto bank – maintained relations with the Bavarian Christian Social Union (CSU), the French Independent Republicans and the British Conservatives. The Christian Democratic Union (CDU) failed to find a viable counterpart among the fragmented Spanish Christian Democrats, ranged across the spectrum from Fraga's Alliance, to Suárez and affiliation with the PSOE. This left the path open for Suárez in May 1977 to create his Union of the Democratic Centre (UCD) out of fifteen different parties, ranging from centrist Christian Democrats to Liberals and Social Democrats. By contrast, the German Social Democratic party's (SPD) influence on the PSOE was significant: it provided funds and advice; as President of the Socialist International since 1976, Willy Brandt ensured that the PSOE remained the sole representative of the International in Spain. The German Trade Union Federation (DGB) helped the Socialist General Workers Union (UGT) to constitute a viable trade union organization, capable of competing with the PCE-dominated Workers' Commissions (CCOO). The elections of June 1977, the first in forty years, saw the emergence of a four-party system at the national level, with regional variations. The UCD received 166 out of the 350, or 47 per cent of the seats in the lower house with only 38 per cent of the votes cast.

THE UCD GOVERNMENTS INITIATE CHANGES IN EXTERNAL POLICIES

There were party political reasons for successive UCD governments' reluctance to chart a clear line in foreign affairs. Areilza's negotiation in early 1976 for the withdrawal of Polaris submarines from Rota harbour by 1979 had postponed debates on the divisive matter of nuclear weapons. Spain resumed diplomatic relations with the Soviet Union and other party-states, as well as with Mexico, which had hosted the government-in-exile of the Spanish Republic since the civil war. Priority was given to achieving consensus on domestic affairs. In October the political parties concluded the Moncloa Pact, which included agreement on the need to overhaul taxation; to move to a more competitive financial system, and an incomes policy. The constitution was ratified by referendum in December 1978, with nearly 88 per cent of the 78 per cent who voted in favour, and only 7.9 per cent against.

Indeed, external relations proved particularly intractable to the politics of consensus. In July 1977 the government lodged its bid for entry to the EC. There were at least two motives in play. In the political culture of the transition, entry to 'Europe' held out the promise of modernization, as well as a recuperation of Spain's lost status and rights. 'Europe' also became synonymous with the EC and democracy (Frey 1988). The other motive was more mercantile. A provisional arrangement adapting Spain's 1970 accord to the first Community enlargement was reached only on 1 July 1977. The EC was expected to offer Spain associate status at the end of the year. Full membership offered a better guaranteee of market access as EC protection against non-members spread from agriculture to fishing, textiles, steel and other sectors. In late summer, Suárez made an initial tour around European capitals, where the message was conveyed that Spain's entry would be less smooth than he may have imagined. Spain thereupon joined the Council of Europe, involving subscription to the European Convention on Human Rights. This was paralleled by a similar emphasis in the United Nations on human rights, with particular reference to Latin America.

How divisive external policy could be was demonstrated in the

Congress debates in March and April 1978 on NATO and the Maghreb: the PSOE and the PCE inclined against NATO entry, and to preference for relations with Algeria over Morocco. NATO membership was postponed to a later date, and made conditional on a 'national debate'.[1] Meanwhile, the murderous campaign of the Euzkadi ta Askatasuna (ETA) against 'the army of occupation' in the Basque Country tempted elements of the armed forces towards sedition. The first serious military coup against the constitutional state was attempted in November 1978. A view gained currency in the Ministry of the Interior, shared by party political leaders including prominent members of the PSOE,[2] that Moscow and its allies supported ETA's violence with a view to prompting a coup d'état from the right. Spain's expected bid to enter NATO would thus be thwarted. Most importantly, sanctuary granted to Basque terrorists in France under French asylum laws allowed the various Basque factions to operate with relative impunity from assured bases. The government's opening in 1979 to the more radical among the non-aligned states, reflecting the expressed preferences of the PSOE and the PCE a year earlier, failed to stop the states' condoning of terror activities in Spain; further alienated the Ministry of the Interior and the Army officer corps; and invited questions in western capitals about Spain's reliability as a prospective member of the Alliance. The Soviet Union favoured Madrid as the venue for the 1980 Conference on Security and Cooperation in Europe (CSCE) in the clear hope of encouraging Spain's neutralist tendencies.

Nor did Spain's relations prosper with France. In the early 1970s, there had been much talk in Paris about the need to expand the 'Latin' membership in the EC, and President Giscard d'Estaing had patronized Juan Carlos by attending his coronation in 1975. Juan Carlos had reciprocated with an official visit to Paris in October 1976 – soon after his June visit to the United States. The French President wanted to establish bilateral relations with Spain, in the manner of Paris–Bonn relations, directly with Juan Carlos. When the Spanish government declined, Giscard d'Estaing then refused to institute the arrangement with Prime Minister Suárez as a counterpart. Suárez's relations with Giscard deteriorated. Worse, Spain's entry to the EC posed a threat to French farmers, and threatened the trade preferences granted to exporters from the Maghreb, and particularly from Morocco, with which Paris cultivated a special relationship. The 'préalable', spelt out by Giscard in a speech at Carpentras in July 1977, was that France would ask for a reform of the EC's 1972 regulation concerning French and Italian fruit, vegetable and wine growers: the implication was that these matters had to be settled first, before negotiations on entry proceded.

French preferences then coloured the Commission's March 1978 'Reflexions' on the Mediterranean enlargement where the fear was expressed that the three new members on entry would generate an EC-wide surplus in cash crops. The initial transition periods suggested by the Commission ranged from five to ten years, but no date for entry was mentioned. The EC budget resources would have to be raised. Spain had to enter the customs union, bringing down its high industrial tariffs and restrictive quotas. In April the Commission indicated that Spain should participate in EC industrial 'restructuring' policies. Import quotas were imposed on Spanish steel exports. Spain was to be granted a three-year transition period to reduce industrial protection. Value added taxes (VAT) were to be introduced on the day of entry to the EC, ending the tax export subsidies available. There were to be no discussions about agriculture or the customs union, until Madrid concurred on the tax issue. A final attempt at a French–Spanish deal came with the French president's visit to Madrid in June 1978. What France in effect was offering was a deal whereby Spain would open up its military, nuclear and electronic markets to France, the implication being that a deal could then be reached on agriculture. The Spaniards refused: their main high technology suppliers were US corporations. Entry talks were officially opened in February 1979. Spain, said Foreign Minister François Poncet, had to accept the 'acquis communautaire'; adaptation had to be achieved on both sides, and 'not by modification of Community rules' (*Le Monde*, 7 February 1979).

After the March 1979 general elections, the cracks in the UCD began to widen. The second oil shock of 1979 prompted a doubling of the trade deficit, and was followed by a world-wide rise in interest rates, prompted by the tightening of US monetary policy in October. Spanish business became alarmed at rising labour and capital costs, as well as the prospect of a PSOE electoral victory. Party and government also faced the displeasure of the armed forces, about subversion and regionalist demands. The Church opposed government positions on education, divorce and abortion. In external relations, no progress was recorded in Spain's negotiations on EC entry. Foreign Minister Oreja announced in June 1980 an accelerated entry of Spain to NATO, in view of the impending renegotiation in 1981 of the 1976 Treaty with the USA.

At the London EC summit of December 1981, the British presidency invited EC member states to moderate their positions on Spain, and favoured Spain's initial entry to the Alliance a few days later. Then in April 1982 the war broke out between Britain and Argentina in the South Atlantic, with the Spanish media and public opinion siding categorically with the Argentinian cause. It was only in the first half of 1982, when Belgium took over the EC presidency, that a 'mini-package' of measures was recorded as the first significant success of Spain's EC negotiations. But President Mitterrand went to Madrid in June, and asked at the July EC summit for the Commission to make a complete inventory of the problems facing the EC on account of the Spanish entry bid. This was the last hint of a French veto, made at a time of maximum political weakness in Spain and Germany. By October 1982, Mitterrand's France faced two new occupants of the chancellery in Bonn and the presidency in Madrid. The election of a Christian Democrat and Liberal coalition in Bonn, favourable to Spain's cause, coincided with the sweeping electoral victory of the PSOE in Spain.

Perhaps the most controversial decision during the whole transition was Spain's entry to NATO, which is the subject of the next chapter. The reasons for the timing involved a complex interplay of domestic and external factors. The 1976 Treaty was due to expire in September 1981, and the new Reagan administration wanted the NATO entry, and the base accords, to be negotiated in parallel. Party political calculations played a role, too. Leopoldo Calvo-Sotelo, who had replaced Suárez, speeded up entry because he anticipated a PSOE victory. The government won the parliamentary debates on NATO entry of October and November, and Spain was invited to become the sixteenth member in December.

The protocol of membership was deposed in Washington on 30 May 1982 – the day that the PSOE recorded a landslide victory in Andalusia. The base accords were signed with the United States in July 1982. Talks were then initiated to create a Madrid NATO command, whereby Spain would hold responsibility for the Canaries–Gibraltar–Balearics axis, outlined in the 1976 Treaty (Rupérez 1986: 189–240, López de la Torre 1987). But the PSOE won their crushing victory in October 1982, with the reputation of wanting to take Spain out. In fact, the party leadership in 1981–82 was highly ambiguous about NATO, stating that it would only accept a definite decision on the subject following a consultative referendum, as foreseen in the Constitution (de Arenal and Aldecoa 1986: 305–78). The base accords were duly ratified, but Spain's membership in NATO was 'frozen', pending the referendum.

MULTIPLE LINKAGES IN REDEFINING EXTERNAL POLICIES, 1982–86

There was much continuity in external policy between the PSOE and the preceding UCD governments. González, like Suárez, quickly moved to a style of presidential government in external relations, inherent to the new constitution (see the appendix). The establishment of regular bilateral summits during 1983–86 with France, the Federal Republic, Italy, Portugal and Britain reinforced the trend. González handled such sensitive areas as the opening of diplomatic relations with Israel, the conduct of relations with the USA, and the definition of Spain's security policy. He allowed institutionalized rivalry between the ministries, but quelled it when it was no longer serviceable. His government was in a much stronger position internally than its predecessors. It enjoyed a majority in the Congress of Deputies and in the country. Its stronger domestic position eased negotiations with the ten EC member states and the Commission. It was not associated with the old regime. The PSOE government also had time on its side. Its domestic and external policy horizons could be stretched well into the future. Whereas its predecessors had hurried into NATO, without being able to trade it for concessions on the EC, the PSOE government could link the promise of a referendum on NATO to progress in the EC talks. The US administration and the EC governments knew that an acceptable package for Spain on the EC could ensure that González put his prestige behind staying in NATO. The PSOE government thus became an indispensable ally for NATO member states in winning over Spain's hostile public opinion.

The PSOE government continued with reform of the armed forces. A new Chiefs of Staff was created in 1984, with the military arm of the state more clearly subordinate to the civilians. This reform was accompanied by further changes in the inherited structure of the armed forces. The professional army's numbers were trimmed. The land army was territorially redeployed from the urban centres to the frontiers, with the constitution of six military regions. The key three regions are at Barcelona, covering the Balearics; the Canaries with their own command; and the Straits, based at Seville (Ministerio de Defensa 1986). The PSOE government also took over and accentuated its predecessor's efforts to modernize Spain's military industries. The Ministry of Defence became a major economic agent. The state's industrial instrument was the Instituto Nacional de Industria (INI), which controlled 70 per cent of arms production in Spain (Daguzan 1988). The PSOE government favoured co-production projects with major US and European armaments corporations, and negotiated offset arrangements with a view to maximizing production in Spain. Production costs were defrayed by sales on world arms markets.

The PSOE government also Europeanized its anti-terror campaign through the CSCE, the Council of Europe and support for the EC Trevi group of Interior and Justice ministers meetings. Bilaterally, meanwhile, Madrid achieved a settlement with Paris. The turning point came in a meeting between González and Mitterrand in December 1983. A month later, González carried his campaign to the Council of Europe in Strasburg, where he called for a united front of the democracies against terrorism. Paris subsequently tightened up on Basque activities launched against Spain from south-west France. EC membership brought Spain into the Trevi group in 1985. Spain participated fully in the accompanying cooperation and exchange of information.

The Socialist government of 1982–86 faced three imperatives relating to economic policy: to win over business confidence, while retaining the government's autonomy to impose unpopular measures; to restructure loss-making industries; and to shift to export-led growth, taking advantage of the US solitary boom as the world's economic locomotive from 1982 to 1986. This required assiduous cultivation of leading Western governments, and welcoming foreign direct investment. Hence, the dispatch with which the PSOE government ratified the July 1982 base accords; and the care that Prime Minister González went to in staging his début in Washington in June 1983. A reform policy in Spain required the assent, not the hostility, of the Western world's leader. Only by staying in NATO could the Spanish government be assured of German or British support for EC entry. That meant wooing PSOE supporters on the grounds that NATO was Europe's prime security club. 'The Community', said NATO's Secretary General Lord Carrington, in Madrid in January 1986, 'is a club which it is worth entering and which is worth defending' (*El País*, 4 January 1986).

González's principal ally in Europe was Chancellor Kohl's government, which moved to vigorous championing of Spain's entry to the EC. In March 1983 the Bundesbank was confirmed as Europe's *de facto* central bank with Mitterrand's decision that month to keep the franc in the European Exchange Rate Mechanism. German diplomacy, with German industrial support, pushed hard to complete the chapters of trade and industry in the Spanish entry negotiations. At the Stuttgart European Council in June 1983, Kohl demonstrated Germany's growing economic and financial weight by linking the availability of new financial resources for the EC budget in a renewed and enlarged Community to ratification by the EC Ten of Spain's and Portugal's accession treaties. There was to be no cash forthcoming for an increase in the size of the EC budget to accommodate the newcomers, until the negotiations on enlargement had been concluded. President Mitterrand, too, switched French policy in a more European direction with his endorsement of the European Parliament's ideas on a European Union, and closer incorporation of European Political Cooperation (EPC) within the Community framework.

London also had its pre-conditions to Spain's EC entry. One was the raising of the blockade imposed in 1969 on access to Gibraltar. At Lisbon in May 1980, Foreign Minister Oreja and the British Foreign Secretary Lord Carrington agreed to seek a solution to all differences over Gibraltar. But it was only with the election of the PSOE government that Madrid took an early initiative to allow passenger traffic across the Spain–Gibraltar border. London though made clear that the condition for a cooperative British stance on the Rock was that the blockade be lifted entirely. Agreement was finally reached in November 1984 between the two Foreign Ministers, Howe and Morán. The accord allowed for talks on the sovereignty question. Britain and Spain granted reciprocal rights of work for Gibraltarians and Spaniards. This accord accompanied an EC–Spain agreement, to raise quotas on car imports into the Spanish markets on which the British government had been particularly insistent. It also enabled Spain to quote the Gibraltar precedent, to little avail, in subsequent negotiations with Luxemburg and the Federal Republic on the free movement of labour within the EC. Not least, the accord raised the British veto on EC entry. Britain kept control of the GibMed command in the Atlantic alliance. The accord opened the way to a normalization of relations between the two countries (*El País*, 24–5 April 1986), exemplified in King Juan Carlos' visit to London in April 1986, and in Queen Elizabeth's visit to Madrid in October 1988.

Spain's relation with Israel was yet another aspect in entry to the EC. Franco's pro-Arab policies on non-recognition of Israel paralleled those of the Vatican. A first step to accommodation was taken in the 1978 constitution, which guaranteed religious freedoms. Article 16.3. stated categorically that no religion would be a religion of state. But the Catholic Church was mentioned alongside 'other confessions', with whom the state would maintain 'consecutive relations of cooperation'. Concordats were later signed between the state and the various religious confessions, notably the Protestants and Jews. A cross-party Spain–Israel Friendship Association was set up. But the PSOE opposed Israel's occupation of Arab territory, and successive Spanish governments gave priority to relations with their major oil suppliers. With the electoral victory of October 1982, González moved quickly to redefine state policy. Contacts between the Spanish and Israeli security forces over terrorism thickened; direct air traffic was opened; political and cultural exchanges intensified. The Netherlands insisted that a condition of Spain's entry to the EC was an exchange of ambassadors with Israel.

The Israeli government wanted an exchange of ambassadors before January 1986, in the hope of tying negotiations on access of non-member countries to EC markets, to the talks between the EC and Spain. But with the NATO referendum hanging over them, and time horizons set, the Ten were in no mood to burden the entry talks by bringing in more complications. Non-members had to be satisfied with the EC pledge in October 1985 to preserve their access. The establishment of full relations between the two states was made at a meeting between Prime Ministers González and Shimon Peres in January 1986 in The Hague, fittingly during the Dutch tenure of the European presidency.

The other strand in redefining Spain's relations with Israel, in the light of EC entry, were González's efforts not to sacrifice Spain's relations with the Muslim world. Gonzalez was concerned that Spain should not be a prisoner of Arab policy. The prime minister spelt out Spain's position on the Middle East in his speech to the UN General Assembly in September 1985:

> A just and peaceful solution in the Middle East would have to be based on Israel's retreat from all the Arab territories occupied since 1967; the respect of the legal rights of the Palestinian people; the right of self-determination and the right of all the states of the area, including Israel, to live in peace within secure and sure frontiers.

He declared in Saudi Arabia that 'The exchange of ambassadors with Israel will occur when it is in the interests of Spain.' Full relations between the two states were thus established in January 1986, after the conclusion of EC entry negotiations and before the referendum on staying in NATO. Spain's terms went beyond the European Council Venice Declaration of June 1980 for a 'comprehensive settlement', in that González stated that 'a just and peaceful solution in the Middle East will have to be based on Israel's retreat from all of the Arab territories occupied since 1967'. The government formally recognized the Palestine Liberation Organization (PLO) office in Madrid shortly thereafter.

The broader canvas of Spain's relations with Latin America are also woven into the diplomacy of Spain's entry to the EC and NATO. The revolution in Nicaragua in 1979, and then the Falklands/Malvinas war in 1982, prompted a renewed European political interest in Latin America. Nicaragua's was a particular crisis that Spain, and the Federal Republic in particular, sought to mitigate. Foreign Minister Genscher feared that a US invasion of Nicaragua, following the controversial introduction of medium-range missiles into NATO Europe in the early 1980s, would prompt a wave of anti-Americanism in Germany; and as

Foreign Minister Morán stated, 'a massive US intervention in Central America would strengthen neutralist and pacifist movements so much that it could endanger the permanence in the Atlantic Alliance of some members, especially Spain'. González raised the matter during his first official visit to the United States in June 1983, and won the support of Speaker Tip O'Neill to work for a peace settlement in Central America. During Reagan's visit to Spain in May 1985, a main topic of discussion with González was reported as the situation in Central America. One of the first manifestations of Spain's full incorporation into EPC between member states' foreign ministries was the October 1984 meeting in San José, Costa Rica, of twenty-one foreign ministers, from Latin America and the EC, as well as the foreign ministers of Spain and Portugal.

Spain, like other western European states, sought both to support and to restrain US global containment policy in order to maintain European security. Spanish–Soviet relations reached a nadir at the time of Spain's entry to NATO, and at the height of East–West tensions. The Soviet Union and allies were accused of supporting ETA, and their fisheries presence in the Canary Islands was curtailed. Yet even in 1981–82, Madrid kept bridges open to the Soviet Union. During the NATO ratification process of April–May 1982, Spain abstained with the Soviet Union on the UN Security Council call for Argentina to withdraw its troops from the Falkland Islands. With the PSOE election in October 1982, the climate of relations improved: in particular, González refused to be drawn into East–West polemics, and in September 1983 used Spain's position as host to steer the CSCE to a conclusion. A high point in relations was King Juan Carlos' visit to Moscow of May 1984, where Secretary-General Chernenko thanked Spain for refusing to host foreign nuclear weapons on Spanish soil. Gorbachev's advent to power in March 1985, seen by González as a historic opportunity to move towards an era of negotiations in East–West relations, meant that the NATO referendum of March 1986 was held in a more relaxed climate of international relations.

Though the Western allies had shown notable reserve about the 1981 Genscher–Colombo proposals to incorporate security matters into EPC, they were more receptive by 1983: the European peace movement had gathered momentum in opposition to nuclear weapons. German and Spanish interests thus converged around an EC relaunch, whereby the EPC agenda would be widened to include the 'political and economic aspects of security', as stated by the European Council at Stuttgart in June 1983. While allied support for EC entry against the French veto could only be assured by Spain staying in NATO, the reverse also held that González could only win the NATO referendum in Spain if the EC was more accommodating to Spain. Holding the NATO referendum in abeyance until satisfaction had been achieved on EC membership thus amounted to a policy of 'deliberate ambiguity'. González finally presented his definition of Spain's complex security policy to the Congress of Deputies in October 1984 in the form of the 'Decalogue' (de Arenal and Aldecoa 1986: 246–50). González stated that Spain belonged to the Atlantic Alliance and participated in its organization. He confirmed Spain's non-nuclear status, and pledged Spain's support for détente and disarmament. While this position was essential to win over a reluctant public opinion to membership in the Atlantic Alliance, there were also significant considerations for external policy. As a non-nuclear country, Spain had an interest in promoting a reduction in the nuclear component of European security, while working for a stabilization of conventional forces.

The multiple strands of the EC entry negotiations began to come together during the French presidency of early 1984. On agriculture, a broad agreement was reached at Luxemburg in June between the French presidency, the Spanish delegation to the Community, and the Commission. It was agreed that fruit and vegetables and beef and milk products should have similar transition periods of seven to ten years, before full inclusion in the customs union. The EC proposed a six-year transition period for industrial products, and Spain proposed seven years. The Luxemburg compromise, as it came to be called, thus incorporated Spain's demands for balance between industrial and agricultural transition periods; for progressivity in the gradual integration of sectors to avoid mutual damage; and for reciprocal concessions in and between sectors. The budget dispute was momentarily settled at the Fontainebleau European Council that June: Community fiscal resources from the levies on farm and industrial imports would be supplemented slightly by increased contributions from the VAT raised in each state, bringing the total EC budget at the time of Spain's entry in 1986 to 1.4 per cent of the EC's GNP. This opened the way for the final round of negotiations, ending in March 1985 under the Italian EC presidency, and including fisheries and social policy. National egoisms triumphed there too. Spain's access to EC waters was limited to 150 boats; free movement of labour into the EC was grudgingly conceded after a seven-year transition, but subject to review after five years. (The details are analysed in chapter 6 on Spain and the EC.)

This cleared the way for the launching of the Commission's programme to achieve the 'internal market' by 1992; and the endorsement of the Single European Act (SEA) by the European Council in February

1986, updating the Rome Treaty. Henceforth, EPC was to deal with the 'economic and political aspects of security'. As Italy's Prime Minister Bettino Craxi stated at the Madrid ceremonies marking the completion of Spain's EC entry negotiations, 'The wills and new energies joining us will have a multiplier effect and will stimulate us to confront our new objectives' (*Le Monde*, 14 June 1985). 'Spain', said González at the June 1985 ceremonies for the signing of the Accession Treaties, 'is ready to advance with those who wish to advance and to wherever they wish to advance' (OID 1985).

COMPLETING THE TASK: 1986–89

The PSOE government had to use all the means at its disposal to win the March 1986 referendum. The easiest task was to draw on the discipline of the PSOE militants: at the December 1984 party congress, 412 delegates voted for, and 126 against, González's argument that Spain had lost no policy autonomy in NATO. Much was also made in the campaign about the 'Europeanization' of security policy. 'It is difficult', González stated, 'to be an active, loyal, effective member of the European Community, and not be in the Atlantic Alliance.' The Atlantic Alliance was the only forum where it was possible 'to oblige United States policy to take a certain European dimension' (*La Vanguardia*, 3 February 1986).

The government also figuratively twisted the arm of the TV networks to field personalities advocating a Yes vote (*El País*, 25 March 1986). There was little that the government could do to win over the extra-parliamentary opposition groups leading the campaign to vote No. It failed to persuade the conservative parties to vote Yes, as the leaders either called for abstention or proposed a free vote. It was essentially cast back on to the argument of the Franco regime reformers, namely that Spain should not be absent from key institutions that decided about its security, whether it was or was not a member. The referendum, won with a 52 per cent majority, was a close-run thing. The PSOE then went on to win the general elections in June, with 184 seats in the 350-seat Congress of Deputies.

The King, in a key speech of June 1986 to the European Parliament, spelt out the main lines of Spain's European policy: a united and free Europe; détente and disarmament; monetary union and the internal market; solidarity between richer and poorer parts of Europe, and of Europe with the world.

A primary task in external policy was to define a Spanish model of participation in the Alliance. This was finally approved by NATO in

December 1988, and held four key components (de Ojeida 1989; López de la Torre 1987): as a non-nuclear state, Spain stayed in the Nuclear Planning Group, where the Europeans consult the USA on US policy; the allies agreed that Spain stay in the Military Committee on the grounds that it functioned more like a diplomatic forum than a military structure; Spanish or allied forces were to fall under each other's direction within their specific territorial zones; further reform of the armed forces and the planning of infrastructure pointed to a *de facto* military integration.

González in his Decalogue had promised to reduce the US forces on Spanish territory. Negotiations for the reduction of the US military presence began in 1985, when the US administration conceded the principle in the hope that it would help the PSOE government win the March 1986 referendum (Marquina Barrio 1991: 51–60). The talks opened in May 1986, and lasted until 1988, with Madrid eventually threatening to allow the existing accords to expire in April 1988. When Washington finally conceded to Spanish demands, negotiations were started on an eight-year bilateral defence pact. The new agreement, signed in December 1988, committed the United States to withdraw the USAF Wing 401 from Torrejón within three years; Rome agreed to base it in Italy. But equally, the eight-year duration of the accords and their lack of military–industrial content pointed to Madrid's intent to act as an ally, rather than as a client seeking to extract the highest possible price for his services from the patron.

The PSOE government also defined Spain's non-nuclear status (Remiro Brotons 1987). During the EC negotiations in 1983 on Spain's joining Euratom, Spain had agreed to sign a specific accord with Euratom and the International Atomic Energy Agency in Vienna to submit its nuclear installations to the same controls as member states. In August 1986, it explicitly recognized Alliance nuclear doctrine on joining the Nuclear Planning Group. But González announced in 1987 a more active role for Spain in the international politics of disarmament through signing the Non-Proliferation Treaty (NPT). Finally, the government was committed to prohibiting the installation, storage or introduction of nuclear weapons on Spanish territory. But as a matter of military policy, the allied nuclear powers deny information on the presence of nuclear weapons in visiting warships or aircraft.

The first three years of Spain's membership in the EC entailed implementation of the tough terms negotiated for the accession treaty. Spain's supportive contributions to European integration were rewarded during the 1988 German presidency when the February 1988 European Council at Brussels agreed on a doubling of the EC regional funds by

1993 – a key objective of the Madrid government to ensure as large a flow as possible of private or public funds into Spain as the trade barriers came down. Such results could not have been achieved without a government capable of implementing *marktkonform* policies, which involved the government in harsh conflicts with its own supporters in the trade unions. The Federal Republic replaced the United States as Spain's first supplier. EC farm producers displaced suppliers from the United States or Latin America. Foreign investment flooded into Spain, with EC investors to the fore. Public opinion, better disposed to the EC than NATO, remained volatile. A central feature of Spanish opinion, shared with political and business leaders, was that EC entry enhanced Spain's status. There was more questioning as to whether it was economically beneficial.

Prior to the 1988 German presidency, González, in a speech in Bonn, proposed a strengthening of EPC and the creation of a European security policy based on prior union between France and Germany (González 1987). Spain's search for a redefinition of relations with the United States thus merged into efforts in the late 1980s to revive the dormant Western European Union (WEU) as the cornerstone of a European security policy.The shock experienced in London and Paris in October 1986, when President Reagan and Secretary Gorbachev nearly bargained away NATO's entire deterrence strategy without so much as consulting the allies, prompted both capitals to revive the WEU, as a fall-back arrangement in the event of a reduced US commitment to NATO. Spain was invited in 1988 to subscribe to the October 1987 WEU document, 'Platform on European Security Issues', that reiterated NATO doctrine on nuclear deterrence and forward defence. But talks were opened only after the European allies had been satisfied that Madrid had settled bilateral relations with Washington. Spain's entry to WEU thus tokened its *de facto* subscription to European NATO strategy (Remiro Brotons 1988); close collaboration with Italy and France on matters relating to security in the western Mediterranean tie Spain closer into the web of bilateral agreements binding western European countries.

The December 1987 Treaty signed in Washington by Reagan and Gorbachev to wind down intermediary-range nuclear weapons opened up the prospect for a denuclearization of Germany and central Europe – a key objective of the new leadership in Moscow. This was followed in 1988 by the unfolding of Gorbachev's policy of decompression in eastern and central Europe, culminating in his December 1988 proposals to the United Nations for comprehensive disarmament, self-determination and self-government in eastern and central Europe.

NATO participation in a major disarmament initiative promised to strengthen Alliance credibility in Spain. It aligned Madrid with Foreign Minister Genscher's position in East–West relations. Madrid favoured confidence-building measures in the conventional stability talks that opened in Vienna in March 1989. Indeed, the move to free elections in Hungary and to the Round Table of talks between Solidarity and the Polish party-state indicated to the Spanish government, during its tenure of the EC presidency, that the communist system was speeding to collapse. Spain's Minister of Culture, with González's accord, insisted that the Polish and Hungarian oppositions be invited to a meeting with his colleagues, held in May. Spain's own transition showed that democratization was the only path to Europe (Semprún 1993: 258–69).

Though priority in Spain's European policy went to alignment with French and German positions to develop the EC, Spain used the presidency as an interested mediator. Madrid's complex of alliances along functional lines was particularly evident in four key areas of EC policy: trade, social affairs, monetary union and institutional development. Spain, France, Italy and Greece, with strong support in the European Parliament, favoured extensive Commission powers for a single bank-licensing policy to third countries. In April, Germany, the UK, the Netherlands and Luxemburg favoured a Commission compromise, leaving the ultimate say on the granting of bank licences with the states in Council and in the Bank Advisory Committee. On the Commission's social policy, Spain's Socialist government could not overtly oppose the Social Charter, championed by France and Germany, but it was well aware that the country's sole comparative advantage in EC markets was low labour costs. The Spanish presidency therefore managed British, and its own, susceptibilities in an ambiguous communiqué that placed social policy within the purview of national governments. In June 1989 Spain agreed to the peseta's joining the EC Exchange Rate Mechanism in a move designed to hold down the peseta and thereby set the measure for future wage negotiations. At the Madrid European Council that month, Spain confirmed its support for Delors' proposal for a European Central Bank, and found a compromise, accepted by Prime Minister Thatcher, to call an inter-governmental conference on monetary union.

One of the major successes of the Spanish presidency was the Community agreement on the joint policing of external frontiers, internal movements across frontiers and cooperation on drugs, anti-terrorist measures and tax evasion. Spain initially joined the Schengen group of France, the Federal Republic and Benelux to end border controls in January 1990, while González expressed support for Chancellor Kohl's idea of a European federal police. Spain's support for a more active EPC role in a Middle-East peace settlement was evident in the subsequent Community statements, and in Madrid's efforts to revive the Euro-Arab dialogue in early 1989. But the major breakthrough for the Community, and for Spain's policy, came with the change of administration in the United States in 1988–89: President Bush's public recognition at the May 1989 Atlantic Council meeting of González's 'leadership' of the West on Central American policy provided González with an opportunity to present his position that the reinforcement of relations between the USA and Europe was beneficial to the process of European unity. At the end of this year, which saw Spain's new international role consecrated, González opted at the Strasburg European Council under the French presidency in favour of the EC's Social Charter, and for monetary union. As Germany accelerated the drive to state unity, González expressed unconditional support for Kohl's conduct of the process.

The confident message from Madrid was that German unity would accelerate European unification. The prime minister's suggestion for the April and June 1990 Dublin European Councils was for the future union to be built on three pillars: monetary union; a common citizenship; and a common and foreign security policy. The proposal received cross-party support, and reflected Spanish public opinion that EC entry had primarily been beneficial to Spain's role in the world.

CONCLUSION

When the great transformation of Europe burst open the world, with the collapse of the communist party-states, German state unity and the implosion of the Soviet Union, Spain was well placed to participate fully in the necessarily prolonged struggle to redefine the boundaries and content of policies framing a new Europe in a post-bipolar world. That was the central triumph resulting from the redefinition of Spain's external policies between 1975 and 1989. The pre-condition was that Spain's constitutional monarchy fulfil the political terms set for full membership in Western institutions. During the process, Spain learnt to exploit all the opportunities available to it. It enjoyed a panoply of bilateral diplomatic relations, as well as membership of the UN and its agencies, and participation in the CSCE; it was a member of NATO, and had retained special relations with the USSR, the Muslim countries and with Latin America. The United States remained a crucial ally. Germany became Spain's principal patron for entry to the EC, in overcoming the French veto. Within the EC, Spain pursued a number of strategies: one was to join the 'lead group' of member states moving the EC towards union; another was to lead a 'Mediterranean' front of like-minded states in the EC to loosen the purse-strings of the richer member states; yet another was to side with the 'Club Med' countries in favour of protectionist measures. As an EC member, Spain had a wider range of external policy options towards the rest of the world, either as a voice in the EC's communal ear for outsiders, or as a significant partner for multinational corporations. The EC presidency confirmed Spain's recovery of status. But as Foreign Minister Fernández Ordóñez stated, 'we are now less naïve and ingenuous on the construction of Europe' (*El País*, 24 June 1990).

NOTES

1 Foreign Minister Oreja's phrase, *Diario de Sesiones del Senado*, 1979, no. 25, p.1048.
2 See the statement by the PSOE leader, Enrique Múgica, 'Hay que denunciar a la gran potencia que apoye el terrorismo', *El País*, 7 June 1980.

4 Western alignment

Spain's security policy

Fernando Rodrigo

This chapter provides an introduction to the changes that have taken place in Spain's security policy since the death of Franco. This is by no means an easy task, largely because of the controversy that surrounded Spain's entry into NATO. This decision aroused passions not only within the political élite, but also in the academic sphere and among the public at large. As a result, essentially political arguments have tended to dominate academic discussion of the issues. This chapter was written when the political debate was over, with the aim of making a contribution to a better understanding of the long and difficult process which, amid great passions, changed Spain's security policy.

The myth-making that accompanied this process resulted in the widely accepted view that during the transition to democracy there existed a fundamental consensus about Spain's foreign policy between the main political parties. A good example of the existence of this myth and its political use is the speech delivered by Felipe González in 1986 in the parliamentary debate which preceded the referendum on NATO membership:

> The UCD and the Suárez government already had amongst their goals Spain's entry into NATO. However, they did not take this step because, firstly, they did not think it was a priority for Spain, as there were clearly other, more urgent goals. One of these was undoubtedly Spain's accession to the European Community. Additionally, they did not want to take the risk . . . of undermining the existing consensus between all parliamentary groups concerning Spain's foreign and security policy. Thus, neither Suárez nor the UCD took the decision to bring Spain into NATO even though this goal was part of their political programme. (González 1986: 188)

The claim that such a consensus existed has been made repeatedly not only by the Socialist party (PSOE 1985), but also by eminent scholars and experts from the left (Yáñez and Viñas 1992: 85). Some have limited the extent and duration of this consensus: 'My conclusion is that, with certain precautions, fragility, and during a relatively short period of time, consensus was a reality in our foreign policy' (Mesa 1992: 152). In this chapter we shall begin with an evaluation of the Francoist legacy in foreign policy and a discussion of the existence of consensus over these questions, or the lack of it, among the main political forces during the transition.

THE FRANCOIST LEGACY IN FOREIGN POLICY AND THE LACK OF CONSENSUS

Spain's major political parties emerged after forty years of dictatorship as divided over foreign and defence policy as they were over reform versus a radical departure from Francoism, monarchy versus republic, and unitary versus federal state. The withdrawal from the Western Sahara at the end of 1975, which coincided with Franco's fatal illness and death, produced a confrontation between the supporters of reform and those in favour of a *ruptura* over the correct foreign policy to deal with the issue; this confrontation existed until the early 1980s. Policy towards the military dictatorships of Latin America was also a source of division between the political forces because the *rupturista* parties were always more radical in their policies toward those countries. Similarly, the policy towards the USA divided them again because the reformers were against the idea of altering the status quo at that time, while the *rupturistas* wanted the immediate withdrawal of US troops and the transformation of Spain into a neutral country (Mesa 1988: 44–51).

Unlike the revolutionary forces in Portugal, however, the major political parties shared a common view of Spain's international position (Opello 1991). They were all very conscious that historically and geographically Spain was a European country and believed it should remain one. Admittedly, Europe meant one thing to the reformists, who thought only in terms of Western Europe, another to the Socialists, who looked more to non-aligned countries such as Sweden, Austria or a neutralized Germany, and yet another to the Communists, who were attracted by the popular democracies of central and Eastern Europe and the 'third way' represented by the Federal Republic of Yugoslavia.

In the mid-1970s, even the EEC was regarded with suspicion by the left, though it was supported by the Socialists and the Communists because they regarded it as:

> a framework for the development and strengthening of a unitary

> working-class policy, represented by class-based parties and unions . . . in other words, the Community could provide a framework for the development of a socialist model in western European countries. (Mesa 1988: 41)

This fundamental disagreement over basic policy options resulted in a growing demand for a public debate on the foreign and defence policy of a democratic Spain (Mesa 1992: 147; Rupérez 1986: 40). During the early stages of the transition, however, far more pressing domestic political issues prevented a proper debate about foreign policy from being held. The formulation of foreign policy was unilaterally determined by successive reformist governments (1975–77), and it was not until late 1977 that Foreign Minister Marcelino Oreja invited the parties represented in the newly elected Cortes to support him in his efforts to implement a series of measures aimed at overcoming the consequences of forty years of Francoism.

It is not therefore possible to speak of a consensus in foreign policy. There was clearly a consensus in the economic sphere represented by the Moncloa Pacts of September 1977, and also in the constitutional arena, leading to the adoption of a new democratic constitution in December 1978. In March 1979, however, in his first speech before Parliament following the elections, Suárez formally announced that 'the consensus is dead'. In the sphere of foreign policy, though, the initiative lay almost exclusively with the government, leaving the opposition little room for manoeuvre. As a qualified expert from the left wrote at the time:

> It is clear, then, that in spite of the government's declaration of intent, foreign policy remains out-of-bounds for the parliamentary opposition when there is disagreement. It is not merely a question of listening to deputies, nor, as the foreign minister has claimed, of 'achieving a consensus on key issues'. Consensus techniques, which are difficult to implement, have proved very useful in the United Nations, but in democratic parliaments issues should be settled by means of debates and votes. (Mesa 1988: 57–8)

Therefore to characterize the foreign and defence policy of Spain during the transition, we should differentiate between various levels. It is possible to speak of disagreement and conflict in some areas (Sahara, Latin America), support in everything aimed at ending the isolation of Spain (diplomatic relations with communist countries, participation in different diplomatic bodies related to human rights and democratic freedoms, membership of European institutions), and, related to NATO, of a 'tacit understanding' not to move significantly towards membership (Viñas 1986: 160).

Nevertheless, it is true that the consensus in the constitutional arena spilled over into foreign and defence policy, preventing the government from moving forward in areas where the obvious disagreements with opposition parties might provoke a conflict. This was specially true of NATO membership, in spite of the statement in July 1977 by Adolfo Suárez's first elected government to the effect that 'The government favours the opening of a debate by the legitimately-elected representatives of the people with a view to examining Spain's possible membership of NATO' (Armero 1989: 73).

This ambition was reiterated by the Minister of Foreign Affairs, Marcelino Oreja, before the Senate Foreign Affairs Committee in March 1978, where he argued that 'participation in the Alliance would undoubtedly entail Spain's formal realignment' (Armero 1989: 94). But still the priorities were consensus in domestic politics and EEC entry in the international arena. Spain's application for EEC membership, submitted in July 1977, was accepted by the Commission in November 1978, and negotiations subsequently began in Brussels in February 1979. When Adolfo Suárez formed his third government after winning the elections of March 1979, it was realistic to assume that Spain could become a member of the EEC in January 1983, before the end of the legislature, as Belgian Prime Minister Wilfred Martens stated during a visit to Spain in March 1980 (Armero 1989: 88).

THE INFLUENCE OF THE INTERNATIONAL FACTOR IN FOREIGN POLICY

It has become commonplace to criticize Suárez's successor, Leopoldo Calvo-Sotelo, for handling the decision to take Spain into NATO 'in an ill-considered, over-hasty and irresponsible manner, destroying the existing consensus between the major parties, without taking into account national interest, and without explaining it adequately to the general public' (PSOE 1984: 80). Serious scholars supporting this view have also had difficulty in understanding the reasons behind this decision: 'The greatest paradox is that it was precisely the Calvo-Sotelo government, the weakest in parliamentary terms of any government since 1977, which took the key decision to take Spain into NATO' (de Arenal 1992: 401). Only the reconstruction of the lengthy process which led to that decision and the analysis of the links between foreign policy and domestic politics can enable us to understand this paradox.

How the link between EEC and NATO was established

By the summer of 1980, the domestic and international situation had changed radically for Adolfo Suárez since the previous elections. The first regional elections in the Basque Country and Cataluña were held with disastrous results for the government. Attempts at containing Andalusian demands for self-government by calling a referendum provoked a reaction which greatly undermined the support for the government in the most important area of Spain in electoral terms. The relationship with the opposition and particularly with the PSOE worsened considerably after González confronted Suárez in May 1980 with a parliamentary vote of no confidence. And as a consequence of all that, the internal cohesion of the UCD broke and the leaders of the ruling party began to seek a replacement for Suárez.

In the international arena, in early June 1980 French President Giscard D'Estaing opened his electoral campaign with a speech to the Assembly of French Agricultural Workers in which he requested 'a pause in the EEC's second enlargement' (*El País*, 6 June 1980). This was a major setback, which forced the Spanish government to reshape its entire international agenda. Suárez was too busy fighting for his political life to react, leaving Foreign Minister Oreja, and the minister responsible for negotiations with the EEC, Calvo-Sotelo, with the task of finding an adequate response.

This answer was formulated by Marcelino Oreja in mid-June 1980 in an interview given to *El País*, in which he linked entry into the EEC to membership of NATO, establishing several conditions and setting up a timetable:

> I want to make the Government's attitude towards the Atlantic option perfectly clear. The Government is totally favourable to Spain's early entry into the Atlantic Alliance. In order to achieve this we require two guarantees and one formality: the guarantee that Spain's process of integration with the EEC will continue, and that there be an Anglo-Spanish negotiation in progress with a view to returning Gibraltar to Spanish sovereignty. (*El País*, 15 June 1980)

However, internal affairs took precedence and at the end of the summer a new government was formed with a new Minister of Foreign Affairs, José Pedro Pérez-Llorca, who stated his intention to continue with the policy established by Marcelino Oreja, but without defining a calendar (*El País*, 23 September 1980). The internal situation worsened during the second half of 1980 and the resignation of Adolfo Suárez as prime minister on 29 January 1981 prevented the implementation of a last-minute decision to proceed with the integration of Spain in NATO (Rupérez 1986: 13–19).

When foreign policy finally took precedence

It was necessary to wait until the resolution of the crisis produced by the resignation of Suárez and the ratification of Calvo-Sotelo as prime minister to give foreign policy a prominent place in the government's agenda. Calvo-Sotelo had more experience than Suárez in the area of foreign affairs and was more aware of the international dimension of politics:

> Those of us who shouldered responsibility for the task which would later be known as the political transition in mid-1976, in the first Suárez government, knew that it consisted of two different elements: one was internal, namely the restoration of formal liberties; the other goal was external: to restore Spain to her rightful place in the concert of nations. (Calvo-Sotelo 1990: 124)

At the same time Calvo-Sotelo had no doubt about the Western alignment of Spain and therefore was very concerned with the consequences of some of the initiatives taken by Suárez personally, which showed his inclination towards a non-aligned foreign policy. His foreign minister, Oreja, had made every effort to conceal this impression before foreign audiences, as his speech of 10 September 1979 to the Belgian Royal Institute of Foreign Affairs illustrates:

> It has been said on occasion that Spanish foreign policy runs the risk of a third worldist or neutralist 'temptation', evidence of which is sought in events such as the president's visit to Havana in September 1978; his recent words in Brazil, in August of this year, rejecting the hegemonic ambitions of the world superpowers; or Spain's invitation to the VIth summit of Non-Aligned Nations in Havana, only a few days ago; or the choice of Madrid as the venue for the second session of the Conference on Security and Cooperation in Europe, to be held in the autumn of 1980. I wish to make it abundantly clear that my government suffers from no such third-worldist or neutralist temptation. (Rupérez 1986: 80–1)

Thus, the main international objective of Calvo-Sotelo as Prime Minister was to clarify the Western alignment of Spain, as his first speech before Parliament on 18 February 1981 indicated, and it is from this perspective that we should look at his goal of integrating Spain into NATO:

> In foreign policy our efforts will be directed at defining a European, western and democratic policy for our country, one that will be clear and irreversible, and that will dispel dreams which may smack of an isolationist temptation with regard to the western framework.
> . . . the government over which I hope to preside reaffirms its Atlantic vocation already made explicit by the Unión de Centro Democrático, and intends to open talks with other parliamentary groups in order to put together a majority, decide the timing and define the conditions and means by which Spain would be able to join the Alliance. (Calvo-Sotelo 1981a: 103–4)

However, the attempted military coup of 23 February 1981 for a while interrupted the normal political process, and many doubts arose about the capacity of a minority government to carry out the integration of Spain into NATO at a time when its need for domestic support was so great.

The discovery of the international dimension of security

Nevertheless, another aspect of Spain's international agenda emerged at this time and pushed the government towards the resolution of the question of NATO's membership: the defence agreement with the USA. For the government, as for all the other democratic parties, the discussion of the defence agreement with the USA was an important and contentious item on the international agenda of Spain. This agreement had been originally signed by Franco in 1953 and established an unequal relationship between the USA and Spain (Marquina Barrio 1986; Viñas 1981). The renegotiation of the agreement was attempted by some Francoist sectors in 1963 and in 1968 without any success, while the opposition demanded its cancellation. Nevertheless, after Franco died this question was off the agenda for five years, because the last Francoist government had negotiated a new agreement, signed in January 1976. Therefore 1981 was the first opportunity for a democratic government to negotiate anew the agreement with the USA. As the Foreign Affairs Minister, Pérez-Llorca, pointed out:

> Spanish foreign policy is at an important crossroads, at a crossroads which we have long been expecting to reach. . . . It is in autumn 1981, as opposition leaders have been reminding us for some time, that Spain will have to face the problems posed by the renewal of its relationship with the West. (Pérez-Llorca 1981)

The negotiations suffered several delays. First, because of the presidential elections in the USA, which made Ronald Reagan president and produced the normal change in the administration. Second, because of the coup attempt of February 1981 in Spain. Therefore, when the new Secretary of State, Alexander Haig, arrived in Madrid in April 1981 the base negotiations had not yet begun, nor had the Spanish government formally decided to take Spain into NATO.

The Spanish government, seeking a formula to give it time to solve the NATO issue, proposed to Washington to negotiate an interim agreement before September 1981, when the treaty of 1976 expired. But the US administration refused and asked for clarification about NATO membership intentions before introducing any change into the bilateral relationship (*El País*, 23 January, 26 August 1981). The negotiations on a new agreement began formally on 25 May 1981, before the Spanish goverment had clarified its position on NATO membership, and were interrupted without any progress made in September, once the decision had been taken (*El País*, 9 April 1981). After the parliamentary approval of Spain's accession to NATO the negotiations began again, and on 2 July 1982 a new agreement was signed which introduced important changes to the bilateral relationship, making it more equilibrated (Viñas 1986: 163–4). Thus Calvo-Sotelo had another reason to explain when asking Parliament to authorize the signature of the Washington Treaty: '. . . and, fifthly, because after several months negotiating the renewal of our bilateral agreement with the US we know that only within the Alliance will we obtain substantial improvements for our defence system' (Calvo-Sotelo 1981c).

The foreign framework of a domestic decision

Calvo-Sotelo's government therefore decided to take Spain into NATO not for domestic concerns but for international reasons, although his political situation discouraged that step. He had tried to rebuild the consensus with the opposition parties over some key policies, such as terrorism and devolution, yet the decision to join NATO was now bound to produce a serious crisis in his government's relations with the PSOE and the PCE.

The scenario chosen to announce the decision, as well as the timetable, also supports this hypothesis. After two months as prime minister, Calvo-Sotelo tried to break the impasse that had existed in the international arena since June 1980, and made his first official trip to the Federal Republic of Germany, which was then governed by a Social Democrat, Helmut Schmidt. There, Calvo-Sotelo, looking for the support of Chancellor Schmidt for the entry of Spain into the EEC, announced the decision to 'take the necessary steps for accession to

NATO as the natural culmination of our European policy, rather than as the outcome of our bilateral agreements with the United States' (Calvo-Sotelo 1981b: 139). The Spanish prime minister was mindful of the forthcoming presidential elections in France at the start of May, and the spring meeting of the Atlantic Council, which on 5 May issued an informal invitation to Spain to join the Alliance. On 31 July the government and the PSOE signed the 'Pactos Autonómicos' to re-organize the process of building the new state, and on 20 August the Council of Ministers decided formally to ask for the authorization of Parliament to proceed with the adhesion of Spain to the Treaty of Washington. After several days of parliamentary discussion on 20 October 1981 the government won the support of 186 deputies against 146, and on 10 December the ministers of foreign affairs of the Atlantic Alliance signed the protocol of adhesion of Spain.

THE DIFFICULT RELATION BETWEEN DOMESTIC POLITICS AND FOREIGN POLICY

Between ideology and the polls

During this time the PSOE had developed a very active policy of confrontation with the government, partly in Parliament where Felipe González had answered the new prime minister promising that: 'if the entry procedure is not submitted to a referendum, if we ever obtain a majority in this Parliament which has voted to take us into NATO, we will propose our departure from the Alliance' (González 1981). The Socialists also took their campaign on to the streets and into the media, organizing a campaign to collect signatures with the aim of obliging the government to hold a referendum in order to prevent the integration of Spain into NATO.

The reasons given by the Socialists for opposing Spain's entry into NATO were many, from alleging a departure from a neutralist tradition in Spain's foreign policy to the loss of autonomy in its international relations. However, the resolution approved at the twenty-ninth PSOE congress in October 1981 gave four reasons:

- NATO does not guarantee Spanish territorial integrity, since the North Atlantic Treaty excludes part of our territory from the Atlantic defence system.
- NATO does not meet our defence and security needs, since our potential areas of risk and threat fall outside what is contemplated in the Treaty.

- Participation in NATO implies an increase in the risk of nuclear destruction for our people.
- The reaction of the other bloc could lead to the strengthening or extension of the Warsaw pact and an increase in the tension and likelihood of war in Europe. (PSOE 1981: 76)

This perception of the Atlantic Alliance contrasts with the evaluation by González four years later, on the eve of the referendum:

> I believe that Spain's interests are best defended by belonging to the Alliance. Our earlier views on the Alliance and its operation were not correct. The member countries of the Alliance are those which enjoy the greatest popular sovereignty, the highest level of economic development, democracy, freedoms, respect for human rights and peace. (*El País*, 17 October 1985)

To explain the Socialists' position on the Atlantic Alliance during the late 1970s and early 1980s several factors should be taken into account. The first is the long experience of the PSOE as an opposition and even an illegal party, led by a small group of young leaders without any experience of government and only with the international experience that meetings of the Socialist International provided .

As a consequence of the lack of experience in government and in foreign affairs the Socialists had an ideological view of foreign policy, and this is the second factor that explains their position on NATO. The PSOE had suffered what González, in a famous interview, called 'una fase de acumulación ideológica extraordinariamente fuerte' (*El País*, 17 October 1985). A good example of this 'ideological accumulation' was the introduction to the foreign policy section of aspects of the programme adopted at the twenty-ninth congress, held just days before the parliamentary approval of Spain's integration into NATO:

> The PSOE, in keeping with the historic tradition of the workers' movement and out of conviction, accepts the internationalist principles of the working class.
>
> With a view to attaining these principles, the PSOE, as a member of the Socialist International, values and regards this organization as an essential element in the encouragement of peace, freedom and solidarity amongst nations. In this sense the PSOE will sustain and develop its link with all socialist and progressive parties, will participate actively in the diffusion of the Socialist International's principles and recommendations, and will support, in so far as it is able to, all initiatives leading to the emancipation of the workers and the oppressed peoples. (PSOE 1981: 147)

Thus, for the Socialists, it was very easy in ideological terms to oppose the government over the NATO issue – particularly during autumn 1981 when the domestic situation was still fragile following the February coup attempt, and the only way to confront the government without destabilizing the democratic system was over matters of foreign policy.

The third factor that helps to explain the Socialist position on NATO is the electoral factor. The campaign against NATO in the second half of 1981 and the first months of 1982 had helped the Socialists to undermine the image of Calvo-Sotelo's government. But on 30 May 1982, after the fifteen members of the Atlantic Alliance ratified the accession protocol, Spain became a member of NATO, presenting the PSOE with an entirely new situation. Spain had assumed very important international obligations, and the idea of withdrawing from NATO was not very plausible. Nevertheless, there were many people who opposed Spain's entry to NATO, around 43 per cent in September 1981 (CIS 1983), and the PSOE could not afford to lose their votes nor leave them to the Communist party which was enthusiastically campaigning against NATO (Morán 1990: 23). As Angel Viñas has stated:

> In the 1982 election campaign the NATO issue played an important role. Many citizens who had been surprised at the way in which the UCD government had carried out the accession, undoubtedly gave their votes to the Socialists, in the belief that the PSOE would take Spain out of the Alliance. (Viñas 1986: 162)

Nevertheless, the Socialist party alone had promised in its electoral manifesto to call a referendum to decide about NATO's membership (PSOE 1982). When the Socialists obtained a landslide victory in the October 1982 elections, the intellectual leader of the campaign against NATO, Fernando Morán, became Minister of Foreign Affairs. On 8 December, at a meeting of the Atlantic Council in Brussels, the Socialist minister announced the Spanish government's intention to stop the negotiations to integrate Spain into NATO's military organization, while remaining an active and loyal partner until an analysis of the strategic interests of Spain had been made and a referendum held (Morán 1990: 23–30).

Defining policies and shifting coalitions

The government formed by González after his victory in the elections was a coalition of people with different views about foreign and defence policy. Although no-one in the government had a clear strategy in relation to NATO at the beginning of 1983, it is possible to identify two sectors. One sector was led by González himself, and included the powerful Economy Minister, Miguel Boyer, the influential Defence Minister, Narcís Serra, and the Secretary of State for EEC Affairs, Manuel Marín, who were concerned mainly about the economic integration of Spain into the EEC and were aware of the obvious connections between obtaining EEC membership and remaining part of NATO.

The other sector of the government was led by the Deputy Prime Minister, Alfonso Guerra, and included the Minister of Foreign Affairs, Fernando Morán, and a number of ministers who were just as committed to Spain joining the EEC, but were not aware of the connection between membership of the Community and of NATO, and were more concerned with ideological principles. As late as 17 July 1983, Alfonso Guerra criticized some Socialists who, after becoming members of the government, had begun to change their opinions about NATO membership. He himself declared: 'I do not think Spain should be in NATO, it should leave' (*El País*, 20 July 1983). Three days after his declarations, some ministers, including Solana, Maravall, Lluch and Campo, agreed publicly with Guerra against Spain's membership in NATO (*El País*, 20 July 1983).

The question of NATO therefore divided the government, but most of the PSOE remained loyal to their commitment to oppose NATO membership, and something similar happened in the Communist party. In Parliament there was a clear division between left and right over the NATO issue, while public opinion was deeply divided as the polls showed. In March 1983, 49 per cent of the people were against NATO membership, 13 per cent in favour and 30 per cent did not respond (CIS 1983).

González did not immediately have a strategy to resolve the NATO problem, and during 1983 the issue was left to different groups of experts while the EEC remained the focus of government policy in foreign affairs. González established a number of personal links with influential leaders of EEC countries, like Kohl, Craxi and Lubbers, who were important in shaping his view of the NATO issue and were also very helpful in supporting Spain's membership of the EEC. Fernando Morán meanwhile established good personal links with Claude Cheysson and other Socialist leaders of France that were very important in overcoming French reticence about Spain's membership of the EC.

The European Councils of Stuttgart in June 1983 and Fontainebleau in June 1984 were decisive for Spain's membership of the EC: in Stuttgart, because Germany linked the solution to the budgetary problems of the Community with the enlargement involving Spain and

Portugal; and in Fontainebleau, because a date, January 1986, was established to proceed with the enlargement.

Meanwhile, a group of diplomats and military officers from the ministries of Foreign Affairs and Defence was established to analyse the range of options available; Morán organized another more restricted group of people, composed only of diplomats from the Ministry of Foreign Affairs and the Spanish delegation to NATO, and prepared a first paper that was sent only to González in June 1984. The document analysed available options and supported membership of the Alliance based on the French model (Morán 1990: 270–3).

This paper, together with analyses prepared by Defence Minister Narcís Serra and the diplomatic adviser of González, Juan Antonio Yáñez, was used to prepare the famous 'Decalogue of Peace and Security'. González presented it to Parliament on 23 October 1984, as the beginning of a dialogue with those opposition parties that had been in favour of NATO membership in October 1981. González said:

> The other great task we face in our foreign policy is the definition of a Spanish defence and security policy which enjoys the support of the Nation. That is, one where there can be a broad consensus over a common denominator. . . .
>
> I hereby promise to start talks, during November, with each of the parliamentary groups, and in December, when we analyse the degree of convergence attained, I will meet all groups so as to explore the possibility of reaching a decision on this common denominator. (González 1984: 423)

González sought a parliamentary debate on the formula aimed at consensus and to use 1985 to explain it to public opinion, before holding a referendum in February 1986. But first he needed to convince the PSOE to change its position and only after a difficult debate did he succeed in doing so at the thirtieth party congress, held in December 1984. The congress authorized the executive council and the government to call the referendum at the most opportune moment, and supported the policy defended by González in Parliament (PSOE 1984).

The decision to remain in NATO without participating in the military structure provoked a second debate within the government, because when the Socialists had frozen the integration in NATO's military structure, Spain was already part of the Defence Planning Committee (DPC), the Military Committee (MC) and the Nuclear Planning Group (NPG). In autumn 1984, Morán sent a second memorandum to González in favour of leaving the situation as it was when the Socialists arrived in office, but expressing some doubts about the participation in the MC, given that it was part of NATO's military structure. However, the Minister of Defence defended the importance for the Spanish armed forces of establishing a link with NATO through the DPC and specially through the participation of the Chief of General Staff in the Military Committee, and González supported his position.

Although González obtained the support of the PSOE for his position, many Socialists were still against NATO, and the opposition parties were not ready to support him in 1985. In December 1985 the Nationalist party of Catalonia, Convergence and Unity (CiU), took the initiative by presenting a motion to Parliament on the NATO question, and this formed the basis of a new consensus among the main parties of the right (Minoría Catalana 1985: 266). In February 1986, when the parliamentary debate to authorize the referendum took place, the same parties refused to support González, who faced a public opinion that was evenly divided on that issue, with 32 per cent against NATO membership, 32 per cent in favour and 36 per cent who did not answer (CIS 1987).

González went into the referendum with a new government, Morán having been replaced as minister of foreign affairs by Francisco Fernández Ordóñez, after Spain's entry to the EEC had been signed on 1 July 1985. The referendum was held in March 1986 and González obtained a great victory, with 52.5 per cent of the voters supporting his position and only 39.8 per cent against.

THE WESTERN ALIGNMENT OF SPAIN

The referendum opened a new period in Spanish security policy. After a decade of doubts and discussions between the main political parties, there was an agenda to integrate Spain into western security. González had established this agenda in his parliamentary speech of October 1984, when looking for a consensus with the main opposition parties.

A new relationship with the USA

One of the key points of this agenda was to change the defence relationship with the USA: not only to negotiate a new defence agreement in 1988 when the agreement negotiated by the UCD was due to expire, but 'to reduce the presence of US forces and bases on Spanish territory' (González 1984: 424). In July 1986, at the request of the Spanish government, new conversations were initiated between the two countries in an effort to find a new framework for bilateral relations and to proceed with the reduction of the American military presence, a reduction that Spain considered should be substantial but without damaging common security. After a year and a half of difficult negotiations – negotiations that took the US–Spain relation to its lowest point – the two governments issued a joint Declaration on 15 January 1988:

> The Governments of Spain and the United States have reached an understanding on the new framework to replace the Cooperation, Defence and Friendship Agreement of 1982.
>
> 1 Following this new defensive agreement, the United States will continue to use the support installations in Spain as well as the authorization to use Spanish territory, sea and air space in times of crisis or war, in support of NATO's reinforcement plans.
> 2 The initial term of the new agreement will be of eight years which can be extended for successive annual periods.
> 3 In fulfillment of the Spanish Government's sovereign decision, the United States will withdraw the Tactical Combat Wing 401 from Spain within three years of the date upon which the new agreement comes into effect.
> 4 No commitment on either side with regard to military or economic aid in the form of credit or a donation will figure in the agreement or be related to it.
> 5 Future cooperation on education, culture or science and technology will be based on new and equitable formulas. This cooperation will be separated from the new defensive agreement. (González 1988a)

The agreement by which Spain obtained the withdrawal of USAF Wing 401 ruled out any form of military or economic help. It was understood that Spain was now a normal ally and therefore the military facilities given to US troops were its contribution to allied defence. The Declaration allowed the two governments to negotiate a new agreement that was signed in December 1988, and established the bilateral relationship on a new and more solid ground as the war against Iraq would show in 1991 (Rodrigo 1992: 99–102).

Integration in NATO: looking for a Spanish model

Another important item on the agenda established by González was to remain in NATO 'without taking part in the integrated military structure' (González 1984: 424). On May 1986, the Spanish ministers of foreign affairs and defence presented in the spring sessions of the Atlantic Council and the Defence Planning Committee a memorandum with nine general points which constituted the basis for the development of Spanish participation in NATO, according to the conditions set by the referendum.

The discussion of these points with the allies lasted from 1986 until January 1988, when Spain was ready to formulate a proposal about its contribution to the common defence effort. The Spanish ambassador to NATO addressed a letter to the Secretary General listing the possible tasks the Spanish armed forces could perform for the common defence. The ambassador's letter pointed out that the Spanish contribution would take place preferably within the limits of the strategic zone of national interest (Rodrigo 1992).

The implementation of the Spanish proposal required the elaboration of several agreements between Spain and the Alliance and before that required the consensus on the general guidelines to be followed by the people in charge of the negotiations. The establishment of these guidelines took almost a year and they were not approved by the Defence Planning Committee until December 1988. Finally, in May 1989, after a year and a half of difficult negotiations, the first two agreements on coordination between the Spanish forces and the allied command were signed. These agreements refer to the carrying out of sea and air operations in the eastern Atlantic and the air defence of Spanish territory. Four other agreements were to follow in the coming years, as Spain became a very cooperative ally taking an active part in NATO activities.

The European option

González had also proposed in Parliament in October 1984 that Spain join the West European Union (WEU), because this was the only European organization with defence competences. Nevertheless, when the negotiations for the accession to the Treaty of Brussels started in The Hague on May 1988, the Spanish decision to ban the installation of nuclear weapons on its territory and the desire to carry out its military contribution to the Alliance, preferably within the area of national strategic interest, were very controversial among the WEU members. The reason for such controversy was that Spanish security policy did not seem to agree very well with the compromises made in The Hague Platform, which committed member states:

- to carry out our share of the common defence in both the conventional and the nuclear field, in accordance with the principles of risk-and-burden-sharing which are fundamental to allied cohesion.
- to ensure that our determination to defend any member country at its

> borders is made clearly manifest by means of appropriate arrangements. (quoted in Cahen 1989: 123)

The clear expression by the Spanish government of its full agreement with The Hague Platform, the Rome Declaration, and the Treaty of Brussels, as well as its willingness 'to participate fully in their implementation', made possible Spanish accession to the WEU together with that of Portugal, on 14 November 1988 (Cahen 1989).

By the end of 1988, Spain had ended the definitional period of its Western alignment. Nevertheless, during the following years it had to work on the consequences of its membership of Western security organizations and the EEC. But soon this process would be mixed up with responses to the great change that shook the Western world following the fall of the Berlin Wall.

5 Spain in the world economy

Keith Salmon

During the period 1975–94 the political economy of Spain became more closely integrated into the world economy. In particular, membership of the European Community altered the pattern of external relations and redefined the position of Spain in the world from a protected national economy to an economy embedded in one of the world's core trading regions and within the corporate space of multinational companies. Integration followed from a general reduction of protectionism, increased liberalization throughout the economy and significant penetration by foreign capital. This was accompanied by the transfer of decision-making to supranational authorities and foreign multinational companies. It exposed the economy to rapid structural change, as the economy was drawn into the rapidly evolving European and global process of restructuring which demanded greater flexibility to maintain competitive advantage. Despite the obvious economic strains involved and the impact on cultural institutions, national identity and sovereignty, the desire to 'modernize' overrode any temptation to revert to national autonomy.

Evolution of the domestic economy can be divided into a period of faltering growth in the mid-1970s followed by a recession at the turn of the decade (see Figure 1). Politically this coincided with the transition to democracy, with economic policy overwhelmingly constrained by domestic political considerations. Slow growth in the early 1980s followed the election of the first PSOE government as Spain prepared for entry to the EC. Membership in 1986 marked a major step towards further opening of the economy, initiating a period of strong economic growth. Growth petered out in the early 1990s as Spain accompanied its European neighbours into recession, slowly emerging from it in 1994. An interesting footnote is that, according to Eurostat, throughout the whole period Spain never regained the real convergence in GDP per capita that it had achieved on the death of Franco in 1975.

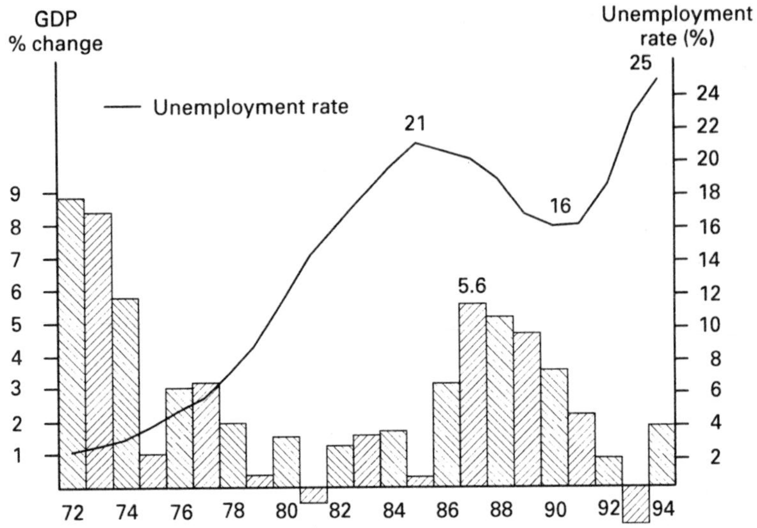

Figure 1 Evolution of GDP and unemployment
Source: Banco Bilbao Vizcaya 1993b

Spain achieved 76 per cent of the EC average GDP in 1991 as against 79 per cent in 1975 (Eurostat 1993a).

From 1975 the macro-economic complexion of the economy was transformed to one increasingly reliant on services, and from one of low tax and low public spending, largely financed internally, to a 'welfare state' of high tax and high public spending relying on external finance (Comín 1988; Segura 1988). One trend that was maintained throughout the whole period was the almost inexorable rise in unemployment (see Figure 1).

Throughout the period the underlying strategic risk was that Spain would be caught between competitiveness based on low labour costs, low technology products and low value added services, and competitiveness based on new technologies and high value added services (Maravall 1987). Hence, the principal strategic goal was to raise competitiveness, restructure the production base and position Spain in the world economy to gain maximum competitive advantage.

This chapter sets out some of the changes in the international context in which the political economy evolved between 1975 and 1994, the changes in trade and investment policy that stimulated increased integration, the forms of closer integration (trade, investment and multinationals) and aspects of competitiveness.

CHANGES IN THE WORLD ECONOMY

The most fundamental process of change permeating the world economy during the period was the increasing integration of national economies into a world economy organized around market principles, strengthening the role of international market forces in determining national economic performance. The most dramatic event in this process was the fall of the Berlin Wall in November 1989 and the collapse of central planning in the former Soviet Union and Eastern Europe. The demise of communism also brought a wholesale reappraisal of defence policy both among NATO countries and in the Eastern Bloc, resulting in a rationalization of the defence industry (the so-called peace dividend). Furthermore, for the European Community it unveiled a whole new region of interest on its eastern border, shifting attention away from the south (a reorientation reinforced by the establishment of the European Economic Area and the accession agreement with the Nordic countries and Austria in 1994). Less dramatic was the continued incorporation of less developed countries (LDCs) into the world economy, especially those of the Pacific rim of Asia, including China with its huge supply of cheap labour and vast potential market.

Not only did the market system expand into countries formally characterized by central planning, but there was also a retracing of the boundary between the public and private sector in existing mixed market economies, illustrated by the process of privatization (Vickers and Wright 1988: 1–30). This shift followed from disillusion in certain circles with earlier economic policies to deal with the economic crisis of the 1970s, coupled with a reassertion of individual freedom over the state. Disenchantment with dirigisme and Keynesianism was bound up in ideological and economic arguments that embraced the perceived bureaucratic inefficiency of the public sector, the appearance of stagflation, the strains of higher public debt, a reaction against the high levels of taxation needed to support weighty public sectors, and the political risks associated with managing a large public sector labour force. The post-war consensus around Keynesian policies to maintain employment levels and prevent recession was broken; in its place came monetarism with its emphasis on controlling inflation and greater reliance on market forces.

Integration, made possible by improvements in transportation and communications technologies and facilitated by more liberal trade and investment policies, allowed companies to organize on a global basis and capital and services to move more freely, opening up new markets and increasing competition. In essence it fuelled the continuing process of international specialization and division of labour. OECD countries experienced varying degrees of de-industrialization and transformation to economies dominated by services, while industrialization, new sources of raw materials and new agricultural export areas continued to develop in LDCs. In this process national governments relinquished some of their power to manage their economies. This was nowhere better demonstrated than in Spain's membership of the Exchange Rate Mechanism (ERM) and the virtual destruction of this system by international capital movements.

In joining the ERM in June 1989 the Spanish government not only lost its previous autonomy over monetary policy but also limited its room for manoeuvre on broader economic policy issues such as economic growth and unemployment. After one year the peseta was trading near the ceiling of its value, a position that it held until midway through 1992. Whereas interest rate policy in Spain was largely dictated by domestic considerations up to 1991, in 1992 it became overshadowed by external considerations and the need to keep the peseta in the ERM and therefore maintain the central plank of Spanish economic policy built around meeting the convergence criteria for economic and monetary union described in the Maastricht Treaty. Thus monetary policy in 1992 was dominated by exchange rate considerations. During the currency turmoil in September 1992 the peseta fell very quickly from the top of the ERM band to the bottom, and the currency was devalued by 5 per cent but remained within the ERM. Continuing downward pressure forced another devaluation in November 1992 (6 per cent) then another (8 per cent) in May 1993. External factors were dictating economic policy (especially the German economic policy of maintaining high interest rates to contain inflation generated by German reunification). High interest rates and clear indications of a tight budget in 1994 were required by the international capital markets as the price of maintaining the exchange rate in the ERM. A stream of economists visiting Spain spoke out about the contradiction of maintaining high interest rates while the economy had entered a recession, inflation was falling and unemployment was over 20 per cent and rising. In August 1993 the ERM virtually collapsed in the face of market pressures. Across Europe interest rates began to fall, in Spain from 14 per cent in March 1993 to 7.5 per cent in May 1994.

Superimposed on the pattern of integration in the world economy there was also a tendency towards segmentation into regional trading sub-systems organized around the core areas of North America, Japan and the EC. Trade, capital flows, information flows and movements of people all intensified between the member states. For example, intra-EC merchandise trade increased from 51 per cent of total EC trade in 1975 to 60 per cent in 1992 (Eurostat 1993b). Trade creation was accompanied by trade diversion into the emerging regional sub-systems.

European integration was fundamental in stimulating measures to liberalize the economy, in harmonizing the regulatory framework of business with that of other member states and in directing the increasing external transactions of the Spanish economy towards the EC. European Community policies spread throughout the Spanish economy, replacing the protectionist system which had been so important in shaping it in the past with a supranational system of protection and a single European market; the cobwebs of autarky and Spanish corporate capitalism were swept away and the market for Spanish goods was transformed from one of 39 million people to one of 340 million. Simultaneously, Spanish industry was confronted with the challenge of competition from the more advanced economies of north-west Europe, with growing competition from other advanced industrialized regions and low cost industrial and agricultural producers emerging in other parts of the world, with exposure to the evolving international division of labour, and with the threat that segmentation of the world economy brought to its special relationship with Latin America.

Driving integration and specialization in the world economy was the continued growth of multinational companies (MNCs) and their now more complex pattern of alliances (Dicken 1992). International production and the new international division of labour within multinational companies became a central structural characteristic of the world economy (United Nations 1993). In the EC, essentially national companies began reorganizing into European multinationals, reinforcing the European economic sub-system (Tsoukalis 1993). As multinationals integrated their operations and accounted for an increasing share of world trade and investment, the locus of control over economic activity shifted beyond the frontiers of many countries, presenting further challenges to national policy makers (Dicken 1994).

No overview of change in the world economy during the period 1975–94 would be complete without reference to the swings in oil prices and their consequences, especially as the Spanish economy was almost wholly dependent on imported oil and gas. Oil prices quadrupled in 1973–74 and then rose again sharply at the turn of the decade (with spot prices touching $40 a barrel). After 1981 prices weakened to reach $28 a barrel in 1985, and then slid to $13 in 1986. In real terms the oil price in 1986 was back to its level in the mid-1970s. In 1986 the oil-consuming countries were estimated to have saved $120 billion on oil purchases compared with 1985, and Spain alone saved $4 billion

(Fanjul 1987).[1] After 1986 oil prices remained weak, apart from a brief interval during the Gulf war. The shock of the oil price rises triggered the economic problems of the late 1970s and early 1980s (contributing to the de-industrialization of OECD countries), transferring resources from the industrialized countries to the oil-producing and exporting countries (OPEC), and recycling resources to the developing countries. Weak oil prices from the mid 1980s contributed to economic growth in the industrialized economies in the late 1980s and to falling rates of inflation in the early 1990s, while concern over 'Third World' debt led capital to seek safer havens in OECD countries, including Spain.

Although membership of the EC dominated the formulation of Spanish economic policy in the 1980s, broader international economic forces lay behind much of the restructuring occurring within Spain. Prior to 1975 these economic forces were managed essentially through national economic policies and decision makers. By 1994 Spain was embedded in a broader European economy and through that in a dynamic world economy, where national economic performance was closely tied to business cycles elsewhere in the world, where national economic policies were overlain by those of the European Union, where the nature of the EU itself was changing and where a significant degree of control over the economy had been shed to the international arena.

TRADE POLICY

Integration was underpinned by changes in trade and investment policy in Spain, initiated with the Stabilization Plan in 1959 and culminating in relation to the EC with the completion of transitional arrangements to the Single European Market at the end of 1992. Further liberalization awaited the implementation of agreements reached in 1993 under the Uruguay Round of the General Agreement on Tariffs and Trade (GATT).

Trade policy in 1975 had evolved on the foundation of the fundamental policy shift made in 1960 as part of the agreement over the Stabilization Plan. Although considerably more liberal in outlook than previous trade policy, it retained a strong protectionist dimension made up of tariff barriers, discriminatory trade regimes and the protectionist element of the special tax on imports (Impuesto de Compensación de Gravámenes Interiores, ICGI) established in 1964, as well as being backed by a plethora of non-tariff barriers that were deeply etched into the fibre of the Spanish economy. Furthermore, the tariff structure was complex, sometimes discretionary in application, subject to frequent changes and to the introduction of protectionist measures (Antonio Alonso 1988).

Although the importance of national initiatives in promoting trade liberalization should not be dismissed, the major steps in liberalization were the result of external pressure. The initial lowering of tariffs followed the commitments made under the Stabilization Plan in 1959 and membership of GATT in 1963. A second round of liberalization followed the preferential trade agreement with the EEC in 1970 (characterized particularly by tariff reductions on imports into the EEC) and a third round of liberalization flowed from the trade agreement with the European Free Trade Association (EFTA) and the conclusion of the Tokyo Round of GATT in 1979. In the late 1970s the tariff structure was graduated to provide higher tariffs on more highly processed goods, and there was a wide variation in the level of effective protection afforded to different goods.

Apart from tariffs, protectionism resulted from the measures subsumed under different trade regimes and from the fiscal treatment of imports. Different groups of products and countries were subject to different trade regimes. As regards the fiscal treatment of imports, imported goods were taxed in Spain, to avoid double taxation. From 1964 the tax applied was the ICGI, which was generally above the level of the principal indirect tax in Spain on domestic products (the cascade sales tax – Impuesto General sobre el Tráfico de Empresas, ITE). Exports were subject to a complex system of assistance throughout the 1960s, 1970s and early 1980s, including lower tariffs on imported intermediate goods that were crucial to exports, favourable tax treatment, export credits, specialized insurance and organizational support.

The process of liberalization was strengthened during the period 1986–94 with measures to harmonize Spanish trade policy with that of the EC and with those designed to create a single European market. From 1986 to the beginning of 1993 import duties between Spain and the EC were lowered in a series of steps to zero. Spain benefited from lower tariffs on its exports to the Community but the impact of reductions was less on exports, since tariffs on many export products had started to be dismantled earlier. Over the same period Spain had to adapt its system of import duties to third countries to bring them into line with the common trade policy of the EC (which in general meant a lowering of duties). As a result of the dismantling of import tariffs consumer goods poured in. For example, from being a negligible part of the market in 1975 the share of the new car market taken by imported cars increased to 11 per cent in 1980 and thence to 45 per cent in 1992 (*El País* 1994).

Hence, on joining the European Community Spain adopted its common trade policy, comprising the removal of barriers to trade within the Community, the Common External Tariff (CET, or variable levy in the case of agricultural produce) and the preferential trade arrangements with certain groups of countries. It also inherited the tensions in world trade involving EC policies.

Outside the EC, trade with the EFTA countries was not subject to major modifications, but it was subject to a significant adjustment in relation to the preferential arrangements governing Community trade with the African, Caribbean and Pacific (ACP) countries under the Lomé Conventions, the Mediterranean countries under the Global Mediterranean Programme (GMP) and the countries subject to the Generalized System of Preferences (GSP). Apart from trade with EFTA (which operated virtually tariff-free) the most preferential treatment was accorded to the ACP countries, which enjoyed a package of trade and aid benefits. These included almost all ACP industrial products being allowed into the EC without tariffs, quotas or reciprocity requirements but with restrictions on agricultural products that competed with those produced in the EC, and the trade-related aid schemes Stabex (stabilization of export earnings) and Sysmin (stabilization of earnings from mineral exports).

By contrast, Latin America was an area with which EC cooperation was notably weak (Archer and Butler 1992). Thus in adopting the common trade policy of the EC (with its attendant implications for development), the historical, cultural, political and economic commitments of Spain to Latin America were threatened. Trade patterns were likely to shift, with manufactured goods and services being more intensively traded within the EC, while the sourcing of primary products switched to the ACP and Mediterranean countries. Spain would therefore need to make serious efforts within the Community institutions to ensure that Latin America's exports reached European countries under the most favourable terms (Nieto Solís 1993).

In relation to capital movements, membership of the EC swept away controls (especially on inward investment) and introduced a timetable for their elimination by 1993. The liberalization of capital markets precipitated an avalanche of inward investment as Spain became the fourth most attractive country in the world for foreign direct investment in the late 1980s (after the USA, UK and France; in 1993 it was fifth among OECD countries).

In sum, the international trade regime was transformed by membership of the European Community. It led to the removal of tariffs and investment controls with other member states and EFTA countries, to a lowering of protection with ACP and Mediterranean countries, and also to a general lowering of import duties with the newly industrializing countries (NICs). It also brought change in the indirect tax system with the adoption of VAT, the ending of ITE and ICGI and hence the removal of the protection afforded by the ICGI. Some exports also lost their advantage gained from the favourable tax treatment of imports of intermediate goods, and became subject to the general provision that exports should not be subsidized by the government. The different trade regimes were abolished in 1986 and replaced by the general import regime of the EC under which all products were included except textiles (covered under the Multi-Fibre Agreement) and agricultural produce (covered under the Common Agricultural Policy). Finally, the process of removing non-tariff barriers to trade in the EC was begun, with such measures as agreements over technical standards, harmonization of trade practices, the opening up of government contracts to companies in other member states and the free movement of factors of production.

EXTERNAL TRANSACTIONS

While trade grew strongly over the period 1975–92, greater integration was primarily a function of an escalation in capital transactions (see Figure 2).

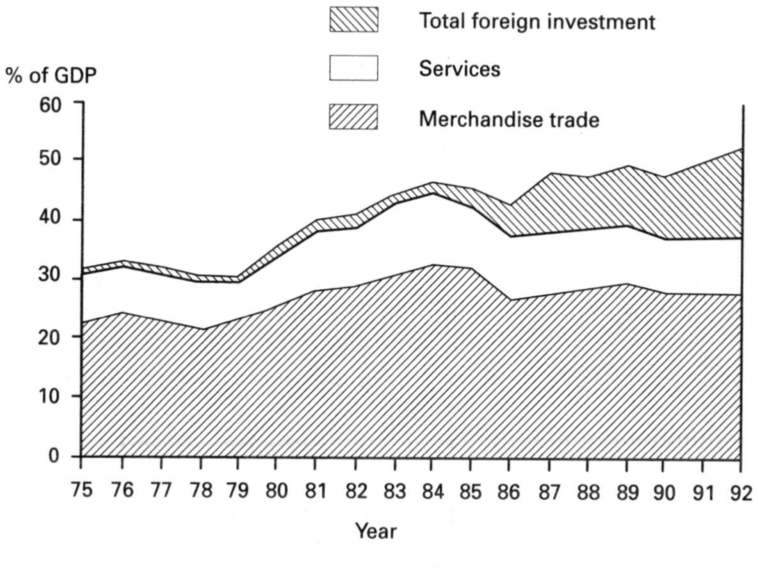

Figure 2 Opening of the Spanish economy
Source: Antonio Alonso 1988; Banco de España 1993; *El País* 1993

Merchandise trade

Between 1972 and 1992 (inclusive) merchandise exports grew twice as fast as exports from all industrialized countries and imports one and a half times as fast (IMF 1993). As a proportion of GDP merchandise trade rose from 23 per cent in 1975 to over 30 per cent in 1993,[2] although merchandise trade as a percentage of GDP in Spain remained one of the lowest in the European Union (OECD 1993).

Apart from the overall growth in merchandise trade, an increasing volume represented intra-industry trade (Bajo and Torres 1992) and its composition changed. Setting aside energy trade, which was a very volatile element (especially imports, varying from 12 per cent of all imports in 1973 to 44 per cent in 1981, thence falling to around 10 per cent in the late 1980s and early 1990s), the principal trend in both non-energy exports and imports from the early 1980s onwards was the increased relative importance of consumer goods, especially consumer durables (notably vehicles). Spanish exports were frequently of lower value added than imports; thus exports of cars concentrated on small vehicles.

Geographically there was an increased concentration of merchandise trade on the EC, especially after 1985 (see Table 1). Imports from Japan and the Asian NICs also increased in relative importance, while there was little relative growth in these areas as export markets. A relative decline of the share of trade with the USA and Latin America included an element of trade diversion, especially in agricultural produce. Nevertheless, the United States remained the fifth most valuable single country source of imports in 1993 and the sixth most valuable destination of exports.

In every year between 1975 and 1993 there was a balance of merchandise trade deficit. The size of this deficit varied with the terms of trade (notably oil prices and exchange rates) and the relative growth of the Spanish economy in relation to other economies. After 1985 the only major EC trading partner with which Spain recorded a consistent trade surplus was Portugal.

Invisible trade

On the invisible account services grew more slowly than merchandise trade,[3] hovering around ten per cent of GDP. From 1975 to 1994 there was a surplus on the account, frequently sufficient to cover the deficit on merchandise trade. However, the surplus began to evaporate after 1985, with import coverage falling from 282 in 1985 to 188 in 1992 (Banco de España 1976 and 1993).

Table 1 Patterns of world trade, 1975–92

Region	*Exports (%)*				*Imports (%)*			
	1975	*1981*	*1985*	*1992*	*1975*	*1981*	*1985*	*1992*
OECD		59.4	69.8	82.4		51.1	56.5	79.0
EC(12)	48.1	45.7	52.1	71.2	35.6	29.4	36.6	60.7
North America		7.6	11.0	5.3		14.6	11.3	8.0
Japan		1.6	1.3	0.9		2.7	3.4	4.7
Rest of OECD		4.5	5.6	5.0		4.4	5.2	5.7
Latin America		7.8	3.8	3.9		9.7	10.1	4.0
Asian NICs		0.7	0.9	1.3		0.9	1.0	2.6
OPEC		14.7	7.2	3.6		30.3	20.3	5.9
Rest of the world		17.4	18.2	8.8		8.0	12.1	8.5
Total		100.0	100.0	100.0		100.0	100.0	100.0

Source: Banco de España 1993; Ministerio de Economía y Hacienda 1977

Travel and tourism accounted for over 60 per cent of income on services and were the source of most of the surplus, the number of foreign visitors doubling from 30 million in 1975 to over 60 million in 1994. Their patterns were even more highly concentrated on the EU than was the case with merchandise trade. Over 80 per cent of visitors to Spain were residents of other EU countries and close to 90 per cent were European. Britain, France and Germany were the key tourist markets. Outside of tourism, the surplus had completely evaporated by 1992.

There was a substantial growth in transfer payments (income and payments), notably between 1985 and 1992 (growing from 1 to 4 per cent of GDP).[4] Throughout the period there was a surplus on the account but the structure of the account changed from being dominated by private transfers (including migrant remittances) to substantial public sector transfers (especially in terms of income).

Investment income grew steadily from the late 1970s.[5] In 1975 it amounted to Pta 77 billion (1 per cent of GDP), in 1985 to Pta 884 billion (3 per cent of GDP) and in 1992 to Pta 2,539 billion (4 per cent of GDP). Throughout this period there was a deficit on the account, growing more pronounced in the late 1980s. This reflected the imbalance between inward and outward foreign investment (Banco de España 1976 and 1993).

Payments under the heading of technical assistance and royalties reflected the technological dependency of Spain. These payments increased from Pta 17 billion in 1975, to Pta 102 billion in 1985, to Pta 358 billion in 1992. As with investment income, throughout the period there was a deficit on the account (Banco de España 1976 and 1993).

Capital flows and foreign investment

Total international private sector investment (foreign purchases and disinvestment plus Spanish purchases and disinvestment abroad) increased from Pta 90 billion (1 per cent of GDP) in 1975 to Pta 836 billion in 1985 (3 per cent of GDP) and thence soared to Pta 8,963 billion (15 per cent of GDP) in 1992 (see Figure 2).

The attraction of Spain as a destination for long-term capital was based on expectations about the profitability of fixed investments, on relatively low labour costs, an expanding domestic market and membership of the EC. Short-term capital was attracted more by interest rate differentials and expectations concerning exchange rate variations, with the currency being underpinned by the floor of the ERM. Neither of these two sets of conditions was likely to be sustained for very long;

hence capital flows were intrinsically unstable, especially portfolio investment.

Foreign investment enhanced total investment in Spain and enabled the Spanish economy in the late 1980s to sustain growth above that of other OECD countries by offsetting the balance of payments deficit (Banco Bilbao Vizcaya 1993a). Between 1987 and 1990 (inclusive) the net inflow of foreign long-term capital was greater than the deficit on the current account. Foreign exchange reserves rose from $5.9 billion in 1975 to $13.3 billion in 1985, soaring to $66 billion in 1991 before falling back to $45 billion in April 1994.

The two outstanding features of private sector investment flows were the escalation of investment after 1986 and the imbalance between foreign investment in Spain and Spanish investment abroad. In 1986 the value of foreign purchases was roughly half that of all foreign purchases between 1970 and 1985 (inclusive). After 1987 foreign purchases continued to grow strongly until in 1991 their value was equal to all the income from services on the current account. Similarly, in terms of net foreign investment (purchases less disinvestment), that accumulated between 1986 and 1992 (inclusive) was four and a half times larger than that accumulated between 1970 and 1985 (inclusive). A similar pattern of growth was followed by Spanish investment abroad, although there was only a one-third increase in Spanish purchases abroad in 1986 and there was a second sharp rise in purchases at the turn of the decade. The imbalance between foreign investment and Spanish investment abroad over the period 1975–92 was illustrated by the fact that net foreign investment was almost six times larger than Spanish net investment abroad.

Apart from changes in magnitude, the other important feature of foreign investment was its changing composition. Growth in foreign investment purchases after 1985 was accounted for by an explosion in portfolio investment and strong growth in direct investment (see Table 2). Until 1985 direct investment was the dominant element, but from 1986 onwards portfolio investment mushroomed to become the largest element of purchases, accounting for almost 70 per cent of the total in 1992. In contrast, property investment remained relatively small and fell away at the end of the 1980s. A somewhat similar evolution was followed by Spanish purchases, although portfolio investment was restrained by regulations which were not fully removed until 1992 and property investment was very small.

Foreign direct investment was the most visible element of foreign penetration of the Spanish economy. From 0.4 per cent of GDP in 1975, foreign direct investment (purchases) increased to 0.7 per cent in 1985

Table 2 Foreign inward investment (purchases) in Spain, 1975–92

Year	*Direct*	*Portfolio*	*Real estate*	*Other*	*Total*
1975	23	7	16	11	57
1980	89	7	43	33	172
1985	194	120	163	53	530
1986	321	507	195	111	1134
1987	444	1483	228	70	2225
1988	691	1211	275	71	2248
1989	806	1774	311	102	2993
1990	1257	1636	259	161	3313
1991	1212	2500	169	75	3956
1992	1053	2716	129	36	3934

Source: Antonio Alonso 1988; *El País* 1993
Note: Figures in Pta billion and refer to long term private capital transactions

and then leaped to 2.5 per cent of GDP in 1990. However, only a proportion of this direct investment was in new production facilities. Frequently, such investment was made to secure distribution channels and markets through the acquisition of Spanish companies.

The geographical origin of foreign direct investment became increasingly focused on the European Community. During the period 1980–85 52 per cent of investment arose in the EC, and this increased to 75 per cent in the period 1986–90 (Banco Bilbao Vizcaya 1993a). In 1992 over 85 per cent of foreign direct investment arose in the EC (*El País* 1994). Similarly, Spanish foreign direct investment focused on the EC (especially Portugal), rising from a little over one-third in 1985 to almost two-thirds in 1992.

External debt

In dollar terms and at current values external debt grew from $8.5 billion in 1975 to $80 billion in 1992 (*El País* 1994). About half the debt in 1992 related to private companies (notable amongst which were the electricity utilities). Increases in external debt reflected the lack of adequate funds in Spain to meet the demands of private and public sector expenditure (for example, as the state sought to meet its social services obligations and all levels of administration sought to finance investment in the late 1980s and early 1990s). Higher levels of borrowing on the international markets were facilitated by the improved international risk rating of the Spanish government and Spanish companies. Higher external debt meant growing debt servicing costs, costs that were sensitive to foreign exchange movements as well as to international interest rates.

Multinationals

Another dimension of integration into the world economy was seen in the growth of foreign-owned multinational business in Spain, visible evidence of the influx of foreign direct investment. In 1975 Seat cars, Pegaso commercial vehicles and Cruz Campo beer were emblems of Spanish-owned manufacturing. By 1992 all of these were owned by European multinationals. Foreign companies were particularly prominent in exports. Nine of the leading ten exporters in 1992 were foreign multinationals. In the tourism industry, foreign inbound mass tourism was controlled from its inception in the late 1950s by a small number of foreign tour operators.

Foreign capital spread throughout the economy to dominate key areas, especially those characterized by a high proportion of exports. In the late 1980s the title of Francisco Jurdao's book 'Spain on Sale' (Jurdao Arrones 1979) could have been applied to almost the entire economy. This represented a significant transfer of control to foreign-owned (especially European) multinational companies and a reorganization of trade such that an increasing proportion occurred within multinational company networks.

In the late 1970s and early 1980s foreign direct investment went predominantly into manufacturing, but from 1986 onwards an increasing proportion of investment went into services, notably into financial services and insurance. The explanation for this shift lay primarily in the liberalization of these sectors and an adjustment in investment flows to reflect the sectoral structure of OECD economies. Investment in services was also attractive in terms of high profitability, market expansion, national market segmentation and the need for close product–client relations, and the link between foreign investment in manufacturing and that in services (Ortega 1993). By the early 1990s the evidence of foreign penetration was clearly visible in the house, on the high street and on the roads.

In contrast to the enormous increase of foreign multinationals in the Spanish economy, there were relatively few examples of Spanish multinationals. Although outward foreign direct investment gathered pace at the end of the 1980s, it was stifled by recession. Investment in distribution facilities (especially in Belgium and Holland) was more common than in production plants. Manufacturing investment was concentrated in labour-intensive activities, especially textiles and shoes, and geographically in the low-labour-cost countries of Portugal and Morocco. The attraction of these countries lay in their geographical proximity, lower labour costs and, in the case of Portugal, a similar business culture. The modest presence of Spanish direct investment outside of Spain was also a characteristic of services, with a few exceptions led notably by the mixed public/private companies Argentaria, Endesa, Iberia, Repsol and especially Telefónica, as well as private companies such as some of the larger banks and hotel groups. In general outward foreign direct investment in services was concentrated in the EC (especially Portugal), followed by Latin America.

The arguments relating to foreign investment are well documented. On the one hand foreign inward investment brought jobs, increased local income, backward and forward linkage effects, the introduction of new technologies and management practices, and access to foreign markets. On the other hand it brought the risks of a 'branch plant economy', the repatriation of profits (Shepherd *et al.* 1985) and the broader concern surrounding the loss of control over decisions (Levitt 1970). Spanish investment abroad raised the spectre of 'exporting' jobs and 'social dumping'.

The long-term problem for Spain was that it lacked major multinational companies headquartered there. (In 1992 there were only four Spanish companies in the *Financial Times* top 100 European companies by market capitalization (*Financial Times* 1994). This may be a significant factor for economic development, since it has been argued that it is at headquarters locations that a complex of high value added activities develop, including marketing, finance, legal, research and engineering activities (Hoggart 1991). In addition, management policy is formed at the home base and is thus strongly influenced by the culture of that base (Porter 1990).

Strategically, the imbalance in foreign investment flows left the country particularly vulnerable to shifts in foreign direct investment patterns. In the early 1990s the volume of foreign disinvestment increased either as part of company policy or as a result of company failures. In some cases companies appeared to be shifting production to lower labour cost regions (for example Colgate Palmolive moving to Portugal, moves by Grundig and Philips away from Barcelona and investment by VW in Eastern Europe). With the completion of the single market, foreign investment strategy was shifting to the rationalization of activities to serve the European, as opposed to the national, market (for example, Gillette closed its plant in Seville). Furthermore, competition for mobile investment was developing in eastern Europe and around the Mediterranean basin, while growth in the Pacific rim of eastern Asia and other 'emerging markets' was exerting an increasingly powerful attraction.

Competitiveness

According to the World Economic Forum (WEF), Spain was one of the least competitive countries in the OECD in 1993, as measured by a series of mainly structural characteristics including those showing a waste of human resources (relatively small numbers in employment), an inadequate infrastructure and technological dependency (World Economic Forum, 1993). Between 1975 and 1992 competitiveness was undermined by the continued protection of traditional industry and institutions, and eroded by rising costs of production (notably labour costs), high rates of inflation, and from the mid-1980s by a high exchange rate. Moreover, investment in research and development remained low (0.7 per cent of GDP in Spain in the late 1980s compared to around 2.5 per cent in the four leading EC countries, the USA and Japan).

In 1975 the economy offered a paradigm example of economic development within a protectionist system. Most sectors were characterized by a multitude of small, family-run businesses. Elsewhere there were powerful monopolies, often controlled by the state through its main holding companies, the Instituto Nacional de Industria, Instituto Nacional de Hidrocarburos and Dirección General del Patrimonio del Estado. Markets were distorted by state regulations and there was a singular concentration on the domestic market, reflecting a business mentality of economic nationalism ('vía nacionalista del capitalismo español', Espina 1992: 213). Stemming from these structural characteristics there was widespread inefficiency, weak management and low productivity.

Oil price rises in the 1970s shook the foundations of traditional industry, with its reliance on cheap energy. Changes in the structure of costs and in demand, together with the rise of the NICs, removed the competitive advantage that Spain had enjoyed in these sectors (Nadal, Carreras and Sudria 1987). In the future, competitive advantage based on low labour costs and low value added products and services would continuously be undermined by competition from NICs; hence the only strategy was to shift the economy towards competitiveness based on new technologies and higher value added activities. This demanded not only changes in the fabric of the economy but a revolution in business psychology matched by an equal leap in industrial policy.

The government response was slower than in many other countries, a result of more pressing political problems and bolstered by continued protection. On the industrial front, when a response came it was principally to promote industrial reconversion (*reconversión industrial*), a term adopted to describe the wide-ranging process of government-sponsored industrial restructuring in Spain in the 1980s (Salmon 1991). Reconversion strategy was designed to establish an industrial base capable of meeting international competition. In practice it amounted to cushioning traditional industries from the full impact of the industrial crisis (including the nationalization of ailing companies such as Seat in 1980), diverting attention away from politically more difficult structural change and delaying the process of international specialization which was taking shape in the world economy.

During the 1980s industrial policy shifted away from protectionism to address the problems of Spain's lack of competitiveness (by emphasizing technology, design, marketing, etc.). Orthodox economic policies such as privatization were adopted. But industrial policy failed to tackle key issues relating to the business environment, including the flexibility of factor markets. Flexibility came to be seen as an important contributory factor both to overall efficiency in the economy and to the ability to exploit competitive advantage (Porter 1990). Where factor markets were subject to international legislation, as in the capital markets, liberalization was achieved. But where the markets were bound by domestic legislation there was much less progress. For example, in the land market new legislation still had not been approved by mid-1994 (*Leyes de Arrendamientos Urbanos* and *Arrendamientos Rústicos*). Most significantly, the PSOE government only confronted the root causes of labour market rigidities with new labour market legislation in 1994 (rigidities that contributed to a combination of wages rising ahead of inflation in a labour market characterized by staggeringly high unemployment).

Heightened awareness of international competition in the early 1990s focused attention on the issue of competitiveness, precipitating a stream of literature (Albi 1992; Segura 1992; *Economía Industrial* 1993a and b; *Papeles de Economía Española* 1993). In general this reiterated the structural weaknesses of the Spanish economy, was critical of previous government industrial policy and preached the orthodoxy of improving human resources, extending liberalization and increasing flexibility in the economy.

By 1994 some progress had been made in restoring competitiveness, notably through a lower exchange rate, new labour market measures and more slowly rising labour costs. But in reality it was perhaps too much to expect that the fabric of the political economy could be completely transformed in the space of only two decades (largely under one political party) and that a country lagging behind in economic development could draw level with the most competitive economies in a dynamic economic environment.

CONCLUSION

During the period 1975–94 the Spanish economy became more fully integrated into the world economy and especially into the European Union. This entailed a new pattern of external relations defined by increased trade, substantial capital flows, extensive penetration by multinational companies, membership of international organizations and by a wealth of cultural contacts. In themselves these were changes that were occurring elsewhere in Europe and around the world. What distinguished Spain among the OECD countries was the speed and the magnitude of adjustments, which were indicative of the pace of economic change elsewhere in the world made possible by mobile capital, the transfer of technologies and information technology.

The external projection of Spain, however, remained small in terms of exports, outward foreign investment and Spanish-owned multinationals. In part this reflected its small size, less than 2 per cent that of the world economy and less than 1 per cent of world population.

Integration was promoted by more liberal trade and investment policies, frequently the result of external pressure and associated with membership of the EC. The most dramatic changes were felt in the capital markets. Elsewhere (notably in services) liberalization was slowed by various forms of continued protection. Reforms to the Common Agricultural Policy and implementation of the agreements reached under the Uruguay Round of GATT imply further integration, especially in agriculture and services.

Trade in goods and services grew, although in relation to GDP they remained relatively modest. From the mid-1980s until 1993 exporters were hindered by a strong peseta, but the weak export performance of Spanish companies was also a reflection of the atomistic structure of many sectors of the economy and a traditional predilection towards supplying the domestic market. Increased competition in the domestic market in future will necessitate a greater export effort supported by foreign policy and diplomacy.

Increased capital flows were the main evidence in the balance of payments of greater integration. On the one hand they contributed to the modernization of the economy. On the other hand greater reliance on external funding exposed the economy to shifts in international investment patterns, and to international interest rate and foreign exchange rate movements. Speculative shifts in capital markets could overturn national economic policy even where that policy had international government support.

Foreign capital spread throughout the economy, incorporating

Spanish business into the corporate space of foreign-owned multinationals. In the process, the locus of decision making shifted away from Spain to the home bases of these companies. A particular weakness was the paucity of MNCs headquartered in Spain. Future specialization in the economy would be less the outcome of government policy and more the result of strategic decisions made by foreign multinationals. Hence, the economy was left vulnerable to shifts in foreign direct investment, which in the mid-1990s had a different set of international horizons to those existing a decade earlier. Outside of Europe, Spanish foreign direct investment targeted Latin America, a high-growth region in the early 1990s but also one of higher economic and political risk. Investment was notably weak in North America and in south and south-east Asia.

Spanish economic policy required some solution to the related problems of balancing external pressures with domestic demands, supporting greater liberalization without sacrificing the economic base of the country, and strengthening national competitive advantage. The strategy adopted from the mid-1980s was to promote an economic environment conducive to private-sector investment, innovation, design and development, while negotiating with Brussels for approval of continued government support of uncompetitive industry, higher levels of structural funding to promote development, and more generally for Community policies that favoured Spain and provided some safeguards concerning the relationships between Spain and Latin America. Integration with compensation was the key policy equation of the new European environment.

The high rate of growth achieved by Spain in the second half of the 1980s suggests that it was successful in positioning itself within the European Community, but the nature of the EC was changing. The challenge for Spain will be to consolidate its position in the evolving European Union, to accommodate any further eastward opening of the EU and to respond to the changing position of the EU in the world economy. In this, foreign policy will have a significant role alongside the business community, which will need to cultivate and exploit competitive advantages as they arise.

At the root of the issues raised by integration were the questions of national identity, cultural integrity and sovereignty: questions brought sharply into focus by recession in Western Europe and the debate over the terms of the Maastricht Treaty and the future political form of Europe. An increasing number of subjects were being regulated by supranational administrative organizations, and strategic decisions were being made by these and by foreign multinational companies.

Securing national advantage in this more integrated world demanded more careful management of external relations, shifting the emphasis from the politics of protection to the politics of persuasion. Perhaps the outstanding question for the rest of the 1990s was whether the commitment to internationalism would be maintained: in Spain, in Europe and elsewhere in the world?

NOTES

1 Throughout the chapter a billion is used to refer to 1,000 million.
2 In the section on trade and capital transactions, GDP ratios were calculated using the GDP at market prices and current values published in Banco Bilbao Vizcaya, 1993b, p. 172.
3 Services cover freight charges and insurance (*fletes y seguros*), other transport, tourism and travel and other services.
4 Transfer payments embrace certain government transactions (e.g. foreign aid, budget contribution to and from the EC, spending on the armed forces abroad) and migrant remittances.
5 Investment income (*rentas de inversión*): income from investments (interest, profits and dividends), which arise when residents of one country own income earning assets in another country.

6 Spain in the European Community

Alfred Tovias

The purpose of this chapter is to survey the record of Spain since it joined the EC in 1986, focusing only on those economic aspects that have not been dealt with in the preceding chapter. Political issues are dealt with in the following chapter. After reviewing and commenting on the terms of accession, this chapter will analyse some direct effects such as the evolution of Spanish trade patterns in the wake of accession. Dynamic effects such as the impact on investment flows and economic growth patterns will then be dealt with. Finally, particular attention will be devoted to the Spanish input in particular areas of EC decision-making in the domain of the EC's external relations. The main conclusion is that entry to the EC has facilitated the modernization of Spain's economy, but has not altered the employment situation nor been instrumental in the reform of Spanish labour markets.

THE ACCESSION TREATY: AIMS, CONTENTS AND TIMETABLE

The Treaty providing for the accession of Spain into the European Community was signed on 12 June 1985, after long negotiations which began in 1979. In fact what had to be negotiated was not reaching common positions between the parties but how and over what period Spain would adjust to the *acquis communautaire* and participate in the EC's budget and in EC institutions. By the mid-1980s the *acquis communautaire* included: (1) the customs union; (2) the Common Agricultural Policy (CAP); (3) a unique system for purchase taxes (i.e. VAT); and (4) external trade agreements. At that time neither European Political Cooperation nor any enabling legislation relating to the 1985 Programme for the Completion of the EC's Internal Market (better known as 'EC-92') were part of the *acquis*. All this would be incorporated later on in the Single European Act agreed upon in 1986 by the enlarged EC, including Spain, and ratified in July 1987. Neither was the European Monetary System part of the *acquis*, so Spain was not obliged to adhere to the Exchange Rate Mechanism (ERM) upon entry.

As witnessed by the length of the three volumes containing the official text of the treaty (Council of the European Communities, *Instruments concerning the Accession of the Kingdom of Spain and the Portuguese Republic to the European Communities*, Vols I–III), 'Operation Enlargement to Spain and Portugal' was rather complex. To begin with, the actual accession in 1986 did not take place in a vacuum. First, the Socialist government took some unilateral measures in advance to prepare the country for entry. Early on it developed policies to increase somewhat the level of flexibility of the economy and it proceeded with the UCD policies of *reconversión industrial*, launched in 1979–80 to restructure ailing industries (Yannopoulos 1989: 52). Among other measures these policies favoured temporary and part-time contracts. Second, upon entry, Spain adopted the VAT system of taxation, not a negligible step given that the old system of Internal Compensatory Taxes and Fiscal Tax Reduction for Exports (*Impuesto de Compensación de Gravámenes Interiores* and *Desgravación Fiscal de Exportaciones*) was indirectly protecting import-competing goods and subsidizing exports. The regular VAT rate was set at 12 per cent, low by EC standards; but it was raised in 1993 to 15 per cent as an outcome of fiscal harmonization plans linked to the completion of the Internal Market. Third, from 1981 Spain received EC aid (through the European Investment Bank) specifically aimed at helping it to adjust to the EC, for example for the restructuring of the fishing fleet. Fourth, there were already important institutional links between Spain and the Community.

To be schematic, the most relevant parametric changes that accompanied Spain's entry into the Community are listed below:

Intra-EC trade liberalization: agricultural products

1 Spain had to obtain free access to the EC for its agricultural products by 1996. For Spain's most competitive products (such as fruit and vegetables) there was a standstill until 1990 followed by six years of transition during which important safeguard arrangements had to operate. This relatively unfavourable outcome of the negotiations for Spain was due to strong pressure applied by France in order to preserve the interests both of the Languedoc farmers and of the Maghreb's agriculture. *De facto*, but for a dozen sensitive products, most of the safeguards were eliminated by 1993.

2 The EC was to obtain free access to the Spanish agricultural markets for most products by 1996 and for a minority of products, such as beef and veal, by 1993. In fact, Spain accepted bringing forward the elimination of all tariffs by that year. Spanish import quotas on dairy products and meat disappeared by 1990.
3 Spain would benefit progressively from all the advantages of the CAP (e.g. it would obtain export refunds, receive guaranteed prices, and so on) until its full integration in 1996. It would also have to respect such common disciplines as production restraints and quality requirements, apply the principle of Community preference and common agricultural prices and be subject to common-responsibility levies (i.e. taxes applied on surplus production). The Canary Islands and Ceuta and Melilla remained outside the CAP. Later on, however, in 1991, it was decided that the CAP would cover the Canary Islands as well.
4 Spain has had to align its agricultural prices with those of the CAP. In the case of fruit and vegetables, this was scheduled to take place only in 1996.
5 Portugal and Spain have had to liberalize progressively their mutual trade in agricultural products, and did actually achieve free trade by 1990.
6 Spain was not yet a member of the EC when the Common Fisheries Policy (CFP) was agreed on in 1983. In the final agreement, trade between Spain and the EC was subject to a seven-year transition period for most fish products, except for a number of sensitive species, for which the transition period was to end in 1996. Only after that date would Spaniards be able to fish in the Irish Box and have all quotas eliminated regulating the number of boats allowed to fish in EC waters. Until then the number would be limited to 300, although only half of them could fish simultaneously. This transition period was later brought forward to 1995 as a result of enlargement negotiations between the EU and northern European countries.
7 Special regimes were provided for several products such as wine and olive oil. For olive oil there was a ten-year transition period, including an initial standstill of five years. Spain, the largest world consumer, did not allow the import of olive oil during the transition period.

Intra-EC trade liberalization: industrial products

1 Spain and the EC had to progressively increase their margins of preference on mutual industrial trade to 100 per cent, attaining a level of free trade in industrial goods by 1 January 1993. It should be noted that the transition period was longer than the one agreed upon

between the UK and the Community in the early 1970s (i.e. five years). But Spain wanted ten years, as for fruit and vegetables, so as to maintain a symmetry between industry and agriculture. In fact, and in view of the tremendous Spanish trade deficit with the EC since 1986, the Community decided in early 1989 to grant duty-free access into the EC to Spanish industrial exports from 1 July 1989, thus re-establishing some equilibrium, if not symmetry.

2 The Community suppressed all surveillance measures concerning Spain's textile exports to EC countries by 1990.
3 Portugal and Spain progressively liberalized their mutual trade in industrial products, achieving free trade by 1990.
4 The Spanish iron and steel industries would be restructured according to European Coal and Steel Community (ECSC) guidelines, and in the case of steel not more than 18 millions tons would be produced per year. The EC also allowed for aid to these industries in line with EC practices. Spain also had to phase out by 1990 its industrial subsidies and align its steel prices for products covered by the ECSC treaty.
5 Spain's state monopolies in petroleum products and tobacco had six years to adapt to EC rules.
6 Spain had to abolish quantitative restrictions on EC-originating imports of cars by 1988. Similar provisions were contemplated for colour TV sets, textiles, some chemical products and arms.

Labour movements

Freedom of movement of Spanish workers was scheduled to take place only from 1 January 1993, except for Luxemburg where the date was set for 1996.

EC trade policy

1 Spain had to adopt its customs duties gradually to the level of the EC's Common Customs Tariff (CCT), and adopt it completely by 1 January 1993 (with the exception of some products for which the deadline was advanced by several years). The Canary Islands, Ceuta and Melilla were excluded from the customs union. However, this changed in 1991 when it was decided that the Canary Islands would be part of the EC's customs union.
2 Spain had to obtain tariff-free access for its industrial exports and preferential status for its agricultural exports in the EFTA and Israeli markets by 1993. In fact, EFTA decided to grant Spanish industrial exports duty-free access from 1 July 1989, following a similar

decision made by the EC. Moreover, Cyprus, Malta and Turkey had to give Spain preferences on its exports.

3 By 1993 all Mediterranean non-members (except for Albania and Libya) and ACP countries had to enjoy free access into the Spanish industrial markets, without any limitations on their exports. Third World countries benefiting from the EC's scheme of the Generalized System of Preferences (GSP) had to obtain tariff-free treatment in these markets, but with limitations. The alignment of tariffs on the EC's preferential rate, which in most cases was zero, was to be made progressively, from 1 March 1986 to 1 January 1993 – for manufactured goods and fish products – and to 1 January 1996 for agricultural exports.
4 Agricultural exports from ACP countries had to obtain completely free access into Spanish markets by the end of the transition period in 1993. Moreover Spain's agricultural imports originating in Mediterranean countries had to benefit from partial tariff preferences, on a much wider scale than under the GSP scheme.
5 Spain had to adopt the EC textile agreements as well as agreements dealing with manioc, sheep and lamb's meat, with several developing countries. More generally Spain had to eliminate all import quotas on non-members' exports by 1993 and integrate the Community's regime. In practice, many quantitative restrictions will be maintained until 1996.
6 Upon expiry, fishing agreements between Spain and third countries had to be replaced by Community agreements with these countries.
7 As an outcome of pressure exerted by Mediterranean non-member countries, alarmed by the prospect of trade diversion in favour of Spain for agricultural products, the EC added new protocols to the agreements concluded with non-members in the mid-1970s. As in the case of Spain, these new protocols provide for the progressive elimination of customs duties on traditional quantities of fruits and vegetables exported to the EC by these third Mediterranean countries. As a quid pro quo, the Canary Islands and Ceuta and Melilla were accorded the same treatment received by other Mediterranean countries under these new additional protocols. These therefore must be seen as part of 'Operation Enlargement'.

Spain's share in EC institutions

Two out of the thirteen members of the Commission, sixty out of the 518 MEPs and one of the thirteen judges at the EC's Court of Justice had to come from Spain, which was given eight votes out of fifty-four in the Council of Ministers. On average the weight of Spain in EC institutions was 11 per cent, which is not surprising given that in 1986 its share in the Community's GDP was about 6.5 per cent and in population 12 per cent. No EC institution was to be established on Spanish soil. However, later on it was decided that the European Office of Trade Marks and Patents would be located in Madrid.

THE IMPACT OF ACCESSION ON SPAIN

The impact on the trade balance and trade patterns

Spain's trade balance with the EC deteriorated sharply from early 1987, as imports increased by 31.6 per cent while exports rose by only 6.8 per cent. Globally, there was a 12.5 per cent increase in the trade deficit, with 1986 exports covering only 77.7 per cent of imports, as compared with 80.9 per cent in 1985. This trend continued throughout 1987, with imports from the Community increasing by 33.9 per cent in that year alone while exports increased by only 16.8 per cent. Between 1985 and 1987 the trade deficit with the Community increased four-fold.[1] The same pattern repeated itself afterwards. This was a combined outcome of: (1) scaling down to zero the Spanish tariff rate applied on EC- and EFTA-originating imports, which was for most products only 25 per cent below the regular tariff rate, which on average was 14 per cent at the time of entry;[2] (2) scaling down the regular tariff rate on non-EC originating imports to conform with a CCT hovering around 4 per cent to 5 per cent; and (3) scaling down to zero the regular Spanish tariff on imports from Portugal and from groups of third countries 'preferred' by the EC, such as ACP, Mediterranean Non-Member Countries or GSP countries. Since overall Spanish protection remained very high by OECD standards, the impact of eliminating tariffs towards selected groups of countries was tremendous.[3]

Not surprisingly, the rate of export growth was lower since enlargement only slightly improved access to EC and EFTA markets: Spain already enjoyed a 60 per cent reduction in the usual EC and EFTA countries tariff rate on industrial imports (except for ECSC products, most textiles and footwear), which was very low already after implementation of the Tokyo Round (i.e. by the end of 1985 the tariff rate on Spanish industrial exports must have been on average about 2 per cent!). The import/GNP ratio rose sharply from 11.6 per cent for the period 1981–85 to 16.2 per cent for the years 1988–89, whereas the export/GNP ratio did not budge. The import coverage declined over the same periods from 110.1 per cent to 78.6 per cent, i.e. from surplus to deficit. The trade deficit would have been larger had it not been for the fact that the price of imported oil dropped in relation to the early 1980s. The EC's import penetration increased substantially from representing 33.4 per cent of total imports in 1984 to a staggering 61.4 per cent three years later and 60.7 per cent in 1992. Germany replaced the United States as Spain's first supplier. Much of the shift may be due to the artificial preference given by Spain to other EC member states, but it was also due to the contemporary drop in the price of crude oil. In primary goods the shift was tremendous. This has been the case particularly for agricultural imports of continental products, which before 1986 originated partly from the US or Latin America and which subsequently were replaced by more expensive French produce. Recent research by Plummer (1991) confirms that negative net trade diversion obtains in the Spanish market ($163 million), about 1 per cent of total trade, mainly in cereals and tobacco, affecting mainly the USA and Thailand. There is also some net trade diversion in iron and steel ($19 million) affecting mainly developing countries. Of course not all was trade diversion. Spain, for instance, had to phase out quotas on highly subsidized beef and dairy imports originating in the EC within a period of four years to 1990, which led to trade creation. All in all, imports of agricultural products from the EC grew by 245 per cent between 1984–85 and 1988.

Spanish exports were diverted to the EC, with the share in total exports passing from 52.3 per cent in 1985 to 63.8 per cent in 1987 and 71.2 per cent in 1992. Here the shift was more marked in industrial exports, pointing probably to a substantial increase in what is called intra-industry trade, which amounted to 43 per cent of the trade flows between Spain and the EC in 1985, a lower proportion than in the rest of the EC, but increasing to 52 per cent in 1987 (Viñals *et al.* 1990: 210). Turning to Spanish agricultural exports, many authors (e.g. Plummer 1991) predict extensive trade diversion regarding agricultural imports of the EC Ten in favour of Spain and Portugal after the transition period in the late 1990s. But, as some have said, for the moment it is the EC which has entered Spain and not the other way round! One reason exports to the EC did not grow initially at the same rate as imports from the Community is that there were still important barriers imposed by the EC in sensitive sectors such as agriculture, in particular until 1990, leaving the possibility of a radical change in the future. Exports to the EC (calculated in ECUs) increased substantially in 1991 (by 19.6 per cent) and 1992 (by 3.9 per cent). In general the slowdown in exports after entry into the EC was mainly related to booming domestic market conditions and also an actual decrease in

Spain's industrial exports to non-EC countries.[4] Thus, other reasons why exports did not grow might be the shift from cascade taxes to VAT and the fact that wages grew much quicker than labour productivity, and that the labour markets are rigid, undoing much of the relative advantage that Spanish industry is supposed to have vis-à-vis the EC.

The impact on Spanish inward and outward investment

Between entry and 1991 it is estimated that about 80 billion dollars entered Spain, half of it in the form of foreign direct investment, as a combined outcome of the enlargement and of the perspective opened in 1985 of completion of the EC internal market of 340 million people. Note that for the foreign investor, enlargement did not only mean easier access to EC, EFTA and Portuguese markets than before, but also reduced political risks. As a result, the presence of multinationals among Spain's largest industrial producers and exporters is overwhelming, sometimes creating resentment, particularly in times of recession (as was the case in 1992–93). Inward tariff-jumping investment which had entered Spain to produce there for local consumption was not justified any more. Foreign investment (FI) originated mainly, but not only, from other EC countries. The EC's share in total FI reached 66.7 per cent in 1991, mostly from the Netherlands, France and the UK. American and Japanese firms also joined the fray, less so Swiss multinationals, which were already well established in Spain. As a result, Spain found it quite easy to modernize its economy by importing massively both embodied and disembodied technology through FI. It is estimated that more than a third of manufacturing investment in those five years came from abroad. The main sectors benefiting from this inflow were chemicals, foodstuffs, paper products and motor vehicles. More than half the investment in electrical and electronic equipment stemmed from FI and these are strong-demand sectors. Of course the import drive extended to consumer goods as well, as a direct result of the double trade liberalization provided for in the Accession Treaty regarding both imports from other EC countries as well as from non-members.

In the late 1980s, FI shifted its attention towards real estate and services, particularly the financial sector, with more speculative, short-term aims, the main one being to reap high short-term interest rates at a time when the peseta was anchored in the ERM (from June 1989). Of course, later on (from early 1992) when investors discovered that the peseta was overvalued given the persisting gap between Spanish and EC inflation rates, many liquidated their investments (see chapter 5 for further explanation of macro-economic developments). FI began to decline in 1991. However, the shock came in early 1992. It is estimated that FI fell a further 22 per cent in the first eight months of 1992 in relation to the same period one year before. Leaving Spain was quite easy since capital controls to be abolished under the Internal Market programme had been lifted by February 1992, ahead of schedule. This put pressure on the peseta, but the Socialist government found it imperative to defend the exchange rate no matter what until September 1992, mainly for political reasons (i.e. to display Europeanism). Holding out against speculative assaults on the peseta was relatively easy given the enormous amounts of reserves amassed by the Bank of Spain during the five years preceding the elimination of exchange controls.

The shift away from manufacturing investment since 1989 may have something to do with the end of the cold war and the emergence of former Comecon countries (including East Germany) as a new pole of attraction for industrial investment, something reinforced by the fact that, after the unions clashed with the Socialist government at the end of 1988, wages began rising at a rapid rate, particularly, but not only, in the service sector. Of course the overvaluation of the peseta hurt industrial exports as well.

Given the tremendous growth in Spanish absorption (both consumption and domestic investment) during the five golden years, it is not surprising that Spanish investment overseas, which was hailed as a new development in the late 1970s and early 1980s, did not make much progress but for the important exception of Portugal. Free trade between the two neighbouring countries led many Spanish firms producing labour-intensive goods to locate in Portugal shortly after accession for export back to Spain. In 1992 Spain invested $640 million in Portugal, the second most important destination country after the Netherlands (12 per cent of all Spanish FI). More recently Spanish investment in Morocco has taken off, jumping from $40 million in 1992 to $125 million in 1993 (first nine months).

The impact on Spanish policy in the EC

The central government's room for manoeuvring was reduced by Spain entering the EC (e.g. in the realm of trade policy). Spain has not been over-enthusiastic about further liberalization of imports from non-EC countries. Obviously Spain has been and seems more inclined toward increasing the support of Mediterranean agriculture within the EC than toward reducing the protection offered to continental products (e.g. grain, meat). This has been accomplished in a roundabout way, for example by securing an increase in structural expenditures from the EC for regions cultivating fruit and vegetables, under the code word 'cohesion'. Shortly after Spain joined the EC, it adopted the view, shared by the Commission itself, that creating an internal market would only increase the economic gap between poor and rich members, and that this tendency should be offset by measures promoting more 'cohesion' within the Community. This sentiment was echoed by Prime Minister González, when he said that he favoured the creation of a social, economic and cultural space in Europe, and not merely the creation of an internal market.[5] Spain, he continued, was already making a tremendous contribution toward 'cohesion' in opening its economy to other EC members by eliminating tariffs and thereby increasing their rate of growth. But the elimination of additional trade barriers on the imports of other EC members without sufficient help to facilitate adjustment would put the Spanish economy in an untenable position.

Thus Spain, backed by Greece, Portugal and Ireland (and sometimes even by Italy), pressed the northern members of the Community to approve new aid to southern members as a reward for the latter's acceptance of new candidates for EC membership (such as EFTA countries) or for association (such as Eastern Europe). Under Spanish pressure, the amount allocated to the three structural funds was doubled in 1988 in real terms from 7 billion ECU to 14 billion ECU (calculated at 1988 prices), representing about 27 per cent of EC expenditure and 0.3 per cent of the EC's GDP. Again at Maastricht (1991), it was agreed that not only a new 'Cohesion Fund' would be created, but that the structural funds would be doubled again over a period of five years to 1997.[6] The recent Cohesion Fund benefits states (not regions) with a per capita income below 90 per cent of the EC average, thus including Spain in the coming years. Total funds available will reach $15.5 billion[7] for the four countries concerned. Although there is no direct support for specific sectors, funds are flowing to agricultural regions in southern Spain (in particular Andalusia) to improve infrastructure and clean the environment. This could in time facilitate exports (e.g. of tourism services).[8]

Another dimension of EC trade policies likely to be influenced by Spain is the Community's multiple trade discrimination policy toward non-members. Spain has been trying to strengthen this policy rather than push the EC toward multilateralism, for this allows it to exert influence by distributing favours and privileges, especially to its former colonies. For instance, Spain has been behind efforts to differentiate between Latin America and other developing countries not covered by the Lomé Convention. It has also pushed forward the idea of singling out Morocco for special favourable treatment.

In the context of the Uruguay Round negotiations which took place between 1986–93, Spain generally backed France's more protectionist positions regarding agricultural trade liberalization (*Boletín Económico del ICE* 1993: 3593) and fought fiercely with France for the exclusion of trade in audiovisual products from the new General Agreement on Trade in Services (GATS) agreement (the cultural exception). Spain was strongly supportive of all new regulations to protect trade marks and fight trade in counterfeit products. Together with other EU members, it had the idea of creating a World Trade Organization approved, so as to circumscribe the use of unilateral measures by the USA. However this did not prevent Spain from simultaneously backing the reform of the decision-making mechanisms regarding the EC's trade policy, which will allow the EC more frequently and effectively to use anti-dumping, countervailing and safeguard measures. In other words, on the one hand Spain has favoured strongly any measure limiting arbitrary measures imposed by the United States, but on the other hand it has supported using more frequently the EC's own economic muscle to impose its will on other trade partners.

Regarding overseas development assistance (ODA), if all of Spain's plans to increase bilateral and multilateral ODA do come to fruition, by the mid-1990s Spain should be able to make its voice heard on EC aid policy. However, the record up to 1991, five years after entry into the EC, was not yet impressive, development aid representing by then 0.23 per cent of GDP, much below the OECD average of 0.33 per cent.

The impact on Spanish economic growth and employment

It is difficult to ascertain whether the good economic record of the Spanish economy in the period 1986–92 is due only to its accession to the EC. For instance, the world recession in the wake of the second oil crisis had been replaced by moderate EC growth and low rates of inflation. The price of oil, on which Spain is so dependent, dropped dramatically in 1986. The Spanish record is anyway impressive, in particular when compared to the poor performance until then (e.g. negative growth in 1981). There was an average of 5 per cent annual GDP growth up to 1990, decreasing progressively to a still impressive 3 per cent in 1991, still one percentage point above the EC average. These above EC average rates helped Spain close the gap, especially the income differential gap, between itself and the EC. In 1985 the income differential between Spain and the EC was 29 per cent; by 1991 it had fallen to 20 per cent. The standard of living rose rapidly between 1985 and 1992. The Spanish GDP per capita grew by 27 per cent in real terms in that period. Unemployment came down from a peak of 21.4 per cent in 1985 to 16 per cent in 1990 (but note that this rate was about the same as the one ten years before when the Socialist party came to power, revealing continuing major mismatch problems in the Spanish labour market and a structural lack of jobs). It is worthwhile noting that instead of the short-term increase in unemployment which was expected to result from trade liberalization,[9] there was tremendous job creation. The main reason for that is, of course, that aggregate demand expanded simultaneously (mostly investment and consumption, less so exports; see above). In fact buoyant domestic demand may have masked serious adjustment problems, which were revealed only after 1991.

The financial balance between the EC and Spain

As required in the Accession Treaty, Spain was a 'net recipient' during the first five years of membership and even in 1992. The EC contribution was equivalent to 0.3 per cent of GDP on average after 1986, before reaching 0.7 per cent in 1991 (although this is a smaller share than the corresponding one received by Greece or Portugal). The Spanish contribution to the budget increased after accession to the EC from Pta 110,000 billion in 1986 to 686,000 billion in 1992. Community payments flow basically from the European Regional Development Fund (ERDF) (Pta 210,000 billion in 1992) and the European Agricultural Guidance and Guarantee Fund (EAGGF) – Guarantee section (Pta 356,000 billion) (*Boletín Informativo* 1992).

THE IMPACT OF SPAIN'S MEMBERSHIP ON EC TRADE POLICIES

In 1986, Professor F. Granell, later a Director General at the EC Commission, suggested that integration into the EC implied Spain's comeback as 'a fragment of a superpower', from being a country playing at best a secondary role on the international scene (*El Periódico*, 1 January 1986). Spain's membership of the EC meant that an increasing share of its human and financial resources had to be put at the disposal of the Ministry of Foreign Affairs and other ministries like Agriculture. Indeed, the Spanish embassy in Brussels is now by far the largest Spanish representation abroad, with much more invested in it than in its Washington embassy.

Spanish input into EC decision-making vis-à-vis Latin America has been more in the domain of atmospherics and consciousness-raising than in operational matters (see chapter 9). Taking the generally prolonged EC decision-making process into account, their modest record to date has only shown the Spaniards that they will need much patience in order to change things in relation to a continent which has been only of secondary interest to the EC thus far.

On the other hand, Spanish input into EC decision-making vis-à-vis Mediterranean non-member countries could objectively be more substantial given French and Italian traditional strong interest in the Mediterranean basin (see chapter 10 on Spanish interests in the Maghreb). However, Spanish policy in Brussels regarding Mediterranean non-member countries was rather short-sighted during the initial years of membership. Spain tried to obtain new concessions from the Community that would not be extended to other Mediterranean countries. If that was not possible, Spain objected to any concession that other EC members wished to confer on non-member Mediterranean countries. What was most important to Spain was that its agricultural products continued to receive preferential treatment over and above that received by Mediterranean non-members, maximizing artificial trade diversion in its favour (Swinbank and Ritson 1988). For instance, although it was agreed that, after a transition period, Spain was to receive full access into EC agricultural markets as compensation for its opening of Spanish industrial markets to EC competition, it does not follow that, by this, Spain was trying to maximize trade creation. There is a huge difference between the level of protectionism built into the CAP and the degree to which Spain opened its economy prior to 1986. Average industrial tariffs in Spain were already much lower than the tariff-equivalent of CAP's non-tariff barriers on fruit and vegetables imports by the Ten. Moreover, the Treaty of Accession compelled Spain to adjust to a low average Common External Tariff, and to eliminate tariffs on imports not only from the EC but also from EFTA, ACP and Mediterranean countries. Last, but not least, it had to adopt the EC's GSP scheme. All this implies that, as far as Spanish industrial imports are concerned, there is a lot of potential trade creation, and that any negative trade diversion effects on third countries should be widely spread out. The reverse is not true for Spanish exports of fruit and vegetables, which by and large are not expected to displace exports after the end of the transition period from France and Italy, which would be trade creation, but rather those of Mediterranean non-members (i.e. trade diversion). Moreover, the negative effects will be concentrated on only a few countries: Morocco, Israel and Cyprus.

In fact, even before accession into the EC, Spain aligned itself with those countries striving to maintain or even enlarge the CAP. For the latter was seen, as in France in the early days of the Community, as 'compensating' the customs union with regard to industrial products. By 1990, however, the Spanish public had learned from the press about the negative effects of trade diversion against the United States in cereals. This led to a re-evaluation of the situation. The line taken has been that EC Mediterranean countries should be granted the same protection for fruit and vegetables that northern Europeans receive for the products of interest to them. In other words, the Spanish government operated under the combined assumptions that CAP was a given, and that agricultural protection had to benefit all EC members equally. Alas, efficiency considerations were strangely absent from the whole approach.

The effects of this philosophy may be seen in a nutshell from what happened between 1983 and 1988. At the end of 1983, the first round of negotiations between the Ten and Mediterranean non-members considered the possible effects of the enlargement on the latter. This did not lead to a proposal from the Commission to the Council of Ministers until July 1985, so that a mandate was not given to the Commission until November 1985, or more than two years after the original negotiations – which was, of course, too late for the Ten to reach any agreement with Mediterranean non-members before Spain's entry into the Community. This delay, initiated by Italy with Spain's backing from the outside, succeeded despite the Commission's desire – supported by the UK and the Federal Republic of Germany – to formulate an agreement before 1986. Italy benefited from the delay because it meant that Spain and Portugal would be sitting in the Council to support the Italian policy of minimizing trade concessions to Mediterranean non-members when it came up for a vote. Both Spain and Italy also wanted to reduce the interval between these negotiations and those on renewal of the Second Financial Protocols attached to Cooperation and Free Trade Agreements with Mediterranean countries, which were expected to take place in mid-1986. For, they thought, linking the two events would put the onus on northern EC members, the idea here being that strengthening the financial component of the Global Mediterranean Policy would oblige northern members to shoulder some of the burden involved in compensating Mediterranean non-member countries.

In March 1986 the Commission asked for an additional mandate. This led to a new compromise, proposed by the (Dutch) President of the Council of Ministers on 17 April 1986, which was vetoed by Spain. For, before it would agree to the compromise, Spain wanted to make certain that Canary Island agriculture would be treated at least as well as that of non-member Mediterranean countries. The Spanish veto acted to block the development of the EC Mediterranean Policy until October 1986. In answer to Moroccan charges that Spain's actions were aimed at increasing instability in northern Africa, Spain replied that it did not question the concessions included in the compromise of April 1986, and that it only wanted to ensure that the Canary Islands would not suffer in comparison with third Mediterranean countries; the real aim was to place the Canary Islands somewhere in between the Mediterranean countries and the Iberian Peninsula with regard to EC agricultural markets. In fact, the Spanish veto aimed at obtaining new concessions for Canary Island agriculture. However, the compensation being offered by the EC to satisfy Spain's requests on Canary Island agriculture was not considered enough. Spain wanted further compensation in the form of new fishing rights from France before it would withdraw its veto. And when this was agreed upon, Spanish Foreign Minister Fernández Ordóñez personally told the Moroccan authorities that a compromise had been reached. This opened the way for renewed negotiations with Mediterranean countries at the end of 1986, which resulted in agreements being signed by the parties involved (except for Morocco and Yugoslavia) some months later. But, here too, Spain linked its signing of these agreements to the conclusion of negotiations on the Technical Adaptation Protocol, the agreement outlining Spain's adoption of the Mediterranean Policy Agreements. Thus, there was a simultaneous signature and ratification of the two types of agreements by the European Parliament at the end of 1987 (except for the important cases of Morocco, for which procedures were completed in mid-1988, and Israel, for which the European Parliament did not ratify the protocols until October 1988 for political reasons).

Thus joint action by Italy and Spain did have a substantial impact on the timing of agreements and quite an impact on the contents as well. But what was achieved fell a long way short of Spain's initial intentions in the years preceding the enlargement. At that time, Spain's clear-cut aim was to obtain the phasing out of fruit and vegetable exports of Mediterranean third countries to the Community over a period of ten years, an aim that was totally rejected by the Commission, which planned to maintain the Mediterranean countries' share in EC imports – an idea that was in turn rejected by Spain. The final compromise between the two sides – that only 'traditional exports' would be preserved – meant that Mediterranean countries would have to forget about fostering economic development on the basis of increased agricultural exports to the EC.

Interestingly, Spain's attitude towards EC policies in the Mediterranean has been changing substantially since 1988. Spain's incorporation into the EC brought the Community into closer geographical contact with the Arab countries and Africa. This has had tremendous implications for the EC since the mid-1980s in view of the intention to complete the EC Internal Market, envisioning among other measures the free movement of labour inside Community borders. This new reality has been an element leading many potential migrants from North Africa to penetrate the huge EC labour market through neighbouring Spain. Some of them have stayed in Spain. It is also the perspective of a harmonization or coordination of immigration and visa policies at the EC level, which will be more restrictive than in the past, that has precipitated migration to the EC (see chapter 11 on Spanish participation in decision-making relating to the 'deepening' process leading to the Maastricht Treaty). Potential migrants are tempted to accelerate the decision to migrate before they think it is too late (e.g. Latin Americans into Spain). Pressure would be even higher, should the EC increase further its barriers against labour-intensive imports originating in Mediterranean countries. Spaniards understand now better than before that the best way to counter undesirable ownward migration is to foster economic prosperity in the southern Mediterranean. Under heavy pressure from two Spanish Commissioners in Brussels, at first Abel Matutes and then Manuel Marín, in 1989 the EC launched a Renovated Mediterranean Policy which does not add much in terms of trade concessions (since Spain does not want to hear about that), but implies an important additional financial effort by the EC (by a factor of 2.7 in relation to the financial package approved in the mid-1980s).

CONCLUSION

The Socialist party, which came into power in 1982, supported entry into the EC mainly for political reasons, i.e. in order to consolidate democracy. As it happens, by 1986 when Spain actually entered the EC, the political goal had been replaced by the economic one of using membership to modernize the economy through further trade and financial liberalization. Moreover, the government tried with mixed results to 'import' from abroad macro-economic orthodoxy. This strategy worked while the economic situation in the USA, Japan and the EC was buoyant, but was seriously tested amidst recession in the early 1990s. What is not yet clear is whether modernization has taken place where it counts, i.e. where it can lead to sustained economic growth, for example in industry and agriculture. The new equipment is in place, thanks in part to massive foreign investment, which flowed to Spain largely as an outcome of accession. It is much less clear whether trade and financial liberalization succeeded in shifting resources to more productive uses. Success is only possible if labour markets are sufficiently flexible and if manpower can make optimal use of the equipment. The latter depends largely on the quality of human resources. The upgrading of human capital could not possibly be obtained by EC membership. In that respect, accession was an opportunity, rather than a panacea. On the other hand if firms have enormous severance costs when they have to dismiss employees, the labour market is not fluid. The laws of minimum wage and social security provisions, apart from increasing unemployment, are an obstacle in the use of Spain as a platform for the export of labour-intensive products based on standard technology – the kind of products for which Spain still has a comparative advantage. The long-term problem is that these are mostly weak- and moderate-demand products (such as ships, cars, etc.) (Viñals, *et al.* 1990: 152). Shifting comparative advantage towards strong-demand products would require probably a total overhaul of the educational system (e.g. more emphasis on technical schools) and of the system of incentives for the promotion of research and development activity. Modern industrial (and even agricultural) infrastructure, which has been largely put into place since accession mostly by foreign MNCs, is a necessary but not a sufficient condition.

It is also rather clear that by joining the EC, Spain succeeded for a while in selling an image of being a serious and stable country, inspiring confidence in potential investors at a time of tremendous turmoil in the rest of the Mediterranean area and in Eastern Europe.[10] Moreover, as a member of the Community, Spain received the key backing of other EC countries for the organization of important projects, such as the Olympics or Expo-92, which were instrumental in maintaining aggregate demand at high levels from 1990 until mid-1992, at a time of recession elsewhere in the OECD.

Lastly, from both an economic and a political viewpoint, there is no doubt that, helped by uncontrollable events, Spain entered the EC at the right time, viewed from its perspective. Economically, positive factors were the decrease in world energy prices and a cyclical expansion in major OECD economies. Politically, it was important for the Western world to have Spain in the EC while the cold war lasted. As with the transition to democracy in the mid-1970s, the international context was instrumental in the success of 'Operation Enlargement'. In the much less favourable circumstances of the early 1990s, Spain is firmly anchored in the EC, which, in spite of its countless crises, continues to be the best vehicle for Spain both to consolidate democracy and to modernize its economy through participation in a technologically-advanced economic bloc.

NOTES

1 *Boletín ICE*, no. 2084, 11–17 May 1987; *Boletín Informativo Banco Central*, no. 440, June 1988. All percentages are calculated on the basis of figures in nominal terms (pesetas).
2 The un-weighted tariff rate was still 19.4 per cent in the mid-1970s. (Yannopoulos 1989: 256).
3 The average effective tariff protection rate was 24.7 per cent, about three times as high as in the rest of the EC (Alonso Zaldívar and Castells 1992: 81).
4 Manufacturing exports to non-EC countries decreased by a cumulative annual nominal rate of growth of 8.2 per cent between 1985 and 1988. See Viñals *et al.* 1990: 206.
5 Speech presented to the Congress of Socialist Parties in the EC, Cascais, Portugal, 5 May 1987.
6 According to *The Economist* (1992), EC aid to Spain will amount to some 7.5 billion dollars a year for the period 1993–97.
7 Billion is here taken as 1,000 million.
8 Note that the Spanish government must contribute with matching funds in European Regional Development Fund (ERDF) projects and with 25 per cent of the total in projects to be funded by the new Cohesion Fund.
9 For instance, Donges and Schatz estimated in 1986 that the short-term (static) job loss in Spain would amount to 0.8 per cent of total employment. Counting on dynamic effects leads the authors to predict a change ranging from –0.2 per cent to +0.8 per cent. All these results were much more pessimistic than proved the case (Yannopoulos 1989: 266).
10 Suffice it to say here that gross manufacturing investment grew by an average annual rate of 26.8 per cent in the period 1986–88.

7 European Political Cooperation

The upgrading of Spanish foreign policy

Esther Barbé

> EPC proved to be a stable system and specific national interests underline the continuation of this system.
>
> Franco Algieri

Twenty-two years after its creation, nobody doubts the usefulness of European Political Cooperation (EPC).[1] Today the second pillar of the European Union, this mechanism of diplomatic accord of the Twelve has grown in importance because of the changes in the international system (the end of the cold war and disappearance of the bipolar logic). The Gulf war, on the one hand, and the many conflicts in Yugoslavia, on the other, have made the diplomatic instrument of the Twelve the centre of interest: it was criticized by public opinion when it was unable to respond to the challenges of the post-cold war era and was a priority subject on the agenda of Community reforms (Dehousse 1991).

In broad terms, EPC – in the process of being formally transformed into the Common Foreign and Security Policy (CFSP) – is a 'stable system' in the sense that its achievements in the sphere of procedures (*communauté d'information*) as well as that of confidence building (*communauté de vues*) have been consolidated. With respect to its action policy (*communauté d'action*), the successes and numerous failures of the Twelve have come to light in the post-cold war era.[2] Nevertheless, there is no reason to believe that its formal transformation into the CFSP will entail a revolutionary change – a new period – in the diplomacy of the Twelve (and more so as the European Union expands first to fifteen or sixteen, and then to twenty or more).

Thus we have an atmosphere of continuity, customarily favoured by the self-interest of the states that form a part of the system. In general, the Community countries have found adequate opportunities for the defence of their national interests in the EPC mechanism – applicable, as we shall see, to the Spanish case. More concretely, the existence of

EPC enables them: (1) to enjoy an international presence otherwise unattainable for small or peripheral countries, partaking thus of greater prestige and leadership possibilities (the presidency of the Community makes the foreign affairs minister in office the representative of a 'world power' and the leader of the Twelve); (2) to place national problems on the European agenda, converting them, in this way, into European problems (the case of the Falklands war is a clear example); and (3) to justify the adoption of unpopular policies to national public opinion on the basis of the existence of a 'European position' (for example, the change in Spain's policy in the Western Sahara from 1987).

SPAIN: FROM OBJECT TO SUBJECT IN EPC

In ten years, from 1975 to 1985, Spain moved from being a topic on the EPC agenda, dealt with by the Working Group on Southern Europe, to becoming one of its designers. Spain participated for the first time in an EPC meeting as an observer on 1 September 1985 (the Treaty of Adhesion to the Community was signed in Madrid on 12 June 1985). From this date until 1 January 1986 when Spain was admitted into the Community, the declarations of Political Cooperation were signed by the Ten plus Spain and Portugal. Thus Spain and Portugal were explicitly associated with EPC before their official entry into the Community. It must be pointed out that before their being incorporated as observers, Spain and Portugal were already receiving information from the very start of the adhesion negotiations (the European Council in London in November 1981 made explicit the will of the Ten to keep Spain and Portugal abreast of EPC work). Thus, the two countries met biannually with the Troika (of preceding, current and future EC presidents) on a ministerial level and twice each semester with the Political Directors (Schoutheete 1986: 201–4, Nutall 1986: 325–6). Before becoming an active subject of EPC, Spain was evidently a matter of concern for its future partners. However, the behaviour of the Nine/Ten was rather discreet with respect to the Spanish political process (execution of anti-Franco militants in 1975, death and succession of Franco, transitional process, the February 1981 coup), and there was absolutely nothing along the lines of an EPC policy with regard to Franco's dictatorship.

The death sentences for five anti-Franco militants in the Burgos trials (1975), constituted the first Spanish problem on the diplomatic agenda of the Nine (Van Praag 1982: 101–4). It will soon be seen how one of the usual cleavages in EPC – idealists/moralists opposed to realists/

pragmatists – was to reappear in the Burgos death sentences, leading the Nine to react late and badly. On a *communauté d'information* level, the Nine interchanged information through the COREU and within the framework of the Working Group on Southern Europe (the group met approximately every six weeks in the second semester of 1975). However, the policy of the Nine in the case of the Burgos death sentences entered treacherous ground when they tried to adopt a common position (*communauté de vues*). Such was the case that the only indication of a common position of the Nine – a secret message sent to the Spanish government on 25 September – was a very mild text in which the Europeans indicated that they did not wish to interfere in Spain's internal matters, but that they requested the revision of the sentences as a sign of clemency. Contrasting with the attitude of the moralist governments (Holland, Denmark) that demanded a reference to be made in the text to the lack of guarantees and the military nature of the tribunals, the Big Three of the Community (West Germany, the United Kingdom and France) imposed a text whose subject-matter was exclusively humanitarian.

The text arrived late – two days before the executions despite the fact that the Dutch government had demanded immediate and conclusive action at the EPC meeting on 11 September – and was followed by a series of blunders. Public opinion in the European countries lobbied in such a way that some governments (British, German, Dutch, Danish and Belgian) condemned the death sentences unilaterally, and finally the Italian presidency condemned the sentences, demanding clemency. However, the presidency was not able to organize joint action (collective withdrawal of the ambassadors). Each country carried out its own policy. Thus, counterposed to Dutch moralism (conclusive action, including the withdrawal of the ambassador) one can talk of French pragmatism (interested in not 'poisoning' relations with Spain).

Despite EPC not being able to decide on any common action with regard to the executions, the Community, on the initiative of the Commission, froze commercial negotiations with Spain within the framework of the Mediterranean Policy. Encouraged by the European Parliament, which on 25 September had voted in favour of freezing relations with Spain until such a time as a democratic regime was installed in the country, the Commission proposed the suspension of Community–Spain negotiations to the Council on 1 October. Finally, the Council adopted a declaration, according to which it was not possible to continue the negotiations 'at that time', in what was the most significant political act of the Nine. The tone of the declaration (which made no reference to suspending negotiations) once again showed the compromise reached between the hardline positions (Holland and Denmark) and those with the greatest interest in an agreement (France and the United Kingdom).

The Working Group on Southern Europe was an ideal framework for interchanging information and opinions on the evolution of Spain at the time of Franco's disappearance from power. Thus, on 30 September, a meeting of the Political Committee expressed the desire of the Nine to adopt a common attitude towards Spain. Implicit here was a certain hope of Franco's successor being the pathway to normalizing relations between the Nine and Spain. As a matter of fact, and despite the manifest will of the Nine, neither Franco's burial nor the coronation of Juan Carlos produced any concerted behaviour from the Community countries in the matter of protocol. Despite the proximity of the dates (the coronation took place on 26 November), the European Council in Rome in December did not address a single line to relations of the Nine with post-Franco Spain.

In reality, the relations of the Nine/Ten with transitional Spain should be seen more in the context of the Community (Spain's adhesion process) than within the framework of EPC, where reference can only be made to specific declarations (such as that of the Council of Ministers on 27 February 1981 congratulating the government on the failure of the recent coup attempt). All the same, in the sphere of EPC (diplomacy) particular mention can be made of the support given by the Nine to Spain's offer to host the third CSCE follow-up conference (to begin in 1980). In this way, the argument that the Nine wished to back the young democracy placed Spain in a privileged international position, enabling Madrid to host an important diplomatic conference (an experience the country had not had since the beginning of the century). The fact that the Nine's support for Spanish democracy through its diplomatic enhancement (Madrid as venue for a huge international conference) was given within the framework of the CSCE is highly symbolic if we bear in mind that this was one of the few frameworks in which one can talk of the existence of a European policy (*communauté d'action* included) (Ghebali 1991).

EPC–SPAIN: LOVE AT FIRST SIGHT OR A DIFFICULT RELATIONSHIP?

Spain's full incorporation in EPC in January 1986 prompted a question. To what degree could Spain alter the difficult equilibrium of European diplomacy of the then Ten? Some of those familiar with both EPC and Spanish diplomacy, such as Philippe de Schoutheete (writer of the

Tindemans Report and Belgian ambassador in Madrid between 1981 and 1985), foresaw difficulties in EPC–Spain relations, and even spoke of the appearance of a 'second Greece'.

To illustrate the fear of a second Greece – whose foreign policy between 1980 and 1986 differed greatly from the 'dominant line' of the other European chancelleries – the effect that Greece's admission had on the Europeans' image of unity in the diplomatic fora must be recalled. Within the framework of the UN General Assembly, Greece's incorporation in the EPC process reduced the degree of convergence in voting among the Europeans. It was feared that the same would occur in the Spanish case. However, the Spanish pre-1986 vote only differed from the dominant European line in a few matters – Palestine, disarmament, human rights and the Western Sahara (Regelsberger 1989: 121) – where Greek (and sometimes Irish) divergence already existed.

The response to the question, to what extent did Spain affect EPC? is complex and requires a review of the main tensions that have surrounded Spain's involvement. From 1986, Spain, like any other partner, was to have an effect on the institutional, organizational and political tensions that marked the development of EPC in recent years (Nutall 1992: 2–4). Later, we will look at how Spain's presence affected these tensions. But to start with, and to counter the argument of a 'second Greece', it must be emphasized that the behaviour of Spanish diplomacy within the EPC framework was totally removed from the image of the *enfant terrible*, as some analysts have pointed out (Regelsberger 1989); if anything, Spain's diplomacy could be qualified as *enfant sage*.

The previous question calls for another complementary one: To what extent did EPC affect Spanish foreign policy? How would Spain's national interests fit in with the demand made by the Twelve for common positions? At the beginning of this chapter, the positive effect that the existence of EPC had on the national interests of its members was mentioned in terms both of diplomatic prestige and of giving greater importance to their specific agendas. Spain, for its part, fell fully within this line of analysis, making EPC an instrument for enhancing its international projection.

We will now broach the two questions, answering the first – To what extent did Spain affect EPC? – in three subsections dedicated successively to the institutional, organizational and political tensions or cleavages. When we talk of institutional tensions, we refer to a conceptual debate that laid the foundations of the entire process of European construction (the old debate between integrationists and inter-governmentalists). When we speak of organizational tensions, we will enter into the sphere of the daily functioning of EPC machinery. Given the fact that EPC matters are dealt with according to the discretion of the rotating presidency, in office for six months, it is clear that each country will establish its own style, particularly during its term in the presidency. Finally, when commenting on the political tensions, we will go into profound issues, and here the line of thought that will enable us to get a grip on the vast agenda will be found in the EPC–US relations which affect the totality of diplomatic activity (especially during the cold war) and which have laid the foundations for European security. There is no doubt that this last point constitutes the key cleavage in the history and development of EPC, a cleavage to which Spain is in no way indifferent.

The second question – To what extent did EPC affect Spanish foreign policy? – will lead on to a final section in which, as has already been mentioned, an attempt will be made to show the empowering effect that EPC has on the role of Spain in the international system.

Europeanism: the great design of the common foreign policy

The Spanish discourse on European construction with respect to its foreign policy dimension places Spain in the group of integrationists as distinct from the group of inter-governmentalists. The point that divides both groups and that has been repeatedly dealt with from the failure of the European Defence Community to the Treaty on European Union, passing through all the important moments of European political construction (Fouchet Plan, Tindemans Report, Genscher–Colombo Initiative, Single European Act), is the option between countries that promote a concerted effort of sovereign states to emit coordinated opinions in foreign policy matters and those countries that want a common foreign policy as an expression of European union.

From the moment it became a member of the Community, the discourse of the Spanish government has been that of the group of integrationist countries that, in broad outline, is made up of Italy, Germany and the Benelux countries, which is counterposed to a group that is clearly inter-governmentalist, made up of the United Kingdom, Denmark and Greece. The French position has changed over time and will be dealt with further on in relation to the Spanish position during the negotiations on Political Union in 1991.

Coinciding with the leading idea of the Davignon Report (1970) which led to the creation of EPC, the Spanish government has argued that a common foreign policy is one of the basic elements of European political construction. More concretely, Felipe González (1988b: 227) established the idea that a common foreign and security policy constituted one of the pillars of European union together with economic and monetary union and European citizenship.

The Spanish position when negotiating the creation of a common foreign and security policy (CFSP) of the Twelve, within the framework of the Inter-governmental Conference (IGC) of 1991, was based on two ideas: first that a common foreign policy is a basic pillar for political union, and second that the European failure in the Gulf crisis is explained by the lack of adequate tools to confront the situation. Thus it was that Spain considered the creation of the CFSP fundamental for achieving European unification and favourable for establishing new mechanisms (diplomatic and military) for the Twelve in the sphere of international policy (Barbé 1992a: 361). With regard to this subject, governmental policy has had the backing of public opinion, favourable to the development of a 'European identity' in the international system. Along these lines, the *Eurobarometer* of February 1991 indicated that 54 per cent of the Spaniards were in favour of the CFSP as compared to 17 per cent who opposed the policy.

In the second place, the Spanish position in the negotiation was 'positively' affected by the internal consequences of the Gulf war. The reaction of public opinion, more 'rational', according to González, than in the past (48 per cent of Spaniards were in favour of Spain's policy of participating in the naval blockade as opposed to 35.4 per cent who were against it) was interpreted by the president himself as 'the end of a century of Spain's isolationism' (González 1991b: 66). This reaction gave the Spanish negotiators a wider manoeuvring margin, less constrained by an internal public opinion set against participation in international organizations of a military nature.

In the difficult negotiations on the CFSP that did not end until the Maastricht summit itself, the Spanish government placed itself in the group of countries in favour of advancing towards a common policy of the Twelve in the international sphere, with its own resources and instruments. Together with Germany, France and Belgium, Spain defended the introduction of qualified-majority voting in the Council for adopting common actions in those areas previously designated as pertaining to the CFSP. With regard to the spheres of action, it must be pointed out that the Spanish government showed itself, in principle, to be partial to including all the spheres of foreign policy in the CFSP (Fernández Ordóñez 1990a: 5088).

At the Maastricht summit, the decision-making mechanism (unanimity or majority) in the sphere of common actions was 'subjected to blocking'. The Franco/German/Spanish desire to advance with majority decision-making clashed with the inflexible stance of the British/Portuguese/Danish. The final result, described by Jacques Delors as 'complex and paralysing', was due, according to Felipe González, to Spanish mediation between the two positions. During a plenary session of the national Congress, González declared:

> I am sorry to say that the formula agreed upon was the one which Spain proposed to find a way out of the impasse as there was no way of reaching an agreement. It was Spain that proposed: Let us at least reach a unanimous accord with respect to the matters that will need qualified-majority decisions. I know this is tantamount to looping the loop, but in the light of the deadlock, this was a formula we used to find a way out of the impasse. If not, there was no way of even the slightest decision being reached unless it were unanimously agreed upon. It is absurd to have it for common actions, above all, in the first phase of construction of a common foreign and security policy; unanimity is inevitable for deciding the direction foreign policy will take, but after that it would be logical to use a qualified majority to develop the common actions. This is what we asked for, but in reality, a great deal of precaution was taken in this respect. (González 1991a: 7788)

With respect to this last point, the Spanish position can be seen as 'careful' if we bear in mind the texts presented by Spain at other times during the negotiation. Thus, for example, we have the common foreign policy proposal that figures, together with other national options, in the report of the personal representatives of the ministers for the Council of General Affairs of 4 December 1990. In that proposal, Spain, which set forth two ideas that were maintained later on (including all spheres of foreign policy in the CFSP, but with mechanisms that would enable specific areas to be selected, and the progressive incorporation of WEU elements in the EC) also behaved prudently with regard to the decision-making mechanism, leaning towards maintaining the consensus. This was seen implicitly and, according to the declarations made by Fernández Ordóñez, as a defence mechanism for Spanish interests in Latin America. It is along these lines that the words of the minister were oriented when he declared in Parliament: 'Spain must be very careful, we run very grave risks that areas of interest to Spain be included in qualified-majority formulae' (Fernández Ordóñez 1990a: 5087).

The clarification at Maastricht – the CFSP would be applied only in predefined areas of foreign policy and Latin America was not included among them (Barbé 1992b: 197) – made it possible for the Spanish position to be more 'generous' with respect to the decision-making mechanism, and to fight for the introduction of the majority vote.

In a word, the Spanish position with regard to the institutional options of the EPC/CFSP can generally be described as integrationist (in favour of having a common foreign policy), while with regard to the mechanism the Spanish position tended towards 'supranational intergovernmentalism' (Keohane and Hoffman 1991), which centres attention on policy negotiation at the highest level (European Council). Politically, this can be seen as Spain pronouncing itself in favour of reinforcing the role of the European Council and the Council of Ministers in the EPC/CFSP, in contrast to maintaining the reduced role of the Commission and Parliament. It is along this inter-governmental line that the proposal of Felipe González (May 1992) to create a Directorate of Powers can be inscribed within the truest of Gaullist traditions. On the whole, one can talk of greater realism in the Spanish conception of the institutional cleavage once it had overcome 'the Europeanist illusion' that came with the homogenization of the 'isolated country' with its European neighbours.

EPC machinery in the hands of Spanish enthusiasm

The fear of a 'new Greece' that existed in 1986 – despite the fact that Spain had already shown throughout the 1980s that, with the exception of the conflicts in the Middle East and the Sahara, it maintained a position very similar to the then Ten in the United Nations – quickly dissipated. From the moment it was incorporated into EPC, Spain could be qualified as active (activism through the EPC machinery and before long it became one of the great 'animators' of the mechanism[3]) – and orthodox (it joined in with the dominant line among the Twelve). Albeit in this last sense, Spain initially enjoyed an especially favourable period for its integration in the EPC machinery since between 1986 and January 1989 (the time of the Spanish presidency) there was no crisis to make the Spanish government choose between its own policy (particularly in Latin America) and the diplomacy of the Twelve. This finally came to pass in December 1989 with the United States' invasion of Panama.

Thus, Spain occupied the presidency of Political Cooperation in January 1989 with the endorsement of the 'European Stamp' for the attitude it had demonstrated from the time of its admission: an attitude that, according to some analysts, had a positive influence on Greece's dissident policy, to such an extent that the Greek vote in the United Nations shifted towards European positions. Thus it was that the third enlargement became a positive factor for regular functioning of the EPC in contrast to what happened with the second enlargement.

From January 1989 Spain exercised the presidency of EPC (together with that of the EC), with the other Community countries doubting its capacity to exercise these functions. The presidency became a 'challenge' for the Spanish government. In terms of organization and coordination, the Foreign Affairs Ministry defined it as 'the greatest task ever undertaken by the Spanish Government and Administration' (Ministerio de Asuntos Exteriores 1989: 1). It was assumed in the *momentum* gathered on democratic Spain's road to modernization and full incorporation into its political environment. The prime minister referred to the presidency in terms of dignity and stressed Spain's will to give the presidency prestige (Kirchner 1992: 105). In the Spanish case, the presidency of the Twelve became what Helen Wallace (1985: 274) has described as 'a distinctive political objective'. This objective involved: (1) orienting the development of EPC in a Europeanist direction; (2) situating Spain, in terms of will and commitment, among the big countries of the Community; and (3) profiting from the prestige of the presidency in its internal politics (with a view to the general elections held in October 1989).

Thus in EPC terms, from January 1989 Spain exercised the functions assigned to the presidency in Article 30 of the Single European Act (initiative, organization, coordination, representation, coherence with the foreign activity of the Community and relations with Parliament) with a Europeanist strategy. This entailed the express insistence on fostering consistency between EPC and the Community's foreign relations (Spain insisted on this in its relations with both the USSR and Romania) and, in a very special way, on improving relations with the European Parliament (an outstanding role was played by the minister, Fernández Ordóñez, who made several appearances during plenary sessions and in Committee). The activity of the entire EPC machinery was particularly important during the Spanish presidency, as we shall presently see.

It must be remembered that Spain took on the EPC presidency in January 1989 after six months of Greek presidency, paralysed by the internal problems of that country and consequently scarcely active. After a 'low profile' European Council (Rhodes), Spain occupied the presidency with an ambitious EPC programme (the subjects of Latin America and the Middle East being high on the Spanish agenda).

Spain's capacity to exercise leadership of the EPC was viewed sceptically by the European chancelleries. The Spanish Political Director wrote with respect to the function of the presidency:

> the presidency plays a fundamental role in the functioning of European Political Cooperation. Since the rule of consensus holds sway, the presidency, obviously, cannot impose a decision on the remaining member countries. However, what it can do is provoke discussions on specific matters, provide the impulse to deal with them, restrain them, orientate them. In general, the presidency has ample space for manoeuvring, but should exercise this activity with prudence in order not to gain the mistrust of any of its Community partners. It not only has great influence, but also an enormous responsibility. The main duty of the presidency consists in complying with its functions in an integrated way by trying to incorporate the points of view and the attitudes of all the member countries in the final decision, before submitting it for approval. If this obligation were not met with, the political credibility of the country exercising the presidency could be seriously affected. (Perpiñá Robert 1989: 49)

Perpiñá Robert may have made very special reference to proper political functioning, but the administrative machinery also played an important role. This explains the process of internal remodelling carried out in the Foreign Affairs Ministry – centred around the creation of a General Secretary for Foreign Policy – to make its structure compatible with the needs of EPC.

It might be of interest to quickly illustrate the functioning of the EPC machinery in order to assess the task carried out by the Spanish administration during its presidency. The EPC mechanism works at different levels. It is based on the permanent interchange of information (Coreus) among the Twelve, its objective being to arrive at a common position on international matters, from formal declarations to joint withdrawals of ambassadors or economic sanctions. It is always directed by the rotating presidency (Spain, during its presidency, received assistance from the Greeks – the previous presidency – and the French – the one that followed – as well as from the Secretariat installed in Brussels). The fact that the troika during the Spanish presidency was of Mediterranean 'sensitivity' facilitated the political task.

On the whole, the Spanish presidency activated the mechanism. It must be remembered that during those six months, Spain convened more than 50 internal meetings (ministerial meetings, political directors meetings and working group meetings) and the EPC produced 3,600 Coreus, 239 diplomatic measures, twenty-five policy declarations, several meetings with third countries (ten of the minister himself, five of the troika and eighteen at lower levels) and eight interventions of Fernández Ordóñez as EPC President in office (Ministerio de Asuntos

Exteriores 1989). Thus it can be said that, in organizational terms, Spain is a country whose attitude fostered the 'day-to-day' development of EPC through what has come to be called the 'coordination reflex' (political) or *esprit de corps* (administrative) or, more simply, *de facto* Europeanization of national foreign policies.

The political agenda: European or Western?

Relations with the United States make up the axis that determines the third cleavage mentioned above. In fact, the bilateral relations between each of the EPC partners and the United States form the basis of the determinant political cleavage between the Nine/Ten/Twelve. Thus the attitude of the Europeans with respect to the EPC mechanism has shifted from a French logic – giving an impulse to the mechanism during the initial stages, precisely because it was considered an alternative to Western leadership by the United States – to a British conduct, desirous of making the American power the 'Thirteenth Partner' of EPC.

The anti-American element in the elaboration of Spanish foreign policy is well known. The demands of Spanish public opinion, linked to the political culture of the party in power from 1982, are illustrative of the fact that although Spain is an ally of the Western defence fora, (proven, for example, by the behaviour of the country in UN votes), Spanish diplomatic options at the time of incorporation in EPC differed symbolically from those of the United States in two prominent conflicts: the Arab–Israeli conflict and the Central American conflict.

However, the principal issue of this cleavage revolves around the concept of European security: the debate between Europeanism (structuring European defence around European institutions) and Atlanticism (around Atlantic institutions). The Spanish government's position in this debate is well known: the referendum on NATO in 1986 involved presenting a detailed programme in which in practice Spain placed itself in the Europeanist group.

This last cleavage was clearly relevant after the end of the cold war and within the framework of Community reforms. In effect, the CFSP negotiations became the ideal moment for determining Spain's position on this political cleavage. This was the time, it must not be forgotten, of the Gulf crisis. From the cumulation of international changes, some provisional conclusions can be drawn with respect to Spanish public opinion: the participative policy of the government during the Gulf war was supported (a will to commit itself internationally); the position with respect to NATO was still not very receptive (42.4 per cent of Spaniards declared themselves to be against and 42.4 per cent in favour of Spain continuing in the organization); a professional army model was defended (72 per cent of the population wanted the army to be made up exclusively of volunteers and professionals); and the idea of a European defence was preferred (according to *Eurobarometer*, of October 1990, 62 per cent of Spaniards considered the creation of a common defence organization of the Twelve necessary). Spanish public opinion, to a large degree, showed itself to be in favour of the creation of highly professionalized intervention forces outside national territory and within the framework of a European defence organization, not an Atlantic one.

The favourable opinion of the Spaniards with regard to the creation of a European defence organization coincided with the endorsement by the Spanish government (together with the French and the German, among others) of the inclusion of the political terms of common security and common defence in the Treaty text. Spain contemplated the creation of a common defence that would complement the other existing security organizations (CSCE and NATO) within the framework of the Twelve. The contention in favour of a 'European defence identity' led to one of the deepest cleavages among the Twelve in Maastricht: Atlanticists opposed Europeanists over defence matters. Forming part of the second group, Spain (together with France, Germany and Belgium against the United Kingdom, the Netherlands and Portugal) proposed within the framework of the inter-governmental conference that the WEU be an 'integral part of the process of European Union and be in charge of getting the security and defence policy under way' ('Conférence' 1991: 1).

In all, it can be remarked that the disappearance of bipolarity 'facilitated' Spain's participation in the debate on European security. In this sense it must be remarked, in the first place, that the NATO reforms (Rome, November 1991) were received positively by the Spanish government. Carlos Alonso Zaldívar, adviser of Prime Minister González on security matters, expressed the pragmatism of the Spanish government in the new international context:

> the creation of multinational units in NATO, among them the Rapid Reaction Corps, does not close the door to creating essentially European units, for example, in the WEU. There is nothing to prevent the WEU from creating its own structure of forces, and each country from assigning the same units to NATO and the WEU. In fact this possibility of 'wearing two hats' is defended by Spain which sees a complementarity between NATO and the EC–WEU and contemplates the possibility of participating in both schemes. (Alonso Zaldívar 1992: 23)

So, after Maastricht and looking ahead to the 1996 revision, Spain endorses a policy that combines pragmatism in the subject of NATO ('double hat') with a militant discourse in favour of the WEU as the 'armed wing' of the EC. In a word, the Spanish situation has been normalized, in that it is now closer to that of other Community countries. The normalization of relations with the United States (1988 agreements) and the new international context (instability in Europe with armed conflicts) are the determining factors in the evolution of the Spanish position regarding European defence. As regards public opinion, the Spanish government's position with respect to the WEU was backed by 71 per cent of the population who favour the creation of a European defence system (according to the *Eurobarometer* of Spring 1993).

PRESTIGE AND INTERESTS: TWO POLES OF SPANISH POLICY

At the beginning of this chapter it was indicated that EPC served to strengthen the machinery, prestige and interests of European diplomacies. This was due logically to the room for manoeuvring that the Twelve had always enjoyed in EPC whenever their national interests were seen to be affected (EPC as the minimum common denominator). The three elements – machinery, prestige and interests – appear when we consider the effect that EPC had on Spanish foreign policy.

In the Spanish case, we have to start by recalling that the common foreign policy (as well as European security/defence) was an important tool in the process of Europeanization initiated by the Socialist government with all that it entailed (an end to isolationism, modernization, etc.). Thus, for the Spanish, unlike other European diplomacies, participating in EPC was historically significant (the 'metapolitical' value, in the words of Fernando Morán (1980: 289), of Spain's admission into the Community). This 'historic settling of accounts' was highly positive for Spanish diplomacy as far as two of the dimensions mentioned were concerned (the machinery and the prestige).

In terms of diplomatic machinery, it is clear that belonging to the EPC process was an important venture for Spanish diplomacy and its communications network as regards quantity (constant information flow through COREU), technical quality (modernization of the equipment in the Spanish Foreign Ministry, made necessary by the 1989 presidency) and political quality (direct and permanent communication with the most important chancelleries of Europe). With regard to decision-making, the habit of permanent consultation favoured the decision-making process in general (supporting the collective positions on situations that were not of great significance for the national agenda, having an *alibi* to justify difficult decisions to internal public opinion on sensitive issues, etc.). Undoubtedly, the most significant achievement in the diplomatic sphere was what has come to be called the coordination reflex among the Twelve, (based on the *communauté d'information*): an achievement in which Spain participated, according to Spanish diplomacy, with its own 'capital' (privileged relations with Latin America that had an important effect on the information channels, the consultation, the personal contacts, etc.).

In terms of prestige, Spain has benefited from belonging to the diplomatic club of the Twelve. In the first place, belonging to EPC has enlarged the Spanish international space to that of the Twelve. In the second place, and more significantly, involvement in EPC opened the doors to the possibility of increasing the country's diplomatic projection. The simple exercise of the presidency fostered it. In the Spanish case, holding the presidency involved the normal managerial function to ensure continuity in subject matters, but at the same time it enabled Spain to bring those questions in which it had a special interest into the limelight, and thus facilitate their international projection.

As has been said, the Spanish agenda for the EPC presidency was an ambitious one. Just before assuming the presidency, Felipe González himself defined the frameworks of action in which the Twelve should maintain a common position: relations with the United States and Canada; reinforcing the Council of Europe; greater opening towards central and eastern Europe through the Helsinki process; reducing military forces in Europe; developing common security; reliance on the WEU; and a cooperation policy for development. He also emphasized the two crisis areas in which the Twelve should take concrete steps – institutionalization of political and economic relations with Latin America and starting a dialogue with all the parties involved in the Middle East conflict – as well as the need to act jointly in the United Nations.

Two questions of great interest for Spanish diplomacy stood out prominently from the Spanish agenda: the Middle East conflict and Latin America. Without touching on specific policies (assigning resources to objectives), it can be said that in both cases the Spanish image was given a boost thanks to diplomatic skill (holding the Middle East Conference in Madrid, 1991) and the country's historical–cultural potential (organization of the Latin American summits and the events of 1992). Spain's international projection, favoured by its membership in EPC, was attained thanks to the remarkable activism and greater international committment (participation in UN peace-keeping forces, a non-permanent seat on the Security Council, participation in the commitment 'Four plus One' initiative in Bosnia). The will to exercise a middle power policy in the international system (based more on prestige than on resources) is apparent.

After having seen how EPC was beneficial for Spanish policy in terms of machinery and prestige, its influence in the sphere of interests remains to be assessed. The two traditional special interests on the Spanish political agenda – Latin America and the Arab world – were prominent in Felipe González's enumeration of the objectives of the Spanish EPC presidency. Spain's strategy with regard to both areas was to place them on the European agenda. In effect, the Spanish presidency stood out by promoting Euro-Arab dialogue and the San José process, and by proposing the creation of a guarantee fund to help the middle-income debtor countries (the majority of which are Latin American). Thus, during the Spanish presidency, the Europeanization of the agenda could be seen as promoting consistency between EPC and the EC's foreign policy (according to Article 30 of the Single European Act), a policy that would combine European (Community) resources with objectives from the Spanish agenda. It met with little success (none in the case of creating a new fund).

The policy developed by Spain on various levels (bilateral, multilateral, Community) in recent years shows us that Spain is attempting to Europeanize its special interests, although a difference in attitude can be observed when dealing with one area (the Arab world) or the other (Latin America).

Spanish policy with respect to the Arab world picked up considerably after the end of the cold war. Europe's displacement towards the East placed Spain in a peripheral position. In the post-cold war era, Spain, influenced by the impact of the Gulf, saw its interests more clearly tied in with the South, making the Maghreb a priority objective inasmuch as it was a risk area for *Spain's global security* (understood as socio-economic security and not in the usual military sense of the term). The strategy followed to defend Spanish interests could be qualified as *pluridirectional* (bilateral, the proposal to hold a Conference on Security and Cooperation in the Mediterranean (CSCM), the Four plus Five Group, pressure for a Renewed Mediterranean Policy) and, with respect to EPC, as a lobby to convert the Maghreb into a common action area within the framework of the CFSP (Lisbon Council, 1992). Thus it could be remarked that Spain unreservedly 'delegated' (Europeanized) its Maghreb policy, based on channelling economic resources towards the region as a preventive measure in favour of Spanish security.

As regards Latin America, the Spanish strategy within the Community framework (foreign relations) could be considered similar to that of the Maghreb (lobbying for a greater flow of resources towards the region), although there was a difference in the sphere of the common foreign policy. Unlike the Maghreb, Latin America constituted *a prestige area* (not a risk zone) and the factor at stake was not security but identity (values). Thus it was that Spanish policy did not attempt the diplomatic Europeanization of its Latin American agenda. On the contrary, Fernández Ordóñez was alert to the need for Spain to retain its diplomatic manoeuvring space in Latin America, confirming thus that Spain was a normalized country in EPC terms: it endorsed advancing towards a common foreign policy so long as it did not clash headlong with Spain's essential interests (for example, perceiving relations with Latin America as part of its own national identity).

NOTES

1 The term 'European Political Cooperation' (EPC) is used throughout the text to refer to the mechanism of diplomatic accord of the Twelve and to the actions that derive from it. The concept of 'common foreign policy' or 'European foreign policy' is associated with general conceptions and not mechanisms or specific actions, whereas the term 'Common Foreign and Security Policy' (CFSP) is used strictly in relation to the negotiations of the Inter-governmental Conference on Political Union and its result, the Maastricht Treaty.

2 The three terms (*communauté d'information, communauté du vues and communauté d'action*) are commonplace among EPC analysts and were coined by Philippe de Schoutheete (Schoutheete 1986).

3 Spanish activism in EPC led the country to occupy the third position as producer of COREUs during the first semester of 1986 (Sabá 1986: 32). According to information collected in the Foreign Affairs Ministry (interview with the European correspondent), Spain occupied the fifth place in 1992 as producer of Mail behind the Big Three and Holland.

8 The autonomous communities and external relations

Caterina García

In our global, interdependent and at the same time regionalized world, there is an increasingly marked tendency for sub-state political entities (regions, federated states and provinces) to participate in international relations. American states, Canadian provinces, German Länder and other European regions provide many examples of such participation.

The case of Spain is no exception. From the moment in which the state was divided into autonomous communities (*comunidades autónomas* – CCAA), and in spite of the limitations imposed by the constitutional framework, the CCAA have slowly conquered their own international space up to the point where their external activity is accepted and regarded as relatively normal. None the less, there is a certain amount of conflict with the central government.

This chapter will begin with an analysis of the legal framework within which the international relations of the CCAA operate (the constitution and the autonomy statutes) and will proceed to examine the doctrine of the Constitutional Court. Once the general framework has been described, it will be illustrated by reference to a specific case, that of a pioneering autonomous community in the sphere of external activity: Catalonia. An analysis will be made of the context in which this external activity is carried out and the political philosophy that inspires it. This will be followed by a description of the external activities themselves. Finally, the chapter will focus on the conflicts that arise, that is, the reactions of the centre to the external activities of the CCAA. Without attempting to be exhaustive, occasional references will be made, where relevant, to information about other CCAA.

THE GENERAL FRAMEWORK

The Spanish constitution of 1978 and external relations of the CCAA

Spain has a recent constitutional text, but one which, from the perspective this chapter is concerned with, was inspired by another text, the Italian one, conceived in a period and context – the 1940s in Europe – that had little to do with the interdependent world of the end of the 1970s. In this sense, the Spanish constitution has been criticized as anachronistic (Jáuregui 1986: 56), as reflecting an archaic conception that does not fit contemporary reality (Remiro Brotons 1984) and, furthermore, as inconsistent with the principle of autonomy contained in the constitution (Mangas 1987). The framers of the Spanish constitution showed a lack of international sensitivity and took refuge behind a tendency to maintain the status quo, with the state at the centre with a strong emphasis on the unity or centralization of the state's external power (González Campos 1990).

The Spanish constitution, by its very nature, grants the state exclusive power in matters of international relations (Article 149.1.3). However, it does not define international relations. Even from a superficial reading of Articles 56.1, 63.2, 94.1 and 97, the state's exclusive protagonism in these matters is readily apparent. All of them specify only those external actions relating to treaty-making power and the right to be represented. No reference is made to a whole series of activities that could have an important international dimension (trade, industry, fishing, cattle-rearing, health, culture, etc.). On the other hand, it may be argued (Mangas 1987: 221) that the framers of the constitution did not refer to all the external actions that imply international relations because some of them are explicitly mentioned in other rules (nationality, immigration, right to asylum, foreign trade, registration of ships and aircraft, and defence of Spain's cultural, artistic and monumental heritage from export and despoliation). If international relations (Article 149.1.3) were to cover everything, there would have been no need to mention some of them explicitly.

On the other hand, it is inconceivable that the scope of the CCAA be restricted to the internal sphere. The enactment of the powers of the CCAA requires activities that go beyond the state's frontiers. Therefore, the question is whether the international dimension of a specific CCAA power could mean, according to Article 149.1.3, its being immediately transferred to the central bodies of the state. Such an interpretation would entail the superimposition of two images of the

Spanish state: a complex one, which internally would be that of a Spain based on CCAA; and another, unitary one, which externally would disregard Spain's organizational subdivision into CCAA.

This latter interpretation would be not only anachronistic but also incongruous with the new structure of the Spanish state, proclaimed and outlined in the Spanish constitution. Besides, with the application of treaty-making power the central state could, through a treaty, take away all the powers of the CCAA. With the introduction of autonomy statutes an attempt has been made to correct this situation on a legal level by introducing CCAA participation in the two phases, the ascending (formulation) and the descending (execution), of concluding international treaties.

The external activities of the CCAA and the autonomy statutes

In general, the statutes go further than the Spanish constitution in externally extending the internal powers of the CCAA, although they do not cover the entire spectrum of external activity. There are four subjects that are broached by the majority of autonomy statutes: (1) the adoption of measures to execute treaties and conventions in those aspects that affect the powers of the CCAA; (2) receiving information on treaties and conventions that the central government negotiates and that affect the autonomous communities; (3) the initiative of CCAA to promote, through the state, the signing of treaties and conventions with other states that have their own linguistic, cultural or historical roots; and (4) the power to recognize by means of a law communities of inhabitants that reside outside the region, in other nations or CCAA.

Thus, the aspects dealt with are those relating to the contracting of international obligations or the execution of obligations taken on by the Spanish state. The importance of this lies, as has already been pointed out, in the fact that the state could, via a treaty, introduce certain policies that constitutionally or statutorily correspond to the CCAA, either exclusively or partially (Pérez González and Pueyo Losa 1982: 13–88). Mangas (1987) has spoken of the 'boomerang effect' when referring to the consequences that the incorporation of EC law might have on the Spanish legal system. Community law has exposed the incoherencies and gaps in Spanish law with reference to the role of the CCAA in international relations. The Community treaties do not consider the constitutional distribution of power nor do they have to respect it. The fact that Community law overrides internal law has favoured central governments (Mangas 1990: 61) since they are the ones that represent the member states in the Council, where they exercise regulatory powers which internally they do not always enjoy.

Thus far, it can be stated that the constitutional and statutory texts do not definitively resolve the wide range of issues that have arisen in the wake of CCAA external activity. The autonomous communities continue to work towards projecting themselves internationally and to overcome *de facto* the restrictive interpretations of the legal texts. The external activities of the CCAA have lent substance to the development of rules with interpretations that have not always been accepted by the central government. The Constitutional Court has witnessed some of the conflicts arising between the state and the CCAA.

The external activities of the CCAA and the jurisprudence of the Constitutional Court

The Constitutional Court has used two criteria in relation to the external activity of the CCAA: one of them broad and flexible, the other restrictive. Without going into the cases in which each of these criteria has been applied, it is worth examining the evolution in the Constitutional Court's doctrine.

From a rigid and centralist idea of the concept of international relations, this High Court has slowly conceded greater space to the external activities of the CCAA. The evolutionary tendency began with the personal vote of the Magistrate Díaz Eimil in the Constitutional Court Sentence (STC 137/89) of 20 July 1989. This vote reflected and embodied the hope of the more flexible Spanish jurists with respect to considering the external dimension of the internal jurisdiction of the CCAA. It stated that a rigid and expansive concept of jurisdiction in Article 149.1.3 meant denying the CCAA any possibility of carrying out activities that, despite a certain international dimension, did not imply exercising sovereignty; nor did they create international obligations, generate responsibilities of the state to others, or affect the state's external policy. This would be tantamount to making decisions without taking contemporary international reality into consideration, and to preventing the CCAA from carrying out certain activities that were necessary for attaining their objectives within the framework of the power conceded to them.

Later sentences have confirmed this doctrinal turn of the Constitutional Court. In the STC of 5 October 1989 it was stated that it could not be permitted that any relation, however remote, to matters in which other countries and foreign citizens were involved, implicitly or necessarily implied that jurisdiction be decided by the 'international relations' rule. Later on (STC of 31 January 1991), the Constitutional Court allowed the Generalitat of Catalonia to promote its cultural values outside Spain, so long as in doing so it did not compromise national sovereignty nor generate state responsibilities vis-à-vis third parties.

With respect to the application of Community regulations, the Constitutional Court has also shown itself to be in favour of greater flexibility (STC 79/1992 of 28 May and 179/1992 of 19 October): activities that derive from complying with Community treaties will be carried out by those within whose juridiction the activity lies. Finally, a sentence of 8 March 1993 confirmed that the external dimension of a matter cannot be used to make an expansive interpretation of Article 149.1.3 of the Spanish constitution which attributes to the state's jurisdiction any measure with a certain external potential, as it would entail a restructuring of the constitutional order itself in so far as the distribution of power between the state and the CCAA is concerned.

There is no doubt that the determination of the CCAA to maintain and increase their external activities has contributed to the doctrinal evolution of the Constitutional Court. Despite the problems of definition that we have referred to, the CCAA carry out the external activities they consider necessary to fulfil their jurisdiction. To cite the most representative examples: First, in 1992, sixteen out of seventeen presidents of the CCAA made a total of 124 visits abroad. Heading the list was an autonomous community with a long tradition in external activities, Catalonia (27 visits abroad), followed by Galicia (22), the latter having spectacularly increased its external projection in recent years, coinciding with the arrival of Manuel Fraga to the presidency of the Xunta of Galicia (regional government). Second, by 1992, ten CCAA had opened commercial offices in Brussels, and some of them had done so in other countries as well (for example, the network of delegates of the Commercial Promotion Corsortium of Catalonia (COPCA) covering twenty-five countries scattered over the five continents). Third, the CCAA have signed numerous cooperation agreements (in 1992, among 11 CCAA, 74 were signed, including 18 by Catalonia and 17 by Andalucía). Most of them were signed with sub-state actors (60 per cent) (*El País*, 10, 18 and 19 January 1993).

These, then, are the most striking examples and the ones that have made the greatest political impact. They are therefore the main and permanent focus of attention (and/or tension) for the central government. However, the external activities of the CCAA go beyond them. They are as diverse as the powers allotted to the different departments of the regional administrations.

CCAA collaboration in the development of the state's external policy

The collaboration of the CCAA in the elaboration of the state's foreign policy is not extensive and is exercised through informal channels of political negotiation. In the foreign policy of the Spanish state, the CCAA act as lobbies – for example, the Canary Islands lobby during the negotiation of Spain's membership of the Community. Their participation in the decision-making process is not institutionalized; all action is taken within the sphere of informal political relations.

Despite this general statement, it must be pointed out that the state and the CCAA have recently acquired some instruments of collaboration. These were created more as a response to the external activity of the CCAA than as the result of the state's will to enable them to participate in the development of foreign policy.

There are three types of collaboration instruments: framework conventions; commissions (*ad hoc* follow-up bodies); and sectoral conferences.

The framework conventions are legal instruments through which the state creates the legal basis that will enable the CCAA to develop their external activities. Thus far, there are only four framework conventions: those signed in 1991 between the Spanish Agency of International Cooperation and the autonomous governments of Andalucía, Asturias, Valencia and the Public Limited Company linked to the government of Madrid, Iniciativas Regionales Madrileñas, SA (Regional Initiatives of Madrid), for carrying out scientific and technical activities with Latin American countries.

The commissions were created as a consequence of the framework conventions and carry out the task of following up the activities that derive from them.

With regard to the sectoral conferences, it must be pointed out that there is only one in existence. The State–CCAA Sectoral Conference for matters related to the European Community was created in 1988 because of the need to find solutions to the problems that arose from having to comply with Community obligations. Its work has steadily increased, from involving frequent contacts to close collaboration. However, after five years of non-institutionalized functioning – the internal regulations of the Conference are still being elaborated – it has still not found definitive formulae for the participation of the CCAA. It is an internal coordination instrument that does not diminish the exclusiveness of state representation vis-à-vis the Community. Without contradicting this principle, occasional direct representation of the

CCAA – always as part of the state representation – has been allowed for some meetings with the Commission when matters that affect them directly are being dealt with.

THE CATALAN AUTONOMOUS COMMUNITY AND INTERNATIONAL RELATIONS

The context of Catalonia's international activity

Catalonia's international activity is developed in an international context dominated by two tendencies – contradictory and/or complementary – that are superimposed: the globalization of relations between different units of the system and the regionalization of these relations. On an international level, this reality was reflected in the slogan 'think globally and act locally'. In this context, international contacts were no longer just a possibility but became necessary for the development of the powers of Catalonia.

As regards the regional context, Catalonia falls within the reality of the Europe of the Regions, a reality in which the regions are acquiring increasingly greater protagonism, precisely because the regional governments, which are closer to the citizens, have a greater functional capacity to resolve a series of problems that the state cannot handle.

There is a regional reality at the EC level that already carries a lot of weight and that is visible in two spheres of activities: on the one hand, the regions act as a lobby in the Community institutions, and on the other, they act together to achieve their objectives through networks of interregional cooperation.

The process of European integration enhances and will reinforce the role of the regions on the basis of the principle of subsidiarity (Llimona 1992: 57). The Union Treaty introduces two novelties. First, for the first time in a Community text, it recognizes the regions as entities wielding a certain political power. The modification of Article 146 of the Treaty of Rome permits a state to send a regional minister to the Council of Ministers when the subject falls within the jurisdiction of the sub-state political entity. Second, the Treaty of European Union foresaw the creation of the Committee of Regional and Local Collectivities which took place in March 1994. In spite of the criticism it receives, the Committee marks an important step forward in the recognition of regional entities.[1] On these two levels, the context acts as a driving force for external activities in all the CCAA. It will be the other context, that of the state, which is responsible for the differences.

Catalonia's external activity is conditioned by the state context of the

Spain of the Autonomies. At this level, there are two basic facts that affect it: a certain positive regional asymmetry and Catalonia's national reality.

Catalonia is one of the 'historic' CCAA of the Spanish state that attained their autonomy by means of the so-called 'fast track'. With 6 per cent of Spain's territory and 15.6 per cent of its population, it represents 20 percent of GNP and 25 per cent of foreign trade.[2] Its economy is based mainly on the service sector (60 per cent of total production). It is a region with a long industrial tradition and a history of contacts with other countries. Its diverse industrial fabric has made it the recipient of a good part of the foreign investment made in Spain.[3]

This situation within Spain leads Catalonia to project itself internationally. To its daily functional reality which involves collaboration with frontier regions is added the reality of long-term strategies. As regards the latter, Catalonia coincides with the interests of the European regions that are leaders in their respective states.

Catalonia is an autonomous community with its own national identity. In general, nationalism encourages the assertiveness of sub-state actors. It is not a *sine qua non* condition but stimulates and reinforces their external activities because not only do they have the will to project themselves externally, but they are united by a capacity to win over the loyalties of those not in favour of the state. The case of Catalonia is no exception. The same is true of Basque and Galician nationalism.

The international concept of Pujolism: Catalonia, open to the world

Personalism is generally a characteristic feature of the initial phases of sub-state external projection. Consider, for example, the direct relation with the increase in external activities of the Xunta of Galicia since its current President, Manuel Fraga, has been head of the government.

In Catalonia, personalism has been of special significance because its protagonist, President Jordi Pujol, has been at the head of the Catalan government since the first regional elections in 1980. The reflections in Pujol's political discourse on the importance of the international dimension were accompanied not only by numerous visits abroad and other acts of an international nature, but also by another aspect that is very characteristic of sub-state international relations: personal initiatives with a high degree of informality.

Pujol considers Catalonia's external projection necessary for developing the two basic axes of Catalan political nationalism: the defence of national identity and the promotion of Catalonia's economic interests.

In the first place, defending Catalan national identity implies quite the opposite of being inward looking; it involves opening up to the exterior. All the same, this claim to being different is accompanied by the declaration, needed to tranquillize Catalonia's interlocutors (especially when they are a state), that the autonomous community accepts the Spanish constitutional order. It is within it that Catalonia must attempt to conquer its own international space.

Pujol is combative and critical of the central administration in his assertion of this international dimension of CCAA activities. There are four factors behind his criticisms: (1) the inefficiency of the central administration in defending some CCAA interests; (2) the dissatisfaction that arises from regional asymmetry, that is to say, the economic differences – positive in the Catalan case, negative in the Galician or Andalucian – between the different CCAA; (3) the systematic opposition to any CCAA activity with an international dimension; and (4) the central government's reactive activities and its emulative attitude in its attempts to put a brake on the external initiatives of the CCAA.

On the other hand, Pujol states that international activity is necessary for Catalonia because of the imperative of international competitivness. The Generalitat has to pursue the modernization of the Catalan economy, and its internationalization is the pathway to achieving it in an interdependent context. As a corollary of this conviction, there is the task of publicizing Catalonia's economic situation: let the world know the competitive advantages of Catalonia, especially those it offers as an interstitial economy, that is to say, one with a flexible industrial structure that adapts to the needs of the market.

On this subject, Pujol emphasizes another characteristic of sub-state external activity: the privatization of roles. It is necessary to concede great importance to private initiatives and to collaborate with them, creating a positive environment for their projection abroad.

With respect to the spheres of privileged relations, Europe is Catalonia's international dimension *par excellence* when we take historical and cultural aspects into consideration. Catalonia has the ideal stage for its economic development and for consolidating its own personal identity in the Europe of the Regions. Another reason for the regional option is the state's inefficiency when compared to the functionality of the regions. All this is advanced without any intention of making the Europe of the Regions a substitute for the Europe of the States.

The external activity of the Generalitat[4]

The initiative in and development of international activity

The Department of the Presidency is the organ that takes the intiative in Catalonia's external activity. This has been due to the role played by Pujol in this field and, currently, because it is laid down by Decree 190/1992, which created the External Activities Committee. This driving-force role of the presidency can be appreciated in the volume of external activity that it generates and the boost it gives to a large part of the external activity of other departments. In this sense, a distinction can be made between the external activities of the presidency, that of the external dimension itself, and those of the other departments, a result of internal responsibilities extending into the external sphere.

The presidency lays down the broad outlines of foreign activity and initiates the framework contacts within which the other departments develop part of their external contacts. This does not imply that contacts outside the broad outlines traced by the presidency are not initiated or developed. On the contrary, exercising their authority, achieving greater functionality and optimizing the resources at hand make it necessary for the different departments to look for the most suitable partners, who may or may not coincide with those suggested by the presidency. In this sense, there are two aspects that complement each other. The first sees external activities as an instrument in the service of a main objective of the Catalan government: the defence of Catalan national identity. Here, a global and political perspective of government action takes precedence. The second, without denying the first, is merely a logical and necessary extension, in today's international system, of its internal jurisprudence to the external sphere. Here, the overriding perspective is specific and functional.

Apart from the global guidelines, two positions can be observed in the definition of objectives: First, the position of those departments which see external contacts as a source of learning and improvement of the methods and instruments for carrying out their tasks; and second, the position of those who see external contacts as a source of more frequent and extensive exchanges with a view to reaping the benefits of cooperation and coordinated activities with other countries and/or regions. With some exceptions, the second perspective requires greater experience and international vocation than the former, which corresponds to the initial phases of external action. On this basis, it can be said that there is a general view that is shared by all, but which translates into an external projection at different speeds.

The process of institutionalizing international activity: the instruments

The presidency also carries out the task of coordination. The increasing number and diversity of external activities has made coordination a necessity. It is the response to this need which has led to a process of institutionalization.

Initially, external activities were coordinated by the Secretariat of Inter-governmental Affairs (1981), attached to the presidency and which in 1984 became the General Directorate. Its task consisted in organizing and coordinating the representative activities (external and internal) of the President and relations with other departments and institutions. The second stage in the process of institutionalization started only in 1990, when a more specific body was created, the External Activities Office. It was assigned the task of coordinating external activities, advocating certain activities and assessing the desirability of specific contacts. The third stage began with the creation of the External Activities Commission, in 1992, of which the External Activities Office became a part.

That same year, Valencia and Navarra created instruments similar to the Commission. Valencia created the Inter-departmental External Activities Commission and, as a support body, the Delegated Technical Commission for External Activities. Navarra created the External Action Service. In all three cases, the functions are similar. In the Basque Country, the General Secretariat of External Action, attached to the Department of the Presidency, carries out the task of coordination.

Finally, in 1994, the Commission was restructured, being organized in two areas: the European Area, and the non-European and Cooperation Area. The External Activities Office has been abolished.

Parallel to this, other tools of internationalization were created in accordance with the objectives and needs of each department. They all have different legal forms and relations with the governmental departments to which they are attached (consortia, entities, companies, etc). The following are the bodies, half-way between the public and private sphere, which on certain occasions have served to avoid interference from the central administration.

Patronat Català Pro Europa: created in 1982 to organize and coordinate all activities concerned with analysing, training and providing information related to the European Community from the perspective of Catalan interests.

CIDEM (Business Development and Information Centre): created in 1985, with an international section whose job is to attract foreign investment. This section is responsible for a territorial network abroad (it has offices in Brussels, Tokyo, New York and Düsseldorf).

COPCA (Commercial Promotion Consortium of Catalonia): created in 1987 within the Department of Commerce, it was soon transferred to the Department of Industry, since its policy of promoting exports complemented CIDEM's policy of capturing investments. Attempts were made to merge with CIDEM but were later dropped because of the reticence of the central administration.

At the time of its creation, this formula for overlapping the public and private spheres was the solution reached after tense negotiations with the central administration. The different interpretations of the consortium's role and the disagreement as to who should be the competent authority for commercial promotion led to one of the biggest conflicts between the two bodies.

The Tourist Promotion Consortium of Catalonia: created in 1986. Although it does not have offices abroad, it does have promoters who use the COPCA offices. Its main objectives relate to promotional and technical assistance activities in the Catalan tourist sector.

Office for Health Cooperation with Europe: created in 1989, this is in charge of coordinating relations between the Health Department and foreign bodies and institutions.

Office for Educational and Scientific Cooperation with the European Community: created in 1988 to promote knowledge of Community programmes.

Commission for Promoting the Teaching of Catalan in Universities outside the Territory of Catalonia: a commission created in 1988 that coordinates assistantships and contributes to the creation of Catalan language departments abroad.

COPEC (Catalan Consortium for the External Promotion of Culture): an independent body attached to the Department of Culture, created in 1991, among other reasons, to promote the presence of Catalan culture in international markets.

Other CCAA have bodies similar in nature and functions to some of the above. Especially noteworthy is the substantial number of bodies dedicated to the commercial promotion and attraction of foreign investments. Many of them, such as CIDEM and COPCA, have mixed legal forms and are attached to the departments of Industry, Commerce, Tourism and/or Economy of the regional governments, combining their international activity with internal promotion. Thus, there is SPRI (Industrial Promotion and Reconversion, PLC) in the Basque Country; in Andalucía, the Institute for the Promotion of Andalucía; in Navarra, SODENA (the Navarra Development Company); in Valencia PROCOVA (Promotion of the Valencian Community, PLC); in Madrid, IMADE (the Development Institute of Madrid); in Asturias, the Regional Promotion Institute; and in Extremadura, SOFITEX (the Extremadura Industrial Promotion Company).

Classification of the Generalitat's external activities

Although it is impossible to describe all the international activities carried out by each and every department of the Generalitat in this chapter, a list can be made of the types of activities based on the responses to questionnaires that covered the entire spectrum of CCAA external activities, including those of regions other than Catalonia.[5]

1 Relations of cooperation within the framework of a specific programme.
2 Relations of cooperation within the framework of a joint declaration, a collaboration protocol or a statement of intentions.
3 Relations of cooperation and exchange deriving from the development of activities specific to the jurisdiction of each department, that do not require formalization.
4 Activities related to promoting the presence of Catalonia in the world.
5 Participation in associations, conferences or other institutions of an international nature.
6 Activities to boost and support the internationalization of private initiative.
7 Presidential visits.[6]
8 Cooperation with the Third World.[7]

Relations between the central and regional government

Two different impressions of the climate of relations between the central and regional administrations were obtained from the responses to the questionnaires used in studying the Catalan case (see note 4) and from a follow-up analysis of the press reports on the subject. In the first case, all the responses obtained coincided fully in pointing out the absence of conflict, whereas the press repeatedly referred to a certain climate of uneasiness and/or a rift between both administrations. The state's discomfort over the external activities of the Basque autonomous community or the declarations of its head of government can also be deduced from the press.[8] In general, the other CCAA have fewer conflicts at this level. A climate of negotiation has surrounded the devolution of powers from the central administration to most regions; greater antagonism is caused by the existence of strong nationalist claims in Catalonia and the Basque Country.

To focus on the Catalan case, the common idea, which can be applied to the other CCAA, is that relations between both administrations have improved in the sphere of external activity. Besides the fact that external activity is no longer a novelty, the decline in conflict may also reflect a general reduction of conflict between the CCAA and the central administration. The *Pi i Sunyer Report on the CCAA, 1991* (Aja 1992: 10) points to, among other reasons, a change in the attitude of the three CCAA that have traditionally been the source of conflict. In the case of Galicia, improvement is attributed to the distinctive personality of its President; in the Basque case, to the scarce trust in the decisions made by the Constitutional Court, which led the Basque authorities to present fewer and fewer issues to the Court; and in the Catalan case, to the good relations of the Catalan group of deputies with the central government in the Congress, especially following the 1993 general election, when the PSOE became dependent on the Catalan nationalists for their parliamentary majority.

As regards Catalonia, the only references of a 'negative' nature are to be found in the speeches of the President of the Generalitat, when he spoke of the reluctance of the central government to accept any CCAA activity with an international dimension, and in the questionnaires of the COPCA and the General Directorate of Commercial Promotion. The latter referred to the problems encountered during the creation of the COPCA in 1987, when there was a clash between the two perspectives (state/CCAA) regarding jurisdiction in the field of commercial promotion. Both questionnaires stress the circumstantial nature of the incidents and their having been overcome; they also mention the good recent relations with the Spanish Institute of Foreign Trade (ICEX).

However, this normalization of relations is not so evident from press sources. In general, the reports on conflicts, tense situations or uneasiness between the two administrations are related to presidential external activities: that is to say, those with more elements of representation and para-diplomacy. Other than some specific matters (such as the refusal of the General Directorate of External Transactions to authorize the monetary transfer needed to hold a promotional seminar in London, the opening of the CIDEM office in Tokyo, and Catalonia's publicity campaign during the Olympic Games in Barcelona) there are sources of tension that are common to all the CCAA. Among them are the presidential visits that have been described as 'ambiguous', and against which the central administration alleges a lack of opportuneness in regard to specific statements made during the visits and the air of official represention that characterizes them. Other complaints from the central administration relate to the number of CCAA offices abroad and the signing of cooperation agreements. Another bone of contention has been the existence of two different political notions of the regional phenomenon, an area in which President Pujol has been particularly active. The positions, albeit different, have been brought closer because the debate has taken place in a European context where regional reality enjoys greater acceptance than traditionally was the case in Spain.

In general, the state wants more information and coordination from the CCAA, and requires that they respect the interests of Spain. The CCAA offered reassurances on this matter: apart from the ambiguous nature of some declarations, independence is totally absent from the discourse of the current autonomous governments.

Despite these areas of tension, it can be said that there has been a certain normalization: the external activity of the CCAA is a living and dynamic reality which cannot be easily halted by central administration intervention. On the one hand, the Generalitat, without renouncing its basic interests, is favourably disposed to resolving any differences. This attitude is beneficial, because if the central government were to feel 'attacked', or feel that the unity of foreign policy was being threatened, it would react by halting or by making external activities difficult. On the other hand, despite the alert attitude of the central government, it must be admitted that it is more tolerant than in previous years: perhaps because the short history of CCAA external relations has eliminated the surprise effect; or because Madrid has had time to study the effects of sub-state activities; or even because the dynamics of the Europe of the Regions have led it to accept as normal a situation that, on a European level, does not provoke negative or alarming reactions in states with internationally active sub-state bodies.

CONCLUSION

It can be said that the CCAA have developed an important amount of international activity in the process of extending their internal activities towards the exterior. This external activity, permitted under Spanish law, takes concrete form in a wide range of actions. Logically, it must be consistent with the state's foreign policy.

On the other hand, the participation of the CCAA in the development of Spanish foreign policy is very limited and above all recent. The incipient collaboration has been a result of Spain's entry to the EC; of the importance of issues that arise especially in connection with Community negotiations on matters that directly affect the activities and interests of the CCAA; and of the application of Community law. The Sectoral Conference created in 1988 is the most stable framework for cooperation between the central and regional administrations. Beyond that, the collaboration channels between the CCAA and the state for developing policy are much more informal (sectoral policy negotiation, lobbying, etc).

The international activities of the CCAA are neither sporadic nor the result of a passing whim; they are expected to continue and grow. The institutionalization of these activities in some CCAA reflects the importance they have acquired and at the same time is a guarantee of their continuity.

This continuity, in turn, is proof of the relative normalization and of acceptance by the central administration, so long as the constitutional framework and the unity of the state's foreign policy is respected. As we have seen, this process of normalization is not devoid of some areas of tension, which are periodically revived but always brought under control.

In general, the CCAA's external presence does not clash with the state's external action. Neither is it particularly cooperative; rather it is a parallel para-diplomacy.

With regard to the content, the activities of autonomic performance are situated at an equidistant position on the economic–political axis, for although there are activities of a clearly political nature, it is also the case that they tend to have an economic dimension, as important or more so than the political. The evidence lies in the numerous CCAA organizations dedicated to commercial promotion and attracting investment.

On the other hand, it must be emphasized that the autonomous governments have given private initiative the space it needs through their external activities, reinforcing thus the tendency to privatize roles, a characteristic feature of today's society. The creation of some of the instruments of internationalization, half-way between the public and private sphere, are the best example. Nevertheless, it should not be forgotten that these mixed formulae were sometimes the means of avoiding clashes with the central administration; they can thus be regarded as a mechanism established with two different objectives.

Finally, Spain's integration in the EC has been of great importance for the consolidation of the CCAA's external presence. Firstly, European regional logic and reality have opened up a new space for international action and had a tranquillizing effect on the central government, which has been able to see how other states accept the external activity of their sub-units. On a Community level, there is no doubt that the Europe of the Regions is no substitute for the Europe of the States. Secondly, the CCAA have been given greater protagonism as a result of the principle of subsidiarity and the application of Community law. Lastly, Community dynamics have encouraged the setting up of the first cooperation links between the state and the CCAA in the matter of formulating foreign policy. The advantage is twofold: an increase in CCAA collaboration in foreign policy without the state feeling its unity threatened in any way.

NOTES

1 The main criticism (Llimona 1992) refers, first, to the Committee's mixed nature (it will be made up of representatives of regional entities and local collectivities). Second, the fact that it has the same organizational structure as the Economic and Social Council and the identical number of members in both bodies is criticized. Third, its powers are considered insufficient as they are limited to a consultative function in five cases.
2 Data for 1991. Source: *Xifres de Catalunya 1993*, Barcelona, Institut d'Estadistica de Catalunya.
3 In 1991, Catalonia received 42.57 per cent of the total investment in Spain (in absolute figures), going down in 1992 to 28.9 per cent (*Catalonia. A Land to Invest in. A Land to Live in*, Barcelona: Generalitat de Catalunya, 1991).
4 To prepare this section, a questionnaire was sent to all the departments of the Generalitat. The questions referred to: (1) the systematic or sporadic nature of contacts; (2) the degree of formalization; (3) the contact regions/countries; (4) the objectives, causes and motivations of external activities; (5) intra- and inter-departmental initiatives and coordination; (6) the degree of conflictivity that the external activities of the Generalitat gave rise to; and (7) the assessment and perspectives of external activities. In addition several interviews were carried out with top officials of the autonomic administration, and supplementary material was provided by the different departments.
5 For a detailed description of all these activities, see García Segura (1993).
6 Between January 1981 and July 1993, Jordi Pujol made 172 visits abroad

to 176 destinations (they are considered different destinations in a single visit abroad if he visits different countries). The priority destination was the European Community (136). The goals pursued were either of a political, economic or cultural type or were related to participation in networks and bodies of European inter-regional cooperation.

7 Since 1986 the Generalitat has been approving a budgetary aid package each year for the Third World which it distributes through non-governmental organizations. It began with 7 million pesetas and in 1993 reached 350 million pesetas. Along similar lines, in 1990 the Basque government created a Managing Commission for Cooperation and Aid to Development of the Third World Fund and a Technical Commission to assist it, to take charge of the management of the cooperation budget (600 million pesetas in 1990).

8 One of the most recent clashes was provoked by claims of the Basque government for their own external policy for relations with the European Union. There was an immediate response from the central government to the Basque claim: rejection on the grounds of being unconstitutional.

9 Spain and Latin America

Jean Grugel

One of the major consequences of democratization for foreign policy in Spain was a policy shift from bilateralism to multilateralism. That is, foreign relations ceased to be based just on country-to-country contacts and began to flow through the organizations of which Spain became a member after the demise of the Francoist dictatorship. Policy came to be influenced by the alliances assumed under the constitutional monarchy. Democratization brought with it the development of a firm and unambiguous commitment to western Europe and the Atlantic axis of foreign policy. The Atlanticist orientation was only made clear by the mid-1980s, however, after the Socialist party (PSOE) won the 1982 elections: entry into the EC and confirmation of NATO membership followed. Earlier, Suárez's foreign minister, Marcelino Oreja, could still speak of 'three axes to foreign policy, the European, the Ibero-american and the Arab' as if they were equally important (Armero 1989: 45).[1] It was only after 1986 that Latin America was explicitly relegated to the status of a 'special relationship'. Our interest here is to analyse how the transformation of Spain's external relations – democratization, multilateralism and Atlanticism – has worked out within the context of Spain's 'special relationship' with Latin America.

The role of Spain's 'special relationships' was a central part of the debate on the direction of Spain's democratic foreign policy, formed by the late 1970s, which focused in particular on how exactly multilateralism should be constructed. For many inside the Foreign Ministry and the Socialist party, it was clear that Franco's reliance on a bilateral relationship with the USA, symbolized by the Pacts of Madrid and the bases deal dating from 1953, had resulted in a weakening of Spain's international presence. Spain had found itself enmeshed in a defensive pact with the USA over which its influence was minimal. For some sectors of the new democratic élite, incorporation into the EC and NATO would remedy Spain's weak international presence. In particular, adhesion to the EC was seen as the main forum through which Spain could defend its national interests. As a result, Spain became an enthusiastic supporter of the European Union and of a common foreign and security policy. The most enthusiastic endorsers of full incorporation into the Western alliance were to propose in the early and mid-1980s subsuming Spain's special relationship with Latin America within the framework of EC/western European relations with Latin America on a region-to-region basis.

For others, however, the place awarded to Latin America within the scheme of multilateralism was rather more significant. Within this school of thought, Fernando Morán's analysis was particularly influential, especially until 1986. According to Morán, the PSOE's first foreign minister, Spain had found itself reduced in the Francoist era to the position of a 'satellite' of the USA in that it lost the capacity for significant autonomous action (Armero 1989). This was in spite of the avowed neutralism of Francoist discourse. But Morán recognized that satellization was not simply a result of Spain's exclusion from a full international role because of the dictatorship. It was an objective problem facing all medium-sized powers in an international system polarized between two superpowers. In Spain's case, her tradition of non-involvement in international conflicts and her weak military presence made the danger even greater. Therefore a central problem facing democratic Spain in external affairs was how to increase her influence abroad and avoid further satellization. 'Special relationships' could play a fundamental role in the pursuit of these aims. Morán argued that Spain's room for manoeuvre within Europe and with the USA would depend on the extent to which it maintained privileged relationships outside Europe and the Atlantic (Morán 1984). By contrast, Fernando Fernández Ordóñez, foreign minister between 1985 and 1993, was to argue first for bringing Spain's policy on Latin America into line with the rest of Europe and then for being able to assume a position of leadership on Latin American issues, a policy orientation continued by his successor in the Foreign Ministry, Javier Solana.

POLITICAL AND CULTURAL LINKS

The idea that an 'Hispanic universe' exists, uniting Spain with the Spanish-speaking territories of the New World in spite of the geographic distance, became the cornerstone of Spain's interest in Latin America after the collapse of her overseas empire. (By extension, Brazil and Portugal can be included in the Hispanic world, which depends essentially on an opposition to Anglo-Saxon culture and politics, posited as dominant and, particularly after the 1898 Spanish–American War, as threatening the autonomy and cultural integrity of Spanish-speaking countries.) This is known in Spanish as *hispanidad*.

Hispanidad, however, found far more outlets for expression in literary and cultural movements than in government-to-government relations. Beyond the élitist circles of the arts in early twentieth century Spain, the most important link with Latin America was through Spanish emigration. News of relatives who had left for Argentina, Cuba, Mexico, Chile and Venezuela kept Latin America very much in the forefront of public consciousness. Emigration to Latin America continued until the end of the 1950s, leading to the establishment of Spanish communities with close ties to Europe. This explains why the reverberations of the Spanish civil war, sometimes perceived as a peculiarly 'European' affair, were felt from Mexico City to Buenos Aires.

But with only a few exceptions – the Franco-Perón protocol of 1946 and the defiance of the US blockade against Cuba in the early 1960s – cultural contacts and migratory flows did not translate into government initiatives on the part of Spain. Francoist policy relied more heavily on contacts with Latin American countries in the absence of other alternatives, at least until the 1960s, but depended mainly on insisting on a common culture with Spain as the 'motherland' and little else. In order to promote ties within the Hispanic world, Franco created the Consejo de la Hispanidad (Council for Hispanidad) in 1940 as a vehicle for cultural penetration in Latin America. Following the defeat of the Axis, Francoist foreign policy went through a reorganization, and in an effort to pacify the Allies, especially the USA, who had been suspicious of the intentions of the Consejo de la Hispanidad, the Instituto de Cultura Hispánica (Institute for Hispanic Culture) was created. Later, in the democratic period, the Instituto de Cultura Hispánica evolved into the Centro Iberoamericano de Cooperación (Iberoamerican Centre for Cooperation) and then into the Instituto de Cooperación Iberoamericana (Institute for Iberoamerican Cooperation, known in Spanish by the abbreviation ICI). ICI was to play a central role promoting Spain's new democratic policies in Latin America, coordinating development co-operation programmes, funding and publishing Spanish research on Latin America and promoting the fifth centenary celebrations in 1992.

The emphasis on *culture* was the key to understanding Spain's relationship with Latin America until 1976 and to some extent even up to 1982. But after 1976, culture as the central link in the special relationship was indelibly and fatally associated with Falangism and Francoism. Emphasizing Spain's cultural links with Latin America was seen merely as a justification for Catholic reaction and dictatorship through the spurious argument of cultural specificity. This was in spite of a reworking of the notion of cultural ties by the Suárez government, especially in terms of linking it to the idea of democratization of 'Iberoamerica' – that is, the Hispanic world as a whole. Although there were some important symbolic gestures on Latin American issues under the Suárez government, strongly supported by King Juan Carlos, these were partial and fragmented (Piñol 1982). After 1982, especially, a new, more realist appraisal of the links between Spain and Latin America was consciously sought. The PSOE tried to interweave Latin American policy into an overall vision of the international system. An increasing North–South focus entered government policy, and, with it, support for western European initiatives towards the region.

THE CONSTITUTION AND LATIN AMERICA AND THE LATIN AMERICAN LOBBY

Spain's interest in Latin America was henceforth postulated on historical links rather than a common culture. The PSOE tried to offer concrete and coherent policies instead of empty rhetoric. First, there was an effort to shape a new agenda of relations, insisting on the promotion of democracy, human rights and economic development. Second, the PSOE government argued for the promotion of new economic ties, in industry, investment and development cooperation, which included mobilizing private sector investment as well as public funds. Third, in the run-up to entering the EC and NATO and in the immediate period afterwards, the idea of a triangular relationship was promoted, between Spain, Latin America and the EC, and the Spanish government offered itself as spokesperson for Latin America in western councils. And fourth, Spain has been active in promoting Iberoamerican summits, a kind of Commonwealth conference of Latin American, Spanish and Portuguese leaders. Summits were held in 1991 (Guadalajara, Mexico), 1992 (Madrid) and 1993 (Bahía, Brazil). After 1993, it was decided to hold them every two years instead of annually. This was partly in recognition of the fact that Latin America's main foreign policy concerns currently centre on the Americas and regional integration and less on Spain and Europe than at the beginning of the decade.

These policies have been underpinned by the recognition of the importance of Latin America to Spain contained in the democratic constitution and by the strength of support for a proactive Latin policy within society. The King performs an important symbolic function in relations with Latin America, one that he has taken seriously, carrying the message of civil liberties, human rights and democracy to Latin

America in a series of official visits since the late 1970s. Royal diplomacy was particularly significant in the run-up to the fifth centenary celebrations in 1992, alongside the promotion of the idea of an Iberoamerican Community, linking Spain and Portugal with Latin America. It is an idea, however, that has merited little interest inside Latin America.

Latin America occupies a unique place on the agenda of Spanish foreign policy in that there are a significant number of agencies and areas within the public arena in Spanish society that are interested in demonstrating solidarity with the region. Political and economic development processes in Latin America, and Spanish and European policies towards Latin America, are hotly debated within Spain's civil society, beyond the closed circles of policy-makers. This is unusual in a society still relatively unaccustomed to participating in international affairs. It is not too difficult to explain why: a sufficient number of Spanish citizens presume that the legacy of culture and history gives Spaniards a unique insight into the working of Latin America and the right to opine on regional affairs. The presence of Spanish citizens, or first-generation emigrants in Latin American countries, and the formation of communities of Latin American citizens – in Madrid and Barcelona in particular – in the 1980s intensified this belief. Public opinion polls revealed through the 1980s an increasing popular acceptance of Spanish diplomatic activity in the region, especially in Central America (Fagot Aviel 1992).

The conditions for the emergence of an influential, though very loose and ideologically heterogenous, 'Latin American lobby' were created by the opening up of the foreign policy process with democratization. Not always directly influential on government policy, the Latin American lobby has none the less been responsible for maintaining Spain's Latin American policies within the public domain. Though not an exhaustive list, the lobby includes the following groups:

- Significant sectors of the universities and the academic world, some of which have close ties of long standing with the Socialist party, the media, the ministries of Education and Culture, and the Foreign Ministry.
- The foreign affairs departments of both trade union federations, the Socialist UGT and the pro-Communist *Comisiones Obreras*, both of which regularly support Latin American solidarity organizations.
- Sectors of the right, especially those tied in some way to the policies of cultural expansion or promotion in Latin America.
- Non-governmental organizations (NGOs), many of which are small and poorly funded but with some influence in the universities, the

political parties and the administration, and privileged in terms of access to development cooperation funding both nationally and through the EU.

- ICI, which is part of the Foreign Ministry, but also plays a prominent educational and cultural role. It hosts public conferences and symposia on Latin American issues; coordinates meetings between Latin American academics, diplomats and ministers and their Spanish and European counterparts; publishes books and reports on Latin American issues; and is an important source of funding for research on Latin America and NGO activity in the region (IRELA 1987). ICI also makes a series of grants available to Latin Americans and Spaniards for academic exchanges. ICI operates as a source of pressure on government and at the same time exists to generate support for government policies.
- The media, in particular the daily papers *El País* and *ABC*, which, from totally different ideological perspectives, regularly and critically assess government action in Latin America and offer space to academics, diplomats and politicians – both Spanish and Latin American. The influence of the media is inevitably difficult to quantify, but there is no doubt that it is immense in terms of shaping public perceptions of international issues.

Throughout the 1980s, Latin American issues – from human rights abuses in Chile, Argentina, El Salvador, Guatemala, Brazil and Peru to trade agreements between Mexico and the USA, and from the South Atlantic war in 1982 to the US invasion of Panama in 1989 – consistently made front-page news and merited long articles of commentary and interpretation, much more so than elsewhere in the European press. The Spanish press has also dealt critically with Spanish arms sales in Latin America, and government responses to ETA activities in Venezuela, the Dominican Republic, Cuba and Nicaragua. It is interesting to note the gap that separates *El País* from *ABC* in their coverage of Latin American affairs. An analysis of editorials in *El País* between 1983 and 1988 reveals a preoccupation with the Central American crisis above all, and underlines the conviction that Spain – and Europe – have a responsibility in the region; democratization, the external debt and Latin America's development crisis were other important topics. *ABC* meanwhile remained concerned principally with Cuba.

We should be wary of attaching too much influence to the lobby upon policy-making. All the interest in Latin America finds only a reduced echo in the parliamentary arena and in party politics. During the initial stages of the transition, the Foreign Ministry came under pressure for greater openness in policy-making, but these demands came mainly from the left. With the PSOE in government and the Communists and ex-Communists in disarray, criticism has become more muted. In addition, at the level of party politics, since Spain's entry into the EC and NATO there has been far more homogeneity surrounding foreign and defence policies, and this again tends to reduce the effectiveness of the Americanist lobby.

SPAIN AND LATIN AMERICAN DEMOCRATIZATION

The transition to democracy in Spain occurred just as dictatorships spread throughout Latin America. This created an opportunity for the democratic élite in Spain to became an important voice in international circles, denouncing dictatorship and supporting Latin American democracy. They were legitimized in this particularly by the success of their own endeavour. At the same time, support for democratization abroad shored up Spanish democracy at home, signalling to the rest of Europe and the USA, as well as to recalcitrant Francoists, that no return to dictatorship would be permitted. The governments of Suárez and González found an important source of support in King Juan Carlos in projecting this new image of Spanish diplomacy, committed to democratization inside and outside the country.

External policies in support of democratization are undertaken for multiple reasons (Goldman and Douglas 1988). In the case of Spain, this policy had two distinct motives, apart from that of seeing Latin Americans enjoy the same system of representation and political liberties that the Spanish themselves were only now experiencing. It brought foreign policy into line with the internal changes taking place inside the country and it created the possibility of renewed influence in Latin America. For Suárez especially, promoting democratization abroad was a way of winning electoral support at home: if the new democracy could not achieve concrete material gains in view of the economic difficulties facing the country between 1977 and 1981, it could at least offer the Spanish electorate the extraordinary sight of a young, dynamic and approachable prime minister consulting with US President Carter, visiting and advising Castro in Cuba and discussing with Latin American leaders how to negotiate the early stages of the transition.

We should distinguish between governmental and non-governmental organizations in the promotion of democracy. Democratization in Spain witnessed a flowering of non-governmental organizations, a majority of which operate in Latin America, coinciding with an increased participation of non-governmental actors in foreign relations internationally through the 1980s. Spanish NGOs tended to spread their resources thinly over the region, eventually concentrating programmes in Central America, and understood economic development as the main path to democratization. Governmental policies in promotion of democracy, in contrast, were centred on the Southern Cone countries of Chile, Uruguay and Argentina. In Chile, where the identification of PSOE leaders in particular with the government of Salavador Allende, overthrown in 1973, had been considerable, Socialist solidarity with the Chilean opposition was notable. The Socialist government also developed a close relationship with the government of Alfonsín in Argentina (the Foreign Ministry having distanced itself from the general west European position on the Falklands/Malvinas war and expressed support for the Argentinian claims over the islands). Not only was the first of Spain's bilateral treaties with Latin American countries signed with Argentina, but Alfonsín was awarded the Prince of Asturias Prize for Iberoamerican Cooperation in 1985. On repeated occasions Spanish government officials denied that they were attempting to 'export' the Spanish model of democratization, citing cultural, geopolitical and development differences (Bayó 1994). None the less, many Latin American politicians have drawn attention to the role the Spanish transition has played in the region, and in particular to the Moncloa Pacts as a symbol both of the possibility of tripartite negotiations during a period of economic difficulty and of a general spirit of discussion and compromise between potentially antagonistic actors in society.

The attitude of UCD governments towards Latin American democratization had been mostly declamatory and dependent on the combined moral weight of Spain and the figure of the King in favour of democracy. The Socialist governments after 1982 chose to try to promote democratization in Latin America in two ways in particular: through policies of economic cooperation and modernization of Latin American economies; and through encouraging the moderation of the Latin American left, through the Socialist International and indeed through the example of the PSOE itself, which abandoned Marxism and embraced capitalist modernization and privatization when in government (Grugel 1993).

Spanish support for democratization through economic modernization is expressed through the promotion of and support for reform of EU policy on Latin America, and through an attempt at stimulating closer economic ties (aid and investment, especially, but also trade) between Spain and those countries of the region engaged in transitions to democracy. Although treaties of friendship and cooperation were signed with a number of Latin American states after 1988, the treaties with Argentina and Chile are those that most clearly bear the hallmark of aid and development cooperation as a form of external support for democracy. They were aimed not only at supporting programmes of export promotion in Latin America and increasing the international presence of Spanish enterprises, but also at supporting democratization in a more direct sense: the treaties are only valid so long as democratic governments are in power – the so-called 'democracy clause'.

In the case of Chile, the Strategic Plan for Cooperation with Chile, drawn up by ICI, identified three strategic objectives, the first of which was 'support for policies of institutional, political and social development of a system based on freedom'. The other priorities were 'supporting economic development and the process of regional integration and cooperation' (ICI 1990: 253). The most important area for non-returnable aid to Chile was social spending channelled through the newly-created Solidarity and Social Investment Fund, aimed at reducing poverty and thereby lowering social tensions which could destabilize the transition (ibid.).

Interestingly, the PSOE government refused to use Chile's external debt as a lever to pressurize the Pinochet dictatorship to democratize. When voting on structural loans to Chile at the World Bank, Spain chose to abstain in 1986 and voted in favour of the loans in 1987 (Portales 1991). In the same way, Spain rejected commercial boycotts as a means of promoting democracy. Spain even continued to sell military matériel to Chile in the 1980s through the Spanish public company, CASA.

The impact of the PSOE's influence upon the Latin American political élites is obviously rather more difficult to document. It is, clearly, much less a case of 'persuasion' than a 'coincidental transformation' taking place among Socialist parties in southern Europe and Latin America. Socialist parties began to take on board the need to incorporate a greater preoccupation with democracy and human rights than in the past. This shift was part of an increasing awareness of the problems associated with the introduction and consolidation of representative institutions amid a profound transformation of leftist doctrine (Barros 1986). In this climate, the PSOE came to be seen as a successful example of the transformation from Marxism to social democracy in that the PSOE's own ideological rethink strengthened the Spanish party system and at the same time offered an attractive formula to the electorate, guaranteeing it victory in four consecutive elections.

The meeting place for Spanish and Latin American socialists was the Socialist International (SI), with the PSOE tending to monopolize European representation on SI committees dealing with Latin American affairs. Indeed, as early as 1978 the SI had recognized the special role of the PSOE in Latin America. In *Democratization in the Iberian Peninsular and Latin America*, the International declared: 'Spain and Portugal are countries which could be said to be in a process of transition between Latin America and the democratic, industrialized Europe. The consolidation of democratic institutions in the two countries . . . is necessary if closer relations are to be established between Europe and Latin America, and it is important in the future institutionalization of democracy in Latin America' (Godoy 1986: 37).

There were some changes in the PSOE's discourse on democracy at the beginning of the 1990s. Traditionally aimed at isolating military dictatorships, the PSOE also began to call on Fidel Castro for democratization in Cuba. The party responded thus to a gradual deterioration in its relations with the Cuban communists, which set in after Spain's entry to NATO and intensified after the embassy crisis of August 1990 (when numerous Cuban citizens entered the Spanish embassy in Havana requesting asylum). A further PSOE motive has been the fear of losing influence in Cuba at the end of Castro's period in office. Cuba is extremely important to Spain for reasons of history. At the third Iberoamerican summit in Brazil, González commented, after a two-hour private conversation with Castro, that he perceived a 'greater flexibilty when it comes to understanding the need for changes in the system of production and to accepting change from the political point of view'. In the same press interview, González was firm in his conviction that the economic crisis was less a result of the US boycott than of the intrinsic errors of Cuban political economy (*El País*, 18 July 1993). Shortly after, the Spanish government took the unusual step of sending to Cuba a team of Spanish economists, headed by the former Minister of the Economy, Carlos Solchaga, to promote economic liberalization.

SPAIN AND THE CENTRAL AMERICAN CRISIS

The 'Central American crisis', which dragged on throughout the 1980s, refers to the series of violent local conflicts in El Salvador, Nicaragua and Guatemala. Following Ronald Reagan's victory in November 1980, Washington decided to support anti-left movements with unprecedented military, economic and diplomatic aid. Reagan's aim was to reverse the victory of the Sandinistas in Nicaragua in 1979 and to prevent leftist movements coming to power elsewhere. Policy was justified through the Reagan Doctrine. Neighbouring countries, especially Honduras and Costa Rica, where no serious guerilla movements existed, also found themselves embroiled in the conflict by US activity in the region. The crisis led to an intensification of contacts and relations between west European governments and political parties and their counterparts on the Central American isthmus. One of the main points of contact for Central American governments in Europe was Spain, where the problems of the region were perceived as a complicated mix of underdevelopment, oligarchical domination, US intervention and civil war, rather than through an East–West lens as in Washington.

Analysing the PSOE government's Central American policies in the period was never easy, especially in view of the low-key approach favoured. Policies were located between, on the one hand, the diplomatic limitations the Spanish government had accepted as inevitable in view of its dependence on the US and the weakness of western Europe as an independent international actor; and, on the other, a genuine sense of solidarity with the promotion of democracy and development in the region. Consequently, despite grand rhetorical denunciations of the dangers of foreign interference in the area (for which read the USA), characteristic of the PSOE in opposition and even in the very early period of the Socialist government, Prime Minister González carefully avoided taking an overtly anti-American line. González was equally wary of assuming a mediating role in the crisis, especially publicly, despite being urged to do so on occasion by both Costa Rica and Nicaragua. Tensions were also evident at times between the Socialist party, committed to more radical policies for the region, and the government, influenced in part by pressure from the Ministry of the Interior which suspected the Sandinistas of harbouring sympathies for the Basque 'armed struggle' independence movement ETA (Story 1991: 69–70).

In the 1980s, in particular, Spain became a focus of Nicaraguan and Costa Rican diplomacy and an important source of diplomatic support for the Contadora group (Panama, Mexico, Colombia and Venezuela), which sought to promote regional dialogue as a way of lessening the possibility of US intervention. The Socialist government was, along with the German Foreign Ministry, the most enthusiastic backer within western Europe of Contadora and of the peace plan which was produced in 1987 by Costa Rican President Oscar Arias. It was also one of the key supporters of the institutionalization of relations between the EC and Central American heads of state via the San José summits which began in 1984. Spanish representation has consistently been at ministerial level, although many west European governments have sent junior representatives from their foreign offices. The PSOE has also occasionally played a low-key negotiating role in the various conflicts in the region, despite González's avowal that negotiation in the region was outside the scope of Spanish diplomacy. In 1985, talks were held at the Spanish Embassy in Managua between the Sandinistas and the opposition Liberal and Social Christian parties; in 1986, Fernández Ordóñez offered the good offices of Spain to stimulate dialogue between the Nicaraguan government and the opposition; Spain sporadically hosted talks between guerrilla forces and governments in El Salvador and Guatemala; and until around 1988, Central America, in particular Nicaragua, was the main recipient of Spanish aid.

One of most significant points of dissension in relation to the Central American crisis between the US government and many west European governments, in particular the PSOE government, arose out of the European insistence that there were two distinct crises in the region, or at least two distinct manifestations of the crisis: the long-term problems associated with extreme inequalities of wealth and power, and the 'low intensity war'. The Socialist Miguel Angel Martínez, then President of the Foreign Affairs Committee in the Congress of Deputies, argued that it was the 'absence of freedom and democracy and national dignity' which led to 'underdevelopment, illiteracy, unemployment and chronic illness' in the region (Martínez 1984: 25). Central America was thus seen to stand in need of a two-pronged strategy: the promotion of economic development and the promotion of democracy. This was in sharp contrast with US government interpretations of the crisis. According to Secretary of State Alexander Haig, the Central American crisis was the result of a Soviet 'hit list . . . for the ultimate take-over of Central America', and according to Reagan, 'a determined propaganda campaign . . . sought to mislead many in Europe . . . as to the true nature of the conflict' (Schoutz 1987: 65).

Spanish recognition of the legitimacy of the Sandinista revolution, therefore, and support for a negotiated end to the conflict, contained the potential for damaging Spain's relationship with the USA. The government of Jimmy Carter had been a firm supporter of Spanish democratization, for which the new political élites were grateful. US investment in the economy was essential, and most importantly of all, the Spanish government was engaged for much of the decade in delicate negotiations with the USA over the future of American military bases. All of this meant that the Spanish government was unwilling to antagonize President Reagan. Moreover, the Reagan government put into operation a diplomatic initiative designed to discourage west European governments from taking too independent a line on the question of Central America. The PSOE, meanwhile, was only prepared to assume a policy towards Central America that won the backing of colleagues in the SI and the EC. Finally, as the decade wore on, the PSOE's commitment to the Nicaraguan revolution wavered, as it evaluated increasingly negatively the internal and external policies pursued by the Sandinistas. As a result of these factors, the government adopted a more moderate line. Express support and the initial admiration for the Sandinistas declined, to be replaced by a more critical assessment. In 1985, Fernando Morán commented: ‘the Nicaraguan Revolution rapidly changed its original principles in 1981. It proclaimed its support for the guerrilla movement in El Salvador, and expelled from power representatives of the liberal middle class, becoming a destabilizing force in the region’ (Morán 1985a: 37).

Critical support for the Sandinistas and a more muted attitude to the US role in the region thereafter became the order of the day, a tendency accentuated when Morán was replaced by Fernández Ordóñez in 1985. The Spanish government began to receive Nicaraguan civilian opposition leaders in the Moncloa, as well as the Sandinistas. At the same time, however, the government cultivated contacts inside the Democratic party in the US Congress in support of more restrained US policies in the isthmus than the Reagan team wished for. The end of the Reagan era brought to a close the most outrageous of US covert operations in the region, and this, along with the Sandinistas losing the presidential elections of 1990 to Violeta Chamarro, paved the way for a lowering of regional tensions. Spain went on to form part of the group of countries that advised the UN Secretary General Pérez de Cuellar when negotiating a peace settlement in El Salvador, and the Spanish armed forces have played an important role in the UN peace-keeping mission in the country since 1992.

SPAIN, LATIN AMERICA AND THE EC

After 1977 the Spanish government’s most important external task was to conclude the difficult negotiations for EC entry. After 1983 its second task was to justify its turnaround on NATO. While EC and NATO issues were being resolved, we can identify little more than a series of *ad hoc* measures in Latin American policy responding to the dramatic events engulfing the region and Spain’s public sensitivity to developments there. After 1986, now under pressure to articulate a clearer regional policy, the government opted for emphasizing the multilateral approach and the idea of a triangular relationship: Spain/EC/Latin America. In an interview in 1987, for example, Fernández Ordóñez discussed Spain’s Latin American policy solely in the context of regional initiatives through the EC (Fernández Ordóñez 1987). The foreign minister’s argument amounted to the proposition that if Latin America were to become an important area for EC activity, Spain should play a key role in constructing the EC's Latin American policy. The government justified this approach to Latin American governments and to its own internal 'Latin American lobby' by arguing that the development needs of Latin America could only be addressed within a multilateral framework. González claimed: 'the only role that we can and should play is that of insisting inside the European Community that the political and economic development of Latin America is enormously important for the Community itself' (González 1989: 148).

Spain's triangular strategy was grounded in the fact that the EC had demonstrated greater interest in Latin American affairs in the early 1980s than at any time since 1945, partly as a consequence of the Nicaraguan revolution and the Latin American debt crisis, and partly as a result of Western Europe's own interest in expanding its international presence. Contadora was well received in Europe; EC initiatives to formalize contacts with Central America date from 1984, before Spain's accession to the EC, and owe much to French and German support for widening the EC's range of international contacts. West European trade with, and aid to, Nicaragua increased throughout the early 1980s until 1985, despite US pressure (Conroy 1987).

Within the EC, Spain consistently promoted deeper relations with Latin America through an expanded aid and development cooperation budget for the region, through encouraging European Parliament contacts with the region and through the institutionalization of region-to-region dialogue. In particular, Spain sought to shape the established dialogues with Central America and the Río Group into European support for Latin American regional integration schemes.

However, the Spanish have failed to increase really significantly the amount of EC aid directed towards Latin America. This is in spite of the fact that it was expressly part of the Spanish agenda (Fernández Ordóñez 1987). Aid to Latin America was 25 per cent of the total EC budget for aid to Latin America and Asia before 1988 and rose to 35 per cent for 1989 and thereafter. One analysis of EC aid policies in Latin America to 1992 commented:

> the progress of cooperation with the region . . . has been slow in a double sense: resources have arrived only gradually, by degree, and moreover, they have not addressed the principal 'hard-core' issues, those upon which Latin American long term development depends: development of strategic human resources, the transfer of key technologies and sustainable development strategies. (ILPES 1992: 72)

One important sign of Spanish sucess, however, was the accession of the Dominican Republic to the fourth Lomé Agreement, effective from 1990. It is significant that the one Spanish-speaking territory to benefit from preferential EC aid deals is located in the Caribbean, and not on mainland Central or Southern America, given the resistance from EC member states, especially the UK, Germany and France, to extend Lomé membership beyond the established areas of Africa, the Caribbean and the Pacific. The Dominican Republic's application to join Lomé, endorsed by Spain, was made in conjunction with Haiti and required protracted and difficult negotiations to bring it to a successful conclusion. In the end, the Dominican Republic obtained a kind of second-class membership, agreeing to remain outside the concessionary protocols for sugar, bananas and rum. In view of all this, it is highly unlikely that Spain would support another application (Grugel 1991). Another, rather more meagre achievement, came in 1991 when Latin America was granted access to funds from the European Investment Bank, an initiative supported not only by Spain but also by Portugal and Italy.

SPAIN, LATIN AMERICA AND BILATERALISM

The PSOE government had undertaken to negotiate in favour of Latin America inside the European Community during the protracted entry negotiations in order to minimize the commercial losses that Latin America would sustain as a result of the enlargement (Marín 1986). After 1986 foreign policy discourse made much of the idea of Spain as an interlocutor or 'echo' of Latin America in the Community. Nevertheless, the concrete gains of the Spain/EC/Latin America strategy were few. It had overestimated western Europe's commitment to the region. EC interest in Latin America remained limited. It reached a plateau towards the end of the 1980s with the insititutionalization of group-to-group dialogue and the signing of the so-called 'Third Generation' Agreements with the larger of the Latin American countries whose economies looked most stable.

The strategy contained another flaw from the point of view of Spanish diplomacy which was to become evident after 1986: Spain is by no means the only possible interlocutor or 'echo' for Latin America in Europe. Many European/Latin American contacts pass through the SI, or the international Christian Democracy movement; and contacts through parties, foundations, economic organizations and development agencies between Latin American countries and Germany, France and Italy had already established the framework of region-to-region relations. British and German NGOs have a long-established important presence in the region. The PSOE government realized that to maintain the 'special relationship' a greater economic presence in the region was necessary. Yet this ran counter to the trend in the direction of Spanish trade. Spain was becoming less important in commercial terms to Latin America as the 1980s progressed: between 1980 and 1986, the value of Spanish/Latin American trade fell by a third, and by 1986 Latin America only represented 3.6 per cent of Spanish exports and only 2.6 per cent of its imports. From 1988 in particular, therefore, efforts were made to strengthen Spain's economic presence in Latin America.

Spain's economic presence internationally has traditionally been weak. In addition, following entry to the EC, Spanish investors concentrated on trying to establish a presence inside Europe. Spanish trade has also tended to be concentrated inside the EC, a tendency we can see emerging from the 1960s. But, coinciding with the economic stabilization and the beginnings of growth in some Latin American countries, the Spanish government consciously decided to foment investment in and exports to Latin America, as part of a drive to internationalize its economy. This has involved rethinking the role of government agencies related to external trade, including the Spanish Institute of External Trade (Insitituto Español de Comercio Exterior – ICEX), and the creation of Sirecox in 1988, a state-owned company whose aim is to help Spanish companies penetrate non-traditional markets. Sirecox started promoting activities in Latin America in 1991 (Freres 1992).

So far, a majority of Spanish investment in Latin America has come from public companies, including Iberia, Telefónica, ENDESA (Empresa Nacional de Electricidad SA) and Repsol. Ninety per cent of all Spanish direct investment in Argentina, totalling 6,200 million dollars, for example, is through publicly owned companies, in the areas of telecomunications, transport and energy. Spanish banks have also started moving into Latin America. Unlike other European banks, they were not affected by the Latin American debt crisis of the 1980s because, at that stage, their investments in the region were limited. Their interest had coincided with the start of recovery of Latin American economies after 1990. For the Central-Hispanoamericano, the Santander and Banesto, investment in Latin America constituted 50 per cent of their investments abroad after this date.

Mexico, Spain's most important Latin American trading partner, is the most attractive country for investment, mainly because of the privatization programme in place since 1986 and the projected growth of the Mexican economy as a result of the North American Free Trade Area (NAFTA). The second most favoured destiny for foreign investment is Argentina. But private investment outside the banking sector has been slower to move in, despite government encouragement through the bilateral treaties signed with Argentina, Chile, Venezuela, Mexico and Colombia between 1988 and 1993 which, though they cover a broad range of issues, refer primarily to investment possibilities and the creation of joint ventures. In percentage terms of new investment in Latin America, the Spanish presence remains small, and trade, even compared with other EU members' trade with the region, is limited.

Bilateral initiatives also encompassed a new approach to development cooperation (Freres *et al.* 1992). To compensate for the failure to increase EC aid to Latin America more significantly, Community policies were complemented by government policies to expand nationally allocated aid for Latin America. Despite its limited quantities (in 1990, Fernández Ordóñez recognized that Spain 'spends a ridiculously low figure on development cooperation', *ABC*, 5 March 1990), the reform of aid policies through the 1980s led to an increase in resources directed towards Latin American countries.

Lastly, following Prime Minister González's failure to encourage western European countries to adopt soft policies towards Latin American debt in the 1980s, the PSOE government adopted a bilateral approach, condoning public debt with some of the smaller Latin American countries such as Nicaragua and Bolivia, and in 1989 rescheduled the Mexican debt in an operation that amounted to an almost 50 per cent debt reduction.

CONCLUSION

The ideological bases of Spain's relationship with Latin America have undergone a profound transformation since democratization. From positing the cultural difference of the Hispanic world and even at times suggesting Spanish leadership within that cultural universe, Spanish policy in the region has come to be formulated within the framework of North–South, region-to-region relations, built on a bedrock of shared history. The agenda of relations was transformed from stressing cultural ties to one concerned with the negotiated end to internal conflicts, democratization and human rights. More recently, the emphasis has shifted again, to a focus on trade, investment and the impact of regional blocs on the relationship.

Latin America remains a key to understanding Spain's separate identity within Europe. But government activity in the region has not always been consistent or coherent. It has followed a kind of pendular movement since democratization. In the first phase, until the accession of the PSOE to power, Spanish policy in Latin America was limited to attempts at rethinking the bases of the Spanish presence in the region, establishing contacts between the new democratic élites in Spain and their counterparts in Latin America, and upholding Spanish ties with Cuba. Foreign policy in Latin America also served an important internal function in shoring up the transition. In the first phase of PSOE government, policy towards the region came to be shaped within the EC/Latin America multilateral mould, and there was excessive optimism about the capacity of Spain to influence the agenda of external relations of the Community. Since 1988, in particular, we can trace the development of a realist policy, based on a realization, first, that Spain cannot shape western Europe's Latin American policy and, secondly, that European policies cannot replace national policy.

NOTES

1 Since the transition in Spain, policy makers and academics alike have increasingly adopted the term 'Iberoamerica' to refer to either Latin America or Latin America plus Spain, or Latin America plus Spain and Portugal. The meaning can usually be deciphered according to the context. Because its use is confined to Spain and because of the ambiguities of the term, I have chosen to use instead 'Latin America'.

10 Spain and the Maghreb

Towards a regional policy?

Richard Gillespie

Relations with neighbouring states in north-west Africa became a priority area for Spanish diplomacy during the 1980s when it was thought that the country's historical 'special relationship' with the Arab world might facilitate a more influential role for Spain in the western Mediterranean. In fact, this purported relationship, although grounded in seven centuries of cohabitation on the Iberian peninsular, had been much undermined over the years by both confrontation and neglect, before being resurrected in the diplomatic discourse of the present century, in part to justify Spain's belated colonial involvement in Morocco.

Unlike France, Spain never had a sustained project of colonial conquest and settlement in the Maghreb, being content (or constrained by financial or military factors) principally to establish coastal footholds (Hillgarth 1976: 253). Even the Moroccan Protectorate established in 1912 had only 90,000 Spanish settlers by 1954, out of a total population of 1.1 million (Fleming 1980). Economic lobbies seeking a more ambitious policy were never strong; more influential over time was the military lobby which saw in north-west Africa some compensation for the loss of the American empire, plus opportunities for action and promotion. Civilian politicians (under the Second Republic) mistakenly saw Morocco as a welcome diversion for the military from intervention in the domestic political arena.

The Moroccan Protectorate itself was entered upon with clearly preemptive motives, namely to prevent France from becoming a southern as well as a northern neighbour. Ironically, Spain owed its Protectorate to support from stronger Western powers, and especially France, a circumstance that gave rise to deference as well as resentment. Spain demurred from greater ambition in the Maghreb partly through fear of upsetting France; only tentatively and briefly did Spanish diplomats engage in more imaginative attempts to exploit the animosity of

Moroccan nationalists towards the French, only to discover that in the long run this nationalism inevitably challenged the Spanish presence too. By 1976 successive withdrawals from the Spanish Protectorate, Ifni and the Western Sahara had reduced Spain's populated territories to the coastal towns of Ceuta and Melilla, both claimed by Morocco.

Of all of Spain's traditional relationships within the Arab world, none has been so crucial as its 'fixation' with neighbouring Morocco (Morán 1980: 96). The Moroccan factor loomed large in the civil war and later Franco and the military resisted calls for decolonization that emanated from the Ministry of Foreign Affairs under Castiella (Criado 1975: 29; Armero 1978: 201–2), only to condemn Spain to a hurried and highly unsatisfactory withdrawal from the Western Sahara amidst the crisis provoked by King Hassan's 'Green March' in 1975. The final decision to give in to Moroccan pressure is often attributed to right-wing Francoist fears about the growth of the radical Polisario movement (Villar 1992: 249–50; Diego Aguirre 1991: 100).

Meanwhile, Spain had pursued a more general policy of cultivating the Arab world. This was initiated in 1946 in response to Western sanctions against the Franco regime. The policy was of some commercial value and it suited the energy requirements of an economy highly dependent on external fuel supplies, but for much of the Franco period Spain was content to develop the policy simply to enlist Arab support when votes affecting Spain were taken at the UN (Hills 1967: 407; Morán 1980: 176). The Arab policy never developed from a Francoist reaction to Western and Israeli hostility (Rein 1993) into a positive and coherent project based upon growing cooperation. Indeed, there was less Spanish courtship of the Arab world once the threat of isolation had been seen off in the early 1950s (Crozier 1967: 245-7), and relations were complicated both by the Moroccan independence process and Spain's eventual siding with the West over Suez (Fleming 1980: 134–6). Later the 'special relationship' with the Arab world was called into question by the American use of its Spanish bases to supply Israel during the 1967 Middle East war.

This brief discussion supports the contention of Fernando Morán, Minister of Foreign Affairs (1982–85) under the first Socialist government, that historically Spanish policy in relation to the Maghreb had lacked vision, a clear perception of Spanish regional interests and a sustained policy designed to serve them (Morán 1980: ch. 9). It should be added, however, that it is hard to develop a regional policy towards an area that, while united by geographical contiguity and cultural elements, as a political entity has always existed more as an aspiration than a reality.

The review of the past also shows that, for all its shared history with the Muslim world, Spain's advantages with regard to the Maghreb were limited and highly ambiguous at the end of the Franco period. It was by no means clear that the Maghreb or a Mediterranean policy would feature so prominently in the foreign policy of democratic Spain. That it came to do so was largely a result of the political ascendancy of the Spanish Socialist party (PSOE), Spain's successful entry into the European Community, the country's strong economic performance in the second half of the 1980s, and a growing domestic realization that the problems of the Maghreb would be ignored at Spain's own peril.

FROM 'EQUILIBRIUM' TO A GLOBAL STRATEGY?

There was certainly something of a post-Franco shift in Spanish strategy towards the Maghreb, but this did not occur with Franco's death in 1975 but rather after the arrival of the Socialists in office in 1982, although there was some anticipation of the new direction in the final stages of Adolfo Suárez's presidency. The strategy inherited from Francoism is generally described as one of 'equilibrium', or sometimes as one of 'alternative compensations' (Morán 1983), while the strategy proclaimed by the Socialist government was described as 'global'.

The strategy of 'equilibrium' took as its starting point the internal rivalries within the Maghreb, especially the disputed hegemony between Morocco and Algeria. Spanish policy supposedly sought to maintain a balance between these rivals by only making a friendly gesture towards one if that were followed up with a comparable initiative towards the other. This was never as straightforward as it sounded. Whereas balance may be a desirable objective in relation to two rivals, policies toward the Maghreb often had to grapple with a more complicated equation in which five African states were involved, as were elements such as Polisario and considerations about the Canary Islands ('Madrid-Argel: Un diálogo difícil', *El País*, 7 June 1978). At times Tunisia or Mauritania were courted as a means of checking the two leading countries. But even when applied just to the Moroccan–Algerian dispute, the subtext behind the Spanish strategy of equilibrium was more often than not concerned with seeking means of containing Moroccan nationalist ambitions, for it was these that most directly affected Spanish interests. It was only Morocco, with its designs upon Ceuta and Melilla, that really had the potential to disrupt the internal politics of Spain, and this could never be ignored by Madrid (Marquina Barrio 1991: 38).

It was partly because the equilibrium strategy collapsed so miserably in 1975 that it lost favour. Faced with Moroccan pressure against the Spanish Sahara, Madrid was unable to enlist the counterweight of Algeria in order to resist Moroccan annexation. Yet there was no immediate change of strategy at this time: 'equilibrium' remained the guiding orientation behind Spain's improvised responses to the crisis in its relations with the Maghreb. Moroccan–Spanish tension persisted, notwithstanding the Tripartite Agreement between Spain, Morocco and Mauritania in 1975, which served Morocco's ambitions. Seeing this agreement as a betrayal of Spanish promises on Saharan self-determination, Algeria meanwhile reacted angrily by allowing the extremist proponent of Canary Islands independence, Antonio Cubillo, to commence anti-Spanish broadcasts from Algiers (*Cambio 16*, 19 December 1976). By means of a relatively passive equilibrium policy, designed to placate both Morocco and Algeria, Spanish diplomacy hoped to avert colonial crises at any price and enable the Suárez government to concentrate on the domestic transition to democracy (Armero 1989: 127).

The alternative 'global' strategy implemented (again only partially) by Fernando Morán after the Socialist victory in 1982 sought to foster good bilateral relations with all the Maghreb states simultaneously, so that it would not be necessary to make successive complementary gestures to Algeria and Morocco in particular. A second hallmark of the policy was Spanish encouragement of the Maghreb states to unite in order to facilitate development and thereby bring more stability to the region. A third feature had already been announced as an ambition in the late 1970s under Suárez: the idea of creating 'a web of common interests' between Spain and north-west African states in the hope that interdependency would bring more stable relations and commercial advantage (*Revista de Política Internacional*, 158, 1978: 252).

Policy instruments also changed under the Socialists. Although accompanied by a military reorganization that was based on the existing assumption that the main threat came from the south, the global strategy involved a new emphasis upon development cooperation as a more enlightened way of countering and reducing this 'threat'. The new use of aid and credit was calculated to assist Spanish exports and encourage the international expansion of Spanish companies, and at the same time contribute towards regional security. For by the 1980s it was recognized that if certain potential crises materialized – above all a Moroccan offensive against Ceuta and Melilla – traditional military defence planning would be of little use. The 'enlightened' policy was to promote development in neighbouring areas and to foster a diverse set of interdependent ties and common interests between Spain and north-west African states. This was pursued initially at the bilateral level and later through the multilateral attempt in the early 1990s to establish a Conference on Security and Cooperation in the Mediterranean (CSCM), partly modelled on the CSCE.

The global strategy proved very difficult to implement and thus served only as an approximate guide to the development of Spanish policy towards the Maghreb after 1982. As Morán stated in 1985, globality requires a degree of solidarity among the states that form the relevant international system; in the absence of that solidarity in the Maghreb, Spanish policy under the Socialists in fact oscillated between globalism and equilibrium (Morán 1986: 315–18, 325–43).

Globalism came up against the persistence of tensions within the Maghreb which after 1982 gave rise to the creation of two rival defence groupings: one formed by Algeria, Tunisia and Mauritania, the other, briefly, by Morocco and Libya. Internal conflicts similarly crippled the development of the Maghreb Arab Union (UMA), proclaimed in 1989. Other impediments to the success of the global approach were the international isolation of Libya as a 'pariah state'; Algeria's domestic crisis, which assumed alarming proportions in 1992 when armed forces terminated a process of democratic reform; and the depth and persistence of Spain's economic recession in the early 1990s. While the global policy remained an ideal, and Spain continued to invest in Moroccan–Algerian cooperation through a project to build a natural gas pipeline from Algeria to Spain via Morocco and the straits, after a decade of Socialist government Morocco was still very clearly Spain's fundamental interlocutor in the Maghreb.

THE PURSUIT OF SPANISH INTERESTS IN THE MAGHREB

Spain's relations with north-west African states are concerned with protecting a number of important national interests and promoting stability in the region. Beyond immediate economic and security concerns are Spanish worries about the huge demographic growth in North Africa, where there seems little prospect of adequate economic growth to support it. If in 1950 two-thirds of the Mediterranean population was to be found in southern Europe, by 2025 this proportion will be located in North Africa, on current projections (Daboussi 1991). Although the Maghreb of the future offers Spanish business the lure of a market of 120 million people, the immediate concerns relate to the Islamist challenge and particularly its violent expressions in Algeria. The fear for the future is of an unstable, crisis-ridden North Africa, with stronger demographic pressures to migrate northwards. This scenario is behind the Spanish insistence that if the internal problems of the Maghreb are not addressed, they will be exported increasingly to Europe, where they threaten to bring political instability.

The Maghreb is of economic importance to Spain, despite representing only a small proportion of her overall commerce. Just over 5 per cent of Spanish exports went to North Africa in 1989, of which 80 per cent went to Algeria and Morocco (Franco, Alonso and Pindado 1990: 43–67). In the late 1980s and early 1990s, Morocco was supplying Spain with 80 per cent of her phosphates, quite cheaply; Algeria was the supplier of 50–70 per cent of Spain's natural gas; about 100,000 Spanish families depended for their livelihoods on the fishing grounds off Morocco, the Western Sahara and Mauritania; and around 15 per cent of Spain's imports of crude oil came from the area (Moratinos 1991: 7–8).

There is also a Spanish cultural interest in the Maghreb. The seven-century Arab presence in Spain saw plenty of conflict, but there were also periods in the thirteenth to fifteenth centuries when Muslim, Christian and Jew lived in harmony, to the benefit of the country's development. Andalusia under the Muslims was a leading European centre of civilization. The cultural pluralism on the peninsula did not survive 1492, the expulsion of the Jews, the forced conversion of Muslims and the introduction of the Inquisition, but history provided a key reference point for the post-Franco PSOE modernizers when later they sought to establish an enlightened and tolerant Spain. Moreover, the colonial legacy included a modest Spanish cultural presence in north-west Africa. Morocco emerged as the leading Spanish-speaking country in Africa, with over two million Spanish speakers by the early 1990s, when Spanish was also adopted as a second language in Algerian schools.

Meanwhile, Spain has experienced a new and growing Muslim presence on the peninsula, with well over 100,000 migrants from the Maghreb living in Spain by 1990, and Moroccans constituting the fastest growing immigrant group. With Morocco's population of 26 million growing at 2.2 per cent per annum, 50 per cent of the population being under 20, and urban unemployment reaching 20 per cent, the demographic pressures behind migration were sure to grow. Algeria's emigrants mostly headed for France, but with 84 per cent of Algerians between 15 and 30 jobless, farming yields the poorest in the Mediterranean, and the socio-economic crisis compounded by the threat from the fundamentalists, there was concern that migration from Algeria to Spain might grow also. Spain had the advantage over France of a relatively small proportion of immigrants to absorb: 38 million Spaniards had been joined by approximately 540,000 legal immigrants (half of them European) and 150,000 illegal immigrants. This meant that integrationist policies introduced in the early 1990s had some chance of success if the numbers of new arrivals were effectively controlled; but for this to happen the cooperation of the north-west African authorities was essential.

Spanish policy towards the Maghreb is also concerned with the preservation of Ceuta and Melilla and with the security and economic viability of the Canary Islands. National interests here were seen by the Socialist government as best protected by means of economic and other forms of cooperation, both bilateral and multilateral, designed to assist economic development and encourage political evolution within the Maghreb. The socio-economic and political problems of the area had to be addressed, not just to control the existing northward migrations, but to prevent the establishment of hostile regimes in the Maghreb, which might make territorial demands and apply pressure. Although isolated threats from Morocco, Libya and Algeria had all been dealt with effectively by post-Franco governments, the nightmare in Madrid was of concerted Arab assertiveness, especially if it arrived on a wave of Islamic fundamentalist sentiment.

In defence of national interests, Spain's regional objectives have been sixfold:

1 To assist the economic development of the Maghreb.
2 To create a context for political and economic interdependence.
3 To promote Spain's cultural and economic interests in the region.
4 To prevent the establishment of hostile regimes.
5 To cautiously encourage pluralism and human rights.
6 To commit the EC to Spain's regional objectives.

Of course, there are evident contradictions between some of these objectives. Support for the development of neighbouring states may be inimical to the development of Spanish economic activity, such as fishing. On occasions the desire to prevent the establishment of hostile regimes may eclipse the work in favour of political change in a pluralist direction. Hence, Spanish policy towards the region has faced some acute dilemmas and has provided ammunition for charges of hypocrisy made by government critics. The Socialist government seemed to be offering its experience of democratization as a model for Latin America and central-eastern Europe, but not for the Maghreb. Spain was no longer different – the Arab world was.

AN UNEVEN REGIONAL POLICY

Despite the pursuit of globalism in her relations with the Maghreb, it did not prove possible for the successive UCD and PSOE governments to strengthen ties with all the Maghreb states. Normal relations with Libya proved impossible for the Socialist government, in spite of Spain's interest in Libyan oil, which is of particularly good quality, unlike that imported from Mexico. Spanish construction firms were involved in major infrastructural projects in Libya until 1984, but then were hit by a commercial crisis when Libya fell behind on payments, owing $90 million to Spanish companies. Spain's exports to Libya had still not recovered almost a decade later. However, Libya was still supplying natural gas and up to 20 per cent of Spain's natural gas imports, and there was a Libyan financial presence in Spain via the Banco Arabe Español and Banco Atlántico.

While critical of the Qadhafi regime, Spain generally counselled against punitive US military responses to Libyan external activities, but from 1986 the Spanish position became less tolerant. Entry into the EC, which led Spain to participate in Community sanctions against Libya, coincided with a deterioration in Spanish–Libyan bilateral relations. Besides the commercial crisis, relations were affected by the involvement of US bases in Spain during the American attack on Libya in 1986, which prompted Qadhafi to threaten that his missiles could reach Spain; and the involvement of Libyan representatives in terrorist activity in Spain. There were several expulsions of Libyan diplomats in 1986, almost leading to a total rupture of diplomatic relations (Armero 1989: 206; *El País*, international edn, 6 January 1986, 28 April 1986, 2 June 1986).

Spain's relations with Tunisia and Mauritania were at this time free of crisis, yet in spite of good political relations, which led to the signing of defence agreements in the late 1980s, these countries were not a high priority for Madrid's diplomacy. There was only a small volume of trade with Tunisia, and since the trade balance strongly favoured Spain it was difficult to expand the commercial relationship (EFE 1989). None the less, Tunisia was valued by Spain as a moderate and comparatively liberal factor in the Maghreb, and González's government sought to strengthen ties by means of a framework agreement on economic and commercial cooperation in 1989. Meanwhile, in poor Mauritania Spain's interests were restricted mainly to an economic interest in fishing rights and a strategic concern about the implications for the Canary Islands if this ethnically-divided country should become unstable. The fact that Mauritania came under the Lomé convention meant that the country received less Spanish help within the EU than did Morocco, Algeria and Tunisia – beneficiaries of the EC Mediterranean policy which was a priority area of Spanish lobbying.

Relations with Morocco

Morocco and Algeria thus remained the crucial interlocutors for Spain in the Maghreb. Contributing to the strengthening of relations here have been the role played by King Juan Carlos in establishing a personal rapport with King Hassan II; the pragmatism demonstrated by the PSOE in office, which did much to allay Moroccan fears that the change of government might thwart national aspirations concerning the Sahara; the enhanced value of a Spanish partner once Spain had entered the EC; and Spain's launching of a coherent, if modest, programme of co-operation during the 1980s.

Spain may have expected to receive more of a pay-off from Morocco following the signing of the Tripartite Agreement on the Western Sahara in the mid-1970s. However, this triumph for Moroccan nationalism was bound to provoke further demands for Ceuta and Melilla, which hampered bilateral relations. Moreover, during the period of UCD government Morocco was rather alarmed by Spanish efforts to placate Algeria over the Sahara issue – including recognition of Polisario by the UCD. Although Morocco helped Spain to overcome the Algerian agitation over the Canary Islands, a distinct improvement in bilateral relations occurred only after the Spanish Socialists came to power.

In 1983 Felipe González made Morocco his first bilateral visit after becoming prime minister, and he quickly demonstrated that his government was committed to close and stable relations with all of Spain's immediate neighbours, regardless of regime type. Spanish–Moroccan relations were diversified and intensified, giving rise from 1990 to annual top-level summits, similar to those initiated with France, Portugal, Germany and Italy. On the important issue of fishing, an agreement offering a degree of security was finally signed in 1983, with Spain acceding to the Moroccan desire to boost its revenues, protect fish stocks and develop a national fishing industry. Part of the financial aid that went with this package was used by Morocco to purchase Spanish arms. Further modifications in the fishing relationship were made in the 1988 and 1992 agreements, now negotiated between Morocco and the EC, although more than 80 per cent of the fishing boats that came under these agreements were Spanish. In terms of the fishing negotiation itself, the transfer of responsibility from Madrid to Brussels was an inconvenience, while in broader terms it was advantageous to Spain, bringing an uncoupling of the fisheries issue from political questions (including pressure on Ceuta and Melilla) and various forms of bilateral cooperation, economic, cultural and military.

Spain's relations with Morocco were complicated by EC membership in other regards too. As producers of Mediterranean products, the two countries were economic competitors, with access to the European market becoming more difficult for Morocco following Spain's entry into the Community in 1986. Spain's membership of the customs union made her representatives adopt protectionist attitudes in relation to non-EC competitors, but her lobbying in the early 1990s in favour of a free trade agreement between Morocco and the EU demonstrated a readiness to regard Morocco as an exception. After all, it was thought that there might be some compensation for Spanish interests in allowing free transit of Moroccan produce through Spain: for example, a lot of citrus fruit grown in Morocco was distributed to European destinations in Spanish trucks.

Besides the cooperation over fishing, Spain strengthened her financial and commercial relations with Morocco, the entry of Spanish banks into the Moroccan market around 1990 being crucial to business expansion, given the close links between banks and industry in Spain. Important military cooperation agreements meanwhile covered areas such as arms sales, co-production ventures, joint exercises, and information and personnel exchanges. Although initially there was still talk of a 'threat from the south' in some Spanish military circles, and particular fears for Ceuta and Melilla when Morocco and Libya signed the Uxda treaty in 1984, that mutual defence treaty was short-lived. While military reorganization and rearmament within Spain reinforced the country's southern defences, the logic behind Madrid's strengthening of military relations with Rabat was that countries to which one supplies electronic weapons systems are less of a threat than countries supplied from elsewhere.

The real turning point in commercial relations came in 1988 when a framework agreement for economic and financial cooperation was signed, and export credit provided for purchases of Spanish goods and services and projects of common interest between 1988 and 1992. By 1990 this had enabled Spain to move up from third to second place among Morocco's suppliers of imports. King Hassan's visit to Spain in 1989 led to the institutionalization of military cooperation (dating from 1983), an agreement to promote and protect Spanish investment, the decision to hold annual summits, and confirmation of another agreement to establish a 'permanent link' between the two countries in the form of a bridge or tunnel. This latter idea was unpalatable to Spain, because of its possible effects on northward migration and contraband in drugs; delays on technical and financial grounds seemed likely.

Two years later, Morocco's relationship with Spain acquired the preferential status associated with a 'friendship and cooperation treaty', of the kind previously only concluded with Latin American countries. This treaty was signed at a ceremony attended by both monarchs, as well as the two prime ministers. A particularly significant feature of the agreement was a mutual commitment to resolve all territorial disputes by peaceful means. Following this, a start was made to bilateral cooperation to combat illegal migration, with Morocco becoming much more involved in repressing this activity along the African coast from 1992.

At the multilateral level, Spain meanwhile strove to achieve for Morocco a much more advantageous deal under the EC's evolving Mediterranean policy. Partly as a result of the activities of Spanish diplomats during 1992, Morocco (followed by Tunisia) was clearly perceived by the Community to be the Maghreb country most worthy of a special partnership agreement, with the potential for gradual moves towards free trade.

Spain remained far behind France in terms of the volume of its trade and cooperation with Morocco, and direct investments in that country. In 1992 France gave the Maghreb as a whole about seven times more aid than did Spain (*El País*, international edn, 6 October 1992). However, helped by tension in the French–Moroccan relationship, Spain reduced the gap (*Financial Times*, survey of Morocco, 3 November 1993) and there was also an important expansion of the area of common Spanish–Moroccan interest fostered by gas pipeline, electrical connection and future telecommunications projects (Moratinos 1991: 16). Of course, further improvements in the Spanish position depended on much more than Spanish diplomatic and governmental efforts. One of the commonest complaints among government officials was of the parochial business culture of Spanish entrepreneurs, over-cautious about international expansion and reluctant to take advantage of the opportunities opened up by Spanish and EC development aid.

Overall, Spain's policy toward Morocco must be credited with a degree of success. The issue of Ceuta and Melilla was shelved for several years, until proposals to grant autonomy statutes to the enclaves provoked Moroccan reactions in 1994; Spain's fishing interests in the region experienced less disruption, although access to Moroccan fishing grounds was gradually reduced as Morocco's own fishing industry was developed with Spanish assistance; economic relations grew very significantly; and the influx of illegal immigrants into Spain ('boat people' at least) appeared to slow down in the early 1990s. However, Morocco's territorial claims and the fishery issues retained the potential to disrupt future relations. Moreover, Spain's plans for continued improvements in bilateral relations were premised on the survival of the Moroccan monarchy, and one could not discard the possibility of its overthrow and replacement with a regime more hostile toward Spain at some stage in the future.

Relations with Algeria

The differences in Spain's bilateral relations with Morocco and Algeria were to some extent a consequence of the very different types of regime that Spain dealt with in each case. In Morocco, the monarchical regime had a traditional basis of legitimacy resting upon the king's role as 'Commander of the Faith' and descendant of the Prophet. It had derived broad support from its expansion into the Sahara, and some success could also be claimed for its policies of marketization in the 1980s and tentative moves in the direction of more representative government. In Algeria, however, the legitimacy derived by the FLN from its independence struggle against the French had been exhausted by the late 1980s by the economic failure of state socialism, compounded by the loss of external allies following the collapse of the Soviet bloc. In retrospect, the attempt at economic reform seems to have been left too late; attempts to defuse the resulting social discontent by bringing in democratization measures ended in the abortion of these measures in 1992, when vested interests in the old regime acted to prevent the election of the fundamentalist Islamic Salvation Front (FIS).

Thus Spain's post-1982 relations with Morocco were informed by Madrid's perception of a significant degree of success and stability on the other side, while relations with Algeria were limited by the uncertainties of dealing with a partner that for a while was deemed to be moving in the right direction, but facing very strong opposition from both bureaucratic interests and the fundamentalists. The style of Spanish diplomacy was also affected by the sharp contrast between the two regimes. Moroccan–Spanish relations benefited from the establishment of strong personal ties between the two monarchs. Royal visits, both by the kings and their heirs, often smoothed the way for important inter-state agreements. The Spanish monarchy played much more of a secondary role in the diplomatic relations with Algeria, which by contrast sometimes had dealings with the PSOE itself as well as with the Spanish government.

Spain's prime interest in its relationship with Algeria – energy – was at the same time an area of difficulty for the Algerian regime, which had allowed itself to become overdependent on oil and gas revenues. Yet, while Spanish–Algerian relations were more troubled than Spain's with Morocco, it may be that they are relatively less vulnerable to a change of regime. Since the relationship with Algeria continued to revolve primarily around energy, which remained the 'blood in the veins' of the Algerian economy, governments in Algiers would find it difficult to disrupt the export of natural gas, even if the FIS were to take power (Dezcallar 1992: 42).

It may have been because of the mutual convenience of this energy link that commerçial relations between Spain and Algeria did not suffer notably in the aftermath of the Tripartite Agreement of 1975, although the Algerians did react with political hostility and the result was a temporary withdrawal of ambassadors in 1977–78. However, trade between Spain and Algeria did come to a virtual standstill in the mid-1980s as a result of Spain being unable to purchase the quantity of gas specified in the 1975 gas agreement, and seeking to negotiate a lower price. Spain experienced the disadavantages of dealing with a centralized economy, in that any sectoral dispute rapidly became generalized and politicized. Eventually the dispute had to be resolved at the political level, with Spain in 1985 giving ground on price but rescheduling its future supplies and paying less compensation than Algiers had demanded. It was not until the early 1990s that trade began to approach the pre-1983 level once more, assisted by a financial agreement signed in 1989, only for political uncertainties to affect future commercial relations after the 1992 coup. As a result of the gas dispute, Morocco displaced Algeria as Spain's main market outside the OECD, exports to Algeria having fallen from $685 million to $15 million between 1982 and 1984 (Morán 1985: 330; *Información Comercial Española*, 28 February 1985, 20/26 February 1989).

From time to time, radical nationalist influences within the FLN made it difficult for Spain to improve its relations with Algeria. While in the late 1970s Algeria sponsored Cubillo's Canary Islands separatism, in an attempt to pressurize Spain into adopting a more assertive line on the Sahara, during the 1980s it was the Algerian attitude to ETA that caused concern in Spain. At the very least, ETA members were given sanctuary in Algeria, and there were Interior Ministry allegations about training camps being located there (*El País*, 10 October 1986). However, as bilateral relations improved slowly after 1985, Algeria collaborated in staging talks between Spanish Interior Ministry officials and ETA leaders, and when these failed in 1989 ETA was finally expelled from Algeria. It is difficult to ascertain what the Spanish gave in return, although in December a military cooperation agreement, long sought by Algiers, was signed. There was already in place an agreement negotiated by Alfonso Guerra in December 1986, under which, in return for the expulsion of *etarras* from Algeria, Algerian oppositionists who went to Spain in 1987 for a meeting of Ben Bella's Pro-Democracy Movement were expelled.

There were clear political and economic grounds for optimism concerning the future development of bilateral relations in the late 1980s, but this mood gave way to pessimism following the resignation of Chadli Benyedid in January 1992. Nevertheless, important business deals went ahead. In June 1992 Enagas and Sonatrach signed an agreement providing for the supply of gas via the projected new Maghreb–Europe pipeline by 1996; if implemented, this would make Spain the second largest importer of Algerian gas, after Italy. Unfortunately, notwithstanding a desire on both sides to continue in this vein, events by late 1992 were escaping the control of governments: the targeting of foreigners by Islamic terrorists forced Spain along with other countries to withdraw its nationals; within Algeria the rising tide of political violence was creating a growing number of asylum seekers; and any thought of improving bilateral relations had to be placed on hold.

POLICY LINKAGES

It is interesting to consider how Spain's policy toward the Maghreb relates to other aspects of her foreign policy, and how the 'foreign policy' element interrelates with domestic policy. For it would be artificial to consider simply the regional policy in isolation when in reality it is influenced by, and influences, other aspects of Spanish policy.

The strongest linkage between Spanish policy toward the Maghreb and other external activity is the relationship to Madrid's European policy. Within the EU Spain attempted with limited success to raise awareness of the problems of the Union's southern flank, and in the early 1990s criticized northern members for being over-preoccupied with central-Eastern Europe at the expense of the Mediterranean. Spain's self-appointed task has been to convince EU partners that the Maghreb is a European problem. It may be primarily a Spanish, French and Italian problem, but the migration and security issues have broader European implications.

In the early 1990s the EU's consideration of a closer relationship with Morocco, and perhaps other Maghreb states, was to a great extent a result of Spanish lobbying. Spain's diplomats were guided by the hope that the country's history and recent activity in the Maghreb would enable them to play a leading role in the development of the European Mediterranean policy, thus influencing a policy of direct relevance and interest to Spain, and at the same time raising Spain's profile within the Union. They thus looked partly to the EU to safeguard Spain's regional interests. Equally, they sometimes found it convenient to 'blame' the EC/EU for policies that were not welcomed in the Maghreb, such as the introduction of visas in May 1991 (*El País*, international edn, 24 December 1990).

Spain's more general credibility in the Arab world, unshaken by recognition of Israel in 1986, enabled the country to play a positive role in the Middle East peace initiatives of the early 1990s. To the traditional Spanish defence of Palestinian rights was added a defence of the right of Israel to exist, resulting in a more balanced posture. Distinct from this Middle East process in the Spanish view was the search for a security framework for the Mediterranean. Here, the greater progress achieved in the western part (the 5+5 initiative) than in the Mediterranean area as a whole (the CSCM proposal) was largely due to the relatively strong bilateral relations that Spain, along with France and Italy, enjoyed with the states of the Maghreb.

In recent years the Maghreb has featured in Spain's bilateral relations with France. Traditionally, Spain resented French influence in North Africa, where Spain gained only the 'skin and bones' of Morocco (as Franco put it) in the form of its protectorate. However, by the early 1990s Spain and France shared a strong apprehension about the implications of the Maghreb's problems for Europe, unless they were urgently addressed. An annual Franco-Spanish ministerial seminar in September 1992 focused almost exclusively on the problems of the Maghreb and recognized the need for Franco-Spanish cooperation in the region, but no joint projects were identified.

To a limited extent, there has also been linkage between Spain's regional policy and its relationship to the USA. The greatest disadvantage to Spain of the American bases conceded in 1953 was that they could be used by US aircraft to assist Israel, as in 1967, and to attack targets in Arab countries (Espadas Burgos 1987: 241). During the Gulf war, Spanish participation in the US-led Western coalition, and the use of Spanish bases for US bomber attacks on Iraq, came close to provoking a real crisis in Spain's relations with certain Arab states, although the threat was offset by Moroccan support for the coalition. González's public criticism of the bombing of the Baghdad bunker, his diplomats' intensive efforts to explain Spain's actions to North African governments, and his government's subsequent readiness to offer more financial aid to the Maghreb, as virtual compensation, all helped to repair the damage at an inter-governmental level; the effects among the people of the region were more difficult to gauge.

The Socialists' determination in 1986–88 to reduce US base facilities in Spain was motivated both by concern over the damage to Arab relationships that might follow American attacks launched from Spanish soil, and by concern over domestic reactions to such attacks from Spanish public opinion. The surviving US military presence still had the potential to cause Spain at least embarrassment in its relations with the Maghreb.

A final external linkage, although somewhat tenuous, is the one between the question of Ceuta and Melilla and that of Gibraltar. Here we are not concerned with historical comparisons of the origins and natures of these disputes: simply to state that a connection is often made in relation to possible solutions. King Hassan has intimated on occasions that he does not think it reasonable for him to press Spain on the North African enclaves so long as Gibralter remains under foreign control (Del Pino 1985). Spanish diplomats concede privately that it would be easier for Spain to contemplate talking to Morocco about the future of Ceuta and Melilla if Gibraltar were returned to Spain: this line of thinking raises questions about whether it is really in Spain's interests to press for the return of Gibraltar (Remiro Brotons 1984: 71). The strategic value of these places may have disappeared, but traditional strategic thinking about military balance still seems to underpin the connection that some political actors and commentators make between the resolution of the Gibraltar and Ceuta–Melilla problems.

As for the linkages between foreign and domestic policy, one must above all emphasize the underlying dual commitments of post-Franco Spanish policy to democratization and modernization. With several events in Morocco having provoked domestic crises earlier in the century, the *memoria histórica* of the Spanish has functioned to counsel great prudence in more recent relations with the Maghreb. Spain's withdrawal from the Western Sahara in 1976 in effect unhinged the Sahara issue from the urgent task of managing the transition at home. Spain has gone to great lengths to keep the issue of Ceuta and Melilla off the agenda and to avoid disputes with Morocco: hence the stoical silence with which Spain responded to Moroccan extensions of its offshore fishing limits or the announcement of new 'security zones' (in 1972, 1983 and 1990), which made life harder for Spanish fishermen.

The modernization drive of the 1980s meanwhile included official encouragement of corporate expansion and the graduation of firms from national to international status. Although Europe is by far the main area of interest for the larger companies, there have been efforts to promote Spanish business in the Maghreb, with a view to the general extension of Spanish influence, the opportunities arising from modernization projects in parts of the Maghreb, and the need to promote development, given the projections of population growth in the region. Spain's economic prosperity in the second half of the 1980s facilitated investment in the Maghreb and the organization of bilateral cooperation, but both were threatened by the recession in the early 1990s. Moreover, Spain's weak tradition of bilateral aid left Spanish companies without the experience to exploit the opportunities associated with multilateral European aid for the Maghreb.

The Spanish economy, however, has a much more strategic interest in the Maghreb, emanating above all from the supply of natural gas. Spain's relations with Algeria have thus been informed by the fundamental decision taken by the first González government to halt the expansion of nuclear energy and reduce Spain's dependence on imported oil by developing a natural gas distribution infrastructure and relying increasingly upon imported natural gas. With the building of the projected new pipeline, natural gas consumption in Spain could triple.

Also relating to the domestic economy is the question of immigration from the Maghreb. It is important to note that, while Spain has introduced stiffer immigration controls for non-EU citizens, there is still in government policy a role for immigrant workers in jobs that fail to attract enough Spaniards (such as agricultural work under plastic, in poor conditions). In spite of national unemployment exceeding 3 million by 1993, the new policy therefore involved negotiating new immigration quotas with North African, and especially Moroccan, officials, with these being based on the perceived requirements of the Spanish economy. There is an evident tension here between Spanish support in principle for a restrictive EU policy on immigration, and a national policy more attuned to the conjunctural requirements of the Spanish economy, together with Madrid's desire for good relations with Rabat.

Immigration represents challenges for social policy within Spain. One view is that, with net immigration being a very new phenomenon, enlightened policies designed to regularize the situation of immigrants and foster their social integration could prevent the introduction of xenophobic movements on the political scene. This effort was made in the early 1990s, but during the course of 'regularization' in 1991–92, about half of the 130,000 migrants who surfaced were Moroccan – this in a country where previously immigration from other European countries had been more common. The 'race card' was not immediately resorted to by any significant Spanish party, but opinion polls did indicate some potential for a xenophobic force to enter Spanish politics in the early 1990s (CIS 1990, 1991). The cultural problems surrounding integration were likely to grow during the decade as migrant workers were allowed to bring their families to join them in Spain.

Finally, since Ceuta and Melilla are regarded by Madrid as integral parts of Spain, the domestic process of devolution may have the potential to provoke tension between Spain and Morocco. It was for fear of a bilateral crisis that the authorities in Madrid delayed the preparation of autonomy statutes for Ceuta and Melilla until long after the rest of Spain had received theirs. Moreover, with this consideration in mind, the PSOE and the centre-right argued endlessly over whether the statutes for Ceuta and Melilla should have a regional or a municipal character. Some Spaniards saw devolution providing Ceuta and Melilla with greater security for the future, others less. With autonomy statutes promised in the 1993 PSOE election programme, this issue remained one capable of disrupting Spain's improved relations with Morocco in the ensuing years.

CONCLUSION

This chapter has explored the difficulties involved in Spain's pursuit of global relations with the countries of the Maghreb. Both the domestic constraints upon such a policy, seen particularly at times of recession, and the extreme complexity of north-west African politics have made it impossible for Spain to follow consistently a global strategy in the region. However, the attempt to do so did bring some benefits for Spain in terms of diversified and growing relationships, at least until the Algerian crisis reached breaking point in 1992. Clearly, for Spain to have some policy guidelines, however problematic, brought more coherence into foreign policy than existed earlier when it was based on improvised reactions to sporadic crises and an unrealistic attempt at equilibrium between countries that could not readily be equilibrated.

The Algerian events of the early 1990s, with the emergence of Islamic fundamentalism as a mass movement capable of taking power, in a way obliged Spanish diplomacy to retreat to its foreign policy approach of two decades earlier. Inevitably, Algeria's crisis enhanced the value of Morocco as a partner for Spain and the EU. Yet by now it was a different Morocco committed to cautious economic and political reforms that was being courted, and the relationship between Madrid and Rabat was now based on a fair degree of interdependence. However, this was not necessarily a sure basis for a stable and trouble-free relationship in the future. Interdependence may work in the Western context among partners whose rationality is based on common cultural assumptions, but it is less easy to apply in countries where religion is centrally involved in political life. Moreover, the relationship between Morocco and Spain involved one country that was within the EU customs union and another that was not, even if greater market access was promised in future to Morocco. Finally, Moroccan irredentism remained an ever-present force. With Rabat all too aware of its enhanced importance for Spain and the EU in view of the crisis in Algeria, Morocco could seek to exploit the situation by pressing its territorial claims to Ceuta and Melilla. Spain and Morocco achieved much in terms of strengthening their economic relations in the late 1980s and early 1990s, but this political obstacle remained in the path of their future relationship.

11 Spain in the post-cold war world

Andrés Ortega

FROM A SPANISH TO A WORLD TRANSITION

By 1989, after fourteen years of sustained efforts and perseverance, democratic Spain had won a comfortable position in the existing European order. It was a full member of the EC, the Council of Europe, NATO and the Western European Union (WEU), and felt increasingly at home within that institutional setting. A good sign was the way it handled, during the first semester of that year, the presidency of the European Community Council, which marked the complete normalization of Spanish foreign policy. But, as Spain was ending its own international transition, a new European and world transition was beginning. The political awareness of this change predated the opening of the Berlin Wall and permeated the Spanish foreign policy apparatus during the whole of that year. It was not the end of history, 'but the end of a certain history and the beginning of another one', as Foreign Minister Francisco Fernández Ordóñez put it in early 1990 (Fernández Ordóñez 1990b: 31). But this time, and in contrast to the previous international mutations of this century, Spain was able to contribute to shape its environment and to be an actor in that change, naturally in proportion to its weight, disposition and newly acquired reputation. In this new setting, Spain's national interests had to be reviewed or redefined. Whether it has managed to fulfil them is a matter still too early to be asserted.

MORE EUROPE

Confronted with a sudden change of the European scenario, Spain focused on preserving and deepening the European Community as the cornerstone of European integration. It was believed that a strong EC should walk hand in hand with German unification and would be a central element of stability for East and West, and even South; and would have positive effects for the internal cohesion – political and economic – of Spain. 'The essential piece of next century Europe is still the European Community, and what we are designing is the next century's Europe and, thus, the European Community is more than ever confronting the problem of its own integration', said Fernández Ordóñez in early 1990 (Fernández Ordóñez 1990b: 31).

German unification did not pose for Spain the kind of political and psychological problems it posed for other European countries such as France or the United Kingdom. Eighty-four per cent of the Spanish population was in favour of unification in November 1989, the highest support in western Europe, a level maintained a year later (Eurobarometer 1990: 20). It cannot be said that German unification was foreseen – especially given the speed with which it happened – but it soon became obvious for the Spanish government that the movement towards unification of the two German states could not be stopped. It was, thus, better to shape it in a European framework – to make a European Germany and not a German Europe, to quote German Foreign Minister, Hans-Dietrich Genscher – taking into consideration the security implications for the rest of Europe and for the USSR.[1] At the time, the security dimension of German unification was thought to be much more important than its economic problems, the latter proving much more troublesome later on.

Fernández Ordóñez also mentioned that, immediately after the fall of the Berlin Wall, Felipe González phoned Chancellor Kohl to congratulate him, being the first European leader to do so. By the December 1989 European Council at Strasburg, Spain was supporting German unification and the entry of the GDR into the EC as part of a unified Germany and not as the subject of a Community enlargement negotiation (although the acceleration of this movement was not foreseen). In May 1990 Spain fully supported at the NATO London Summit the 'unity' of Germany. This position contributed to enhancing the good relations which prevailed between both governments.

Spain viewed the new situation as a unique opportunity to create a political Europe, or a Political Union (González 1992/93: 7–21) and a new European architecture on which working groups in the Ministry of Foreign Affairs had been focusing even before November 1989. A major Spanish foreign policy priority was thus defined, one that would lead to the Maastricht Treaty. The basic aim was 'to make Europe and to have Spain in it'. Or, in other words, to place Spain among the *core countries* participating in the main political and economic frameworks of the European Union (including WEU). It was seen as the best way to prevent the risk of a *peripherization* of Spain.

Deepening European integration was also necessary, from Spain's point of view, to ensure that the inevitable enlargement of the EC would not distort Spain's European policy objectives. In this almost simultaneous process of widening and deepening the European Community, Spain's position after 1990 was guided by three criteria (Ortega 1994: 227). The first was the need for efficiency and cohesion. The European Union could not be built if the economies of its member countries did not function properly. It was also true that this common project could not work if the rich countries grew richer while the poor ones grew poorer. Thus, it was important to reinforce the policy of economic and social cohesion. The second criterion was democracy and effectiveness, in the sense that the EU had to stress the democratic character of its institutions and preserve the relative political weight of its member countries. Third, the EU had to have the capacity of international initiative: it needed to be able to act internationally. This has been a priority of the Spanish government since Spain joined the EC, and the need for it has been felt in view of the unpredictable evolution of Europe and the world. This capacity, according to the official Spanish perception, had to be reinforced through the creation and development of a genuinely common foreign and security policy, a single currency, and a consistent policy of development aid, among other instruments. In this way the EU could create increased stability within itself and in its geopolitical environment, developing a policy of solidarity, in particular in its neighbourhood, i.e. not only in the East, but also the South and in particular the Maghreb countries.

It was in this frame of mind that Spain's leaders participated in the Maastricht negotiating process. Major changes had taken place in Europe since June 1989 (European Council in Madrid) and even before, and every country had to re-evaluate its positions. For the first time, Spain as a full member was able to have its say in the reform of the EC treaties; it made contributions to all of the main chapters and participated with Bonn and Paris in launching major initiatives.[2]

Maastricht's central provisions deal with monetary union, planned to come into being at the earliest on 1 January 1997 and – in theory – at the latest, and automatically and irreversibly, on 1 January 1999. Spain insisted on postponing these decisions to facilitate the achievement of a single geometry Europe. But to reach the goal of being able to participate in this monetary union, Spain's economy had to converge in nominal terms. For Spain, this meant redoubling its efforts, as it was only just coming out of the transitional period of adaptation to the EC, and the supplementary process of preparing for the Single Market, and now it had to prepare its economy for monetary union. Thus, after Maastricht, what in 1991 was a foreign policy issue – negotiations on conditions for moving on to the third stage of economic and monetary union – became domestic policy. To accept Maastricht implied accepting a certain economic policy – which, according to the government, Spain needed with or without Maastricht – and this led to a divergence, for the first time in recent Spanish history, on the issue of European integration. A part of the left-wing coalition Izquierda Unida came out against the Treaty.

Spain managed to obtain parallel agreements on economic and social cohesion to facilitate convergence work towards a more equitable European Union. The most specific measure was the establishment of a Cohesion Fund, a review of the operation and amount of structural funds, and a system of contributions to Community coffers based to a greater extent on the relative prosperity of each member state. These measures were later articulated in the definition of the EU financial perspectives for the 1993–99 period, with Spain expecting to gain net transfers from the EC of around 2.4 per cent of Spanish GDP (compared with around 0.7 per cent by 1991).

Spain also championed the idea of European citizenship in the European Union Treaty, rights and duties which would be added to those derived from national citizenship (such as freedom of movement and residence throughout the Community; the right to vote and be elected in one's place of residence in local and European elections, regardless of nationality; the right of petition to the European Parliament (a Community Ombudsman was also created); and the right to diplomatic and consular assistance in third countries where the citizen's country has no representation).

The Common Foreign and Security Policy (CFSP) was another of the main subjects discussed at Maastricht, and in this Spain participated actively (based on its 26 November 1990 proposal). The agreement envisaged 'systematic cooperation' and joint actions by the member states. The CFSP, as supported by Spain, is global in scope and progressive in implementation, and it includes 'the eventual framing of a common defence policy', which over time could lead to a 'common defence'. Meanwhile, the Western European Union (WEU) became an integral part of the development of the European Union and was charged with the elaboration and implementation of decisions and actions that had defence implications. It was also agreed at Maastricht to reinforce the powers of the European Parliament, to bring new areas within the scope of the Community and to strengthen inter-governmental cooperation on judicial and police matters.

The Congress of Deputies ratified the European Union Treaty on 29 October 1992 by a huge majority: 314 votes in favour, three against (of the Basque extremist Herri Batasuna), and eight abstentions (from a part of Izquierda Unida), plus some significant absences. The parliamentary ratification of the Maastricht Treaty coincided in Spain with the first signs of economic recession. For Spain, the simultaneous experience of further European integration and economic crisis was a novelty, which, coupled with the mismanagement of the Yugoslav crisis by the EC/EU and its member states, and the results of the referenda on the Maastricht Treaty in Denmark (first referendum) and in France, created a certain sense of frustration in the Spanish public. According to a poll carried out in the spring of 1993, public support for the Maastricht Treaty in Spain was more dubious: 37 per cent would have voted yes in a referendum (the lowest in the EU after the UK), 17 per cent were against (also one of the lowest rejection positions) and 45 per cent were undecided (*Eurobarometer* 1993: 4). None the less there was great support in Spain for a single currency (68 per cent), a common foreign policy (66 per cent), and a common defence (71 per cent), and 65 per cent thought that belonging to the EC was a good thing for Spain (13 per cent were against).

But Spain's position seemed to wobble somewhat in 1993 when two succesive monetary storms forced the devaluation of the Spanish peseta (which, however, managed to stay in the Exchange Rate Mechanism of the EMS). This new situation, coupled with the effects of the economic crisis and the difficulties of economic convergence, and the perspective of a rapid enlargement of the EU, seemed to cast shadows over Spain's European policy. None the less, even in what seemed an adverse situation, Spain did not react in an anti-European way – quite the contrary.

In the course of 1993–94, the enlargement negotiations with Austria, Sweden, Finland and Norway led Spain to defend very concrete national interests (in particular relating to fisheries) and more importantly to fight to retain its weight in the Council, i.e., preserve its capacity for minority blocking. The threat to minority blocking was foreseen in 1990 when the Spanish administration, while approving the principle of the EC enlargement, thought that this process – with Turkey, Cyprus and Malta pressing to join, followed in the near future by the central and eastern European countries – had to be carried out without denaturing the European common integration project, without undermining the relative position of Spain within the EU, and without undermining the relations of the EU with geographical areas of priority attention for Spain.

After joining the EC, Spain developed a new kind of policy, a European policy (Ortega 1994), which now covers EU and other matters and is not foreign policy of the classical type. This European policy also covers the bilateral relations of Spain with other EU member states. These changed dramatically after Spain joined the EC, and even before, with France, Portugal, Germany and Italy in particular becoming countries with which regular bilateral summits are held. But in the post-cold war era, and given the relative renationalization of some foreign policies in Europe which it provoked; and with the economic recession, and the merging of some differing perceptions of the national interests, those bilateral relations went through a phase of lesser brilliance during 1993.

INCORPORATING THE EAST

Spain's relations with the central and eastern European countries and with Russia had been traditionally scarce. The Soviet revolution of 1917, the outcome of the Spanish civil war and the establishment of communist regimes in Eastern Europe considerably froze those relations. None the less, towards the end of the Francoist regime, as Spain sought international recognition, small steps were taken in relation to these countries.

It was only when democracy returned to Spain that this country started to look again towards the East. During the early months of 1977 diplomatic relations were established with all the eastern European countries (with the GDR in 1973; Albania had to wait until 1986). For the first time in January 1980 a Spanish minister of foreign affairs visited Moscow.

But the real discovery of the East by Spanish foreign policy, and even public opinion, started with the policy of perestroika launched by Gorbachev in the USSR. An excellent working and personal relationship was established between Gorbachev and González during their first official meeting in Moscow in 1986. Gorbachev travelled to Madrid in October 1990, and Spain opened a credit line for the USSR of $1,500 million (later redesigned in view of the break-up of the USSR), within the context of a friendship and cooperation agreement, signed between the two countries when González travelled to Moscow in July 1991; it was renewed in 1994.

The Spanish government openly bet on Gorbachev, as a guarantor of a peaceful and orderly change, and of the maintenance of a certain unity of the USSR. As González stated in 1990: 'We must invest in perestroika.' González thought that a solid centre was needed in the USSR to prevent the eruption of violence. In conversation with Gorbachev on 26 October 1990, González, according to the Russian version, is reported to have said that 'there is not in the world a single political leader who would consent to the division of the national territory. We cannot imagine a worse situation if it happened in the Soviet Union' (Poch 1993).

The Spanish government reacted immediately in support of Gorbachev during the coup attempt in August 1991. But it soon recognized that the break-up of the USSR was a fact of life. It welcomed the Alma Ata agreements of December 1991, given their peaceful and negotiated nature, reflecting the will of the parts of the old USSR to cooperate with each other under the Commonwealth of Independent States. According to Fernández Ordóñez on 23 December 1991, the disintegration and dissolution of the USSR did 'not constitute any surprise, because it has come about gradually. It is a fact of enormous political, economic, social and security consequences. It is a fact with historical repercussions for Europe and for the whole world' (Fernández Ordóñez 1991: 89).

Spain, together with its EC partners, recognized the new republics, opened new embassies in the area (for example in Kiev) and subscribed to bilateral agreements with several of the new states. A new treaty of friendship and cooperation with the Russian Federation was signed in April 1992 when Fernández Ordóñez visited Moscow and held an interview with the Russian President. (On that same occasion, Fernández Ordóñez travelled to Kiev.) Boris Yeltsin was invited to visit Spain during the Barcelona Olympic Games and the Universal Expo in Seville, but he declined the invitation, apparently for internal reasons. The visit finally took place in April 1994, when there was a renewed interest by Yeltsin in Spain's transition experience. Actually, this experience of peaceful and successful change has been, and probably will continue to be in the near future, an important Spanish asset in its dealings with the former communist countries.

The change in the East gave rise to a certain feeling of anxiety in Spain, a fear that the energy needed to reconstruct these countries and the whole area would deprive the EC of energies that would otherwise have been invested in southern Europe, the Maghreb or even Latin America. None the less, the Spanish government soon decided that 'incorporating the East' into the Western European structures was a main European challenge for the 1990s (Serra 1991). From this perspective, Spain, despite being in theory one of the countries in most direct economic competition with the new democracies, accepted the association agreements ('European Agreements') of the EC with most of these countries, and pushed for other forms of cooperation, such as the development of the North Atlantic Cooperation Council, the Partnership for Peace initiative and the European Stability Pact. A series of official contacts and visits reinforced Spain's bilateral relations with those countries in the early 1990s. Meanwhile the East, in the process of change, also discovered Spain and its successful transition to democracy and to a decentralized state model.

Meetings of the Spanish ambassadors to the Eastern European countries, to promote the Spanish activity and coordinate approaches, were held regularly at the Ministry of Foreign Affairs in Madrid in 1990, 1992 and 1994. The General Directorate for Europe within the ministry was reinforced, modestly, during these years. From the start, Spain took part in the PHARE and other EC programmes towards Eastern Europe, providing 8 per cent of the EC aid, and contributing 3.4 per cent of the capital of the European Bank for Reconstruction and Development.

But the worse experience, for Spain as for the rest of the West European countries, was the violent break-up of Yugoslavia. Two basic considerations guided Spanish policy at the beginning. First, it was desirable to preserve some kind of unity in Yugoslavia; second, only if united could the Twelve and the EC/EU have some influence on events. When these two principles entered into contradiction – given the German attitude and the reality on the ground – Spain opted for saving the unity of the Twelve, considering that it was the only way for the EU to preserve a mediation and pacification capacity. Spain, like other EU members, recognized Slovenia and Croatia, and later on, Bosnia-Herzegovina.

Confronted with the Balkan conflicts, Spain decided to participate actively in the UN humanitarian and peace-keeping operations, opening thus a new page in Spanish military history (which had started to be written in the course of peace-keeping and peace-making operations in Namibia, Angola, Mozambique and Central America).

The original reasons for Spain's active military involvement in former Yugoslavia were basically humanitarian; of international responsibility (particularly as Spain was going to have a seat in 1993–94 on the UN Security Council); European (to 'make Europe' while helping to solve a dispute or at least to control it); and of good relations with the Muslim world.

Spain's military presence in former Yugoslavia, which started in July 1991 (participating in the EC military mission), increased in earnest in

October 1992 – with the detachment of a tactical group (some 1,150 men) – and by spring 1994 stood at some 1,400 men (mainly professional soldiers in the area of Mostar, but also in other places and at UN forces headquarters), plus some 50 civil guards participating in the supervision of the embargo on the Danube, and two frigates and a logistic vessel in the Adriatic from July 1992.

Public opinion reacted positively to the participation of Spanish troops in these missions, in spite of the loss of the lives of Spanish soldiers (11 by December 1993). In May 1993, according to an opinion poll, 79.8 per cent of the Spanish population were satisfied with the way Spanish troops were developing their mission in the former Yugoslavia. This support would have changed drastically, according to the poll, if the situation switched to Spanish participation in a military intervention.[3]

The processes opened by the end of the cold war also had an internal dimension when the debate on self-determination erupted again in some sectors of Basque and Catalan nationalism. It started promptly with the case of the Baltic countries, whose independence process was supported 'pragmatically and without provoking the USSR' (Fernández Ordóñez 1990: 30). But it can also be said that the energy of the self-determination wave was lessened by the Maastricht Treaty and, perhaps, by the effects of war in the former Yugoslavia. The Basque Nationalist party (PNV) discourse, for instance, was relativized, in the sense that with the perspective of European Union, the notion of Basque independence was losing meaning (although, conversely, the President of the PNV, Xavier Arzallus, said in July 1993 that 'if the European project fails, I shall defend independence'). In the account of his conversation with Gorbachev in October 1991, González is reported to have said: 'I do not feel on the part of the autonomous communities, Basque, Catalan and other, the pressure that you receive, but there are some analogies' (Poch 1993). If González had thought that 'the phenomenon of centrifugal forces is inevitable in the process of democratization' (Poch 1993), he also gave a clear warning at the Helsinki summit in 1992 that 'exacerbated nationalism is the great peril of the present Europe'.[4]

TOWARDS A NEW SECURITY POLICY

By 1989, when the old order changed dramatically, Spain had established the basic elements of a 'peace and security' policy, as it was labelled by the government: its own particular model of participation in NATO; new and different defence relations with the United States; a clear stand taken on nuclear issues and on major disarmament and détente questions; a relative modernization of its armed forces; and a doctrine favouring the 'Europeanization of European security'. Spain had also successfully negotiated membership in the WEU. The government had been insisting on the Twelve playing a greater role in building and managing European security, which, in its opinion, could be done without prejudice to Spanish commitments to NATO. This was merely a declaration of good will, but there were few other options before 1990, when, after the fall of the Berlin Wall, entirely new horizons began to open up for European security.

The new European security architecture was a main concern of Spanish diplomatic and security planning, even before the fall of the Wall, as has been mentioned. This has more to do with the place of Spain and its weight in Europe than with the perception of a specific threat. A large majority, over 76 per cent, of Spaniards do not perceive any external threat to the peace of their country (Del Campo 1992: 109). Spanish security perceptions, taking into consideration that this country felt it lived to a great extent away from the cold war, partly explain some of Spain's attitudes and its adaptation to the post-cold war world in 1989–92. In this general rearrangement of European security, Spain's policy sought to preserve a steady link between the United States and Europe; to keep the Atlantic Alliance as a factor of stability in the transition, although keeping in mind the perspective of a probable disappearance of the Warsaw Pact; and not to create supplementary security problems for the ex-USSR (Ortega 1991). Spain supported the control and reduction of nuclear weapons, and actively participated in the CFE (Conventional Forces in Europe), though from the very beginning argued that this process should come under the Conference on Security and Cooperation in Europe (CSCE) umbrella so as not to limit it to agreements between two military alliances and, thus, to facilitate the transition in Europe. Spanish diplomacy was not very keen on creating new schemes or institutions – such as the European Confederation proposed by the French President Mitterrand – but rather on reforming and improving the existing frameworks.

The attitude of Spain towards the CSCE process changed over time. At the start of the post-cold war era, Spain's diplomacy attached great importance to the development and use of the CSCE. Earlier, the CSCE had been a source of international recognition for Franco's regime in its latter years, especially with Arias Navarro's presence in 1975 to sign the Helsinki Final Act. But it can also be said that the CSCE process contributed to training a number of diplomatic and military experts in East–West relations – from which Spain was distant – participating thus in the so-called 'Helsinki circle' (Fuentes 1988). In the middle of the

Euromissiles crisis, the new democratic Spain performed a considerable mediation at the CSCE review conference which opened in Madrid in September 1980 (with a UCD government and Spain outside of NATO) and closed three years later (with a PSOE government and Spain in NATO).

In the post-cold war, Spain at the Paris summit of 1990 supported the reinforcement and cautious institutionalization of the CSCE as the 'necessary frame of reference to overcome the division of Europe and shape the future of Europe's security' (Fernández Ordóñez 1990b: 532). None the less, the membership of some twenty new states in post-cold war Europe also showed the CSCE's practical limitations. From the Spanish perspective, the CSCE is no more the 'great white hope', as Prime Minister González had put it, even though it has an important role to fulfil in terms of regulating minority rights and in preventive diplomacy and peace missions. At the CSCE Helsinki summit meeting of July 1992, the European map had been substantially altered, and González expressed the need for the CSCE to develop 'its own capability in conflict prevention and crisis management'. The CSCE was also the best umbrella for a necessary process of disarmament and arms control in Europe, as has already been mentioned. González also called on the CSCE to pay attention to another kind of transatlantic relation, or 'the prolongation of Europe beyond the Atlantic' – Latin America – while also recalling the importance of the Mediterranean.

In these years, the Spanish government meanwhile favoured and actively participated in the progressive adaptation and transformation of NATO, through different decisions at consecutive meetings. Clearly, the CSCE was not enough to satisfy or respond to Europe's security challenges in the mid-1990s. Thus, at NATO's Brussels summit in January 1994, Spain supported the idea of creating first the North Atlantic Cooperation Council, to open a new channel of communication with the West's former enemies of the Warsaw Pact. Later, in 1994, Spain backed the US initiative of Partnership for Peace – bilateral agreements between NATO and all the European non-member states – considering that, at this stage, going for a formal enlargement of the Atlantic Alliance might not solve the security problems of the central and Eastern European countries that were willing to join; could have debilitated NATO; could also have created more security problems in Europe; and at the same time could have contributed to Russia's sense of isolation, thus further endangering the process of reform in that country.

These agreements complemented those adopted by NATO at its previous Rome summit in 1991, where it was agreed that NATO should evolve into a lighter, more flexible, more multinational organization, with a lower nuclear and more European profile. The NATO summit in January 1994 also recognized the importance of a 'European security identity', a process traditionally backed by González's government (Ortega 1991) which considered that this identity could not be constructed against NATO. This identity, already spelled out in the Maastricht Treaty, was deemed more necessary with the end of the cold war and the partial but important military withdrawal of the US from western Europe.

This European identity started to develop mainly through the WEU, which was also in a process of transformation. In 1993 Spain named a Permanent Representative (ambassador) to the WEU, distinct from the one in NATO, and actively participated in its development. From the start, Spain argued that the creation of multinational units within NATO should not prevent the WEU from setting up its own forces, nor any country from assigning the same units to NATO and the WEU. This 'dual-hat', and 'separable but not separate' concept, fitted Spain's position. In this respect, and in order to reinforce the complementarity between NATO and the WEU/EU, Spain stated its readiness to take part in both structures. Along these lines, at the end of 1993, the Spanish government also announced that it would assign units to the Eurocorps which France and Germany had launched earlier. Spain was thus contributing in practice to the setting up of interlocking institutions of security in Europe, which implied not replacing one by the other, but rather making them work together.

In foreign and security policy, Spain's reaction to the post-cold war situation was also to defend a further enhancement of the UN system, and in particular of the Security Council. Democratic Spain had found in the UN one of the most useful instruments for the often difficult task of harmonizing principles and interests in international politics. Spain's diplomacy worked hard to have Spain seated on the Security Council as a non-permanent member for 1993–94, the second time that democratic Spain had achieved that goal.

One area of UN affairs where Spain has put words into action has been in peace-keeping operations. Although Spain did not participate in this kind of operation until 1988, it did so with such determination that, until the dispatch of Blue Helmets to Yugoslavia and Cambodia, it had a larger officer contingent than any other country. This was a major change for a country that experienced not so splendid isolation during the previous 200 years, and it marked a major new direction for Spanish security policy. Active participation in UN peace missions was well received by Spanish public opinion: 58.6 per cent of the electorate approved in 1992, according to an opinion poll (Del Campo 1992: 118). It also contributed to a radical change in the perceptions of the Spanish armed forces, boosting their morale and finding a new mission for them.

LOOKING SOUTHWARDS

As stated already, by 1989 the theoretical framework of Spain's new security policy had been defined. But in 1990, with Iraq's invasion of Kuwait, the government was, for the first time, forced to assume the practical consequences of its security policy. The Gulf crisis affected Spain in several ways (Alonso Zaldívar and Ortega 1992; Alonso Zaldívar and Castells 1992): dependence on large supplies of oil at reasonable prices; the need to respond to the requests for soliditary by the United States and some of its Community partners; the impact of the crisis on the Arab world, and in particular the Maghreb; opposition to the change of international frontiers by force (especially when Spain's borders in Ceuta and Melilla are disputed by Morocco). Spain also stressed the need to act on the basis of UN Security Council resolutions, and called for a political consensus among the Twelve and a coordination of their military action in the WEU.

The other question the government had to bear in mind was the reaction of public opinion. There is a long and deep-rooted tradition in Spain of non-participation in international military conflicts. The isolationist psychology, which is part of this tradition, was just as strong as rational analyses of national interest. The government's management of the crisis during most of the conflict was supported by a narrow majority of public opinion, a majority that grew when it came to an end. There were difficult moments, such as when it was made public that the air base at Morón (Seville) was being used by American B-52 bombers. The favourable trend in public opinion was undoubtedly helped by a broad consensus among parliamentary groups. The goverment's aim was four-fold: to contribute to the cohesion and effectiveness of the anti-Iraq coalition; to take into account a public opinion that lacked historical experience in these matters; to favour a European security identity; and to avoid a negative impact on bilateral relations with the Maghreb countries. For these purposes, the government combined three key courses of action: full logistical support for the allies; coordination of Spanish naval participation within the framework of the WEU; and non-participation in direct combat operations.

Spain offered logistical support – 'all that we can', as González promised – to some EC partners, such as France and the United Kingdom; to third countries, such as Turkey and Czechoslovakia; and especially to the United States. Details of this support were kept secret during the crisis for security reasons. This caused an adverse domestic reaction which faded when the information was made known after the war. Thirty-five per cent of the total US air deployment used bases in Spain, transporting more than 200,000 tonnes of matériel and some 100,000 men and women. The B-52s flew some 300 missions from Morón, and 237 American ships were received at Spanish ports. Theory had become practice. This experience convinced the American administration that the new bilateral agreement – which had provided for the removal of the 401 Wing from Torrejón – was not the fruit of anti-Americanism, but an instrument that had done away with historical mortgages and established a new form of cooperation. Some time later, President Bush described Spanish support during the Gulf war as 'rock-solid'.

As mentioned above, the Spanish government tried, from the very beginning, to coordinate its response with its EC partners and sought to bring it under the WEU umbrella. It did so no doubt to increase public acceptance and because it thought that the Gulf crisis might turn out to be a test case for the coherence of the Common Foreign and Security Policy in the making. Accordingly, and although the government had decided to contribute actively to the embargo against Iraq since the beginning of August, it waited until the WEU ministerial meeting on the 21st of that month to announce its decision to send a frigate and two corvettes into the Gulf. These ships, twice relieved, carried out some 3,000 missions. The Spanish government stressed at all times that its forces in the Gulf region would not enter into direct combat. Since part of the military personnel aboard Spanish ships were conscripts, participating in direct combat in the Gulf could have presented serious problems. Public reaction to possible casualties was an unknown and sensitive factor. Nevertheless, Spain did send land forces (professionals and volunteers) after the war, as a part of the humanitarian operation to help the Kurds in northern Iraq.

The Spanish government's handling of the crisis, Saddam Hussein's intransigence, and the brevity of the war, may account for the success of this tricky transition from security theory to practice. By the end of the war, a large majority of the general public (62 per cent) backed the government's position. Naturally, some minority groups had further distanced themselves from the government, and the debate on whether to retain compulsory military service or introduce a professional army became a major public issue which influenced later decisions to reduce compulsory service to nine months and move towards a half-professional army. The idea of setting up a Rapid Intervention Force as soon as possible also gained ground.

Spanish diplomacy proved capable of maintaining a frank dialogue with its Maghreb neighbours during the crisis which had an obvious Mediterranean dimension. The events led the Spanish government and administration to elaborate or develop ideas that had already been sketched for the area. It can also be said that Spain's position of 'double confidence', having established diplomatic relations with Israel (in 1986) while preserving its support for the Palestinians, was a decisive factor in the selection of Madrid as the venue for the opening on 30 October 1991 of the Middle East Peace Conference.[5]

Long before that conference, Spain's diplomats had been working on the idea of applying the CSCE methods to the Mediterranean. The CSCE methodology had yielded positive results in Europe, contributing to generate a process of change and détente. The Spanish administration thought that a similar method – by 'baskets' (security, humanitarian issues and economic cooperation), by confidence-building measures and by generating a process – could be applied fruitfully to the Mediterranean. Thus Spain, jointly with Italy, launched in 1990 the plan for a Conference on Security and Cooperation in the Mediterranean (CSCM).[6]

From the Spanish perspective, the idea of a CSCM was, and is, not a point of arrival but a point of departure: an instrument. It had to be gradual in implementation, integral in content, global in its scope, and universal in relation to participants (Ministerio de Asuntos Exteriores 1991). The Spanish aim was to help to create the conditions that would make possible such a conference. Obviously, a precondition was the solution of the Arab–Israeli conflict.

The idea was being shaped before the Gulf war. However, this conflict, and the Middle East negotiating process put in motion by the USA immediately after the war, persuaded Spain to keep the CSCM project in relative hibernation for a while, so as not to interfere with the Middle Eastern peace process. None the less, Spain had been forced to launch the idea as the Italian Foreign Minister, then Gianni de Michelis, suddenly pressed publicly for the project. The USA was not keen on the idea initially, but modified its position. The idea is not dead. It is simply waiting for a proper time. Meanwhile, a number of initiatives have been launched in this field, some in the eastern Mediterranean, some in the western, some for the whole Mediterranean. They could eventually come together in a CSCM framework.

The CSCM, however, must be analysed in a wider context: Spain's efforts to develop more intense and fruitful relations with the Mediterranean and Maghreb countries. As this policy has been described in the previous chapter, there is no need to go into detail here, except to place it in the general framework of the post-cold war era. Spain's Mediterranean policy is the other side of the coin of its European policy. The political, economic and cultural revitalization of the southern Mediterranean countries would create an area of greater prosperity and stability which would greatly benefit Spain and its position in Europe. On the other hand destabilization and the economic backwardness of the Maghreb would put Spain in the uncomfortable position of inhospitable frontier and of being pushed towards a peripheral position in Europe. Furthermore, one of Spain's major concerns was and is that the opening of the East would distract European efforts away from the South. In fact in 1993 the EC was devoting yearly 2.5 ECU of aid to each inhabitant of the Maghreb and 7 ECU per inhabitant of the central and Eastern European countries. Spain therefore strongly encouraged the definition in the EC of a new Mediterranean policy (through the Ordóñez and the Matutes documents) and later the establishment of a Euro-Maghreb Partnership. It also succeeded in bringing the attention of NATO to problems in the South, as seen at the January 1994 summit meeting.

RETHINKING THE FUTURE

The new situation following the cold war – Spain's contribution to the resolution of the Gulf crisis; participation in the UN Security Council and in UN peace missions, especially in former Yugoslavia; the change in Nicaragua; Spanish efforts to bring a peaceful and orderly transition in Cuba, etc. – helped to conclude the normalization of Spanish foreign policy, at the same time that it became more Europeanized, while retaining a degree of autonomy. But it can also be said that the dynamic consensus on which democratic Spain's foreign and security policy has been built – from the neutralist temptation of the first UCD government, to the 'decalogue' of González – has led to a new situation and a new kind of public opinion consensus based on initiatives such as Spanish participation in UN peace missions, the Europeanization of security policy, closer relations with Iberoamerica and the Maghreb, and international cooperation in the fight against terrorism and drug-trafficking, as reflected in public opinion polls (Del Campo 1992: 63)

In these years of dramatic change, the interest of Spanish public opinion in foreign affairs has grown (Del Campo 1992: 92), in particular with Spain's direct involvement in the Maastricht Treaty negotiations, in the Gulf war, in the former Yugoslavia, in the Middle East peace process, and in the discovery of the East while this part of Europe was changing profoundly. All these issues had a reflection in parliamentary debates, mainly in the foreign affairs, defence and European affairs commissions of the Spanish Parliament, although to a lesser degree (except after European summit meetings) in plenary sessions. It should also be said that the spectacular growth of Spanish foreign policy activity has been achieved despite a shortage of funding and means for a policy on which increasing demands are made.

Summing up, we can conclude that by 1994, Spain had managed to travel through the troubled waters of the post-cold war change. None the less, Spanish foreign policy still has to face difficult tasks. The first one may be to have to walk on the tightrope separating the concept of the *small Europe* and the *large Europe*. Within this framework, it has to overcome the difficulties of setting up an EU Common Foreign and Security Policy without paralysing the national foreign policies of its member states. In this context, Spain was also making major efforts to include areas of Spanish interest, mainly the Mediterranean and Latin America, in the CFSP. This implied, above all, preserving its weight within a European Union engaged in a process of enlargement and deepening; on the horizon lay the crucial inter-governmental conference scheduled for 1996, after the second Spanish presidency of the EC/EU in 1995.

But Spanish foreign policy in this post-cold war era does not finish in Europe, nor even in the European framework. Some current developments, such as the evolution of the Maghreb (in particular Algeria), the globalization of the economy and its impact on foreign policy, the setting up of NAFTA, the economic rise of Pacific Asia, the positive evolution of Latin America, the process of change in Russia, and the transformation of eastern Europe, may call for a major rethinking of Spanish foreign policy in this *entresiècles* (Ortega 1994: 17–18).

NOTES

1 Fernández Ordóñez declared on 16 November 1989 that 'reunification is not on the agenda', adding that 'if in the long term the peoples of both (German) states show their will to unite, it will be very difficult to prevent it' (Fernández Ordóñez 1989:315).
2 For example, in the French, German and Spanish foreign affairs ministers' meeting in Paris on 11 October 1991 to impel the negotiating process and the development of the WEU and of a Common Foreign and Security Policy.
3 Poll by the Centro de Investigaciones Sociológicas (CIS) as reported by *Diario 16* on 13 March 1994.
4 In an interview Felipe González said: 'I believe self-determination as a

principle ought to be a matter that is only agreed to and regulated internationally. Otherwise, it will an extremely dangerous situation for Europe, because there will be no end to the splintering. If we enter into a process of unlimited change of boundaries in Europe, we will be entering a period of tremendous risks'. And he added: 'It is not a question of self-determination or no self-determination. It is a question of limits. And, in Spain, self-determination is limited by the Constitution. If anybody wants to change the Constitution, they must change it constitutionally, not by force.' (González 1992: 50–4).

5 Madrid was chosen 'for its history, tradition and good relations of Spain with both parts', said US Secretary of State James Baker.

6 Fernández Ordóñez referred to it internationally for the first time on 12 February 1990 at the 'Open Skies' Conference in Ottawa, and then formally at the CSCE meeting on the Mediterranean in Palma de Mallorca on 24 September 1990.

12 Perspectives on the reshaping of external relations

Richard Gillespie

This volume has drawn attention to the importance of the redefinition of a country's external relations for the establishment and consolidation of a new democracy. Democratic transitions may be seen as a series of transitions affecting the political regime, economy and external relations. Studies that focus largely upon domestic developments in an attempt to account for democratization are of limited value. Those that analyse both domestic and international factors, and even discuss linkages between the two, provide a much more satisfactory explanation, yet all too often they are marred by a tendency to see the basic dynamic as an internal one, merely influenced by, and rarely influencing, an external environment. It is the contention of this book that the redefinition of a country's external relations is an integral part of the process of democratization. While external events and international developments clearly play a greater role in initiating some democratic transitions than in others, a reshaping of external relations based on a realistic assessment of the international scene and the potential and interests of the country in transition will normally feature prominently in the process of consolidating a new democracy.

One of the keys to Spain's successful transition was the economic and cultural 'opening' of the country to the Western world during the last two decades of Francoism. This transformed the country to such an extent that, by the time of Franco's death in 1975, even many members of the Francoist élite accepted the need for change, including the establishment of a more representative governmental regime and entry into the European Community. There was clearly a period in the late 1970s when the political élite in Spain was engrossed in the internal reordering of political structures and external relations were addressed with little urgency. Yet once the new constitution was in place, and as domestic politics became more routine, the new arrangements were given more permanence by the reshaping of Spain's external relations during the 1980s, most notably through entry to the EC and NATO. The story, however, is not one of Spain being simply 'absorbed' into the dominant power bloc formed by democratic Western powers: within the European arena, Spain has sought – with a degree of success – to commit its partners to Mediterranean and Latin American policies that are in Spanish interests, while in the case of NATO domestic reservations about entry were used as a bargaining counter to achieve a redefinition of Madrid's military relationship with Washington. Meanwhile, Spanish diplomacy achieved a number of bilateral successes, improving relations with the neighbouring countries of France, Portugal and Morocco, and establishing a dialogue with the UK over Gibraltar.

At the start of this volume, four perspectives were introduced by Jonathan Story as possible ways of focusing upon Spain's external relations during the period of democratization. These were: (1) Spain as part of an international system of states; (2) Europe as a society of states, to which Spain sought readmission; (3) Spain's external relations as part of a web of political and market interdependence; and (4) the domestic political perspective. The contributors to this volume were well aware of each of these perspectives but were left at liberty to analyse their subjects as they thought fit, so long as they focused upon the interplay of domestic and external factors. Their chapters suggest that a combination of different perspectives is necessary to do justice to the complex processes involved in the reshaping of Spain's external relations during the course of democratization.

The value of the international system perspective is seen in several chapters of this book. Before 1989, the bipolar nature of the system placed great constraints upon the reshaping of Spain's external relations, while also generating strong popular pressures to terminate Spain's military link with the USA, seen by many as inimical to the country's national interests and defence requirements. The persisting desire to normalize relations with the established Western democracies counselled against an 'excessive' Spanish commitment to relations with the Third World – a tendency present in the PSOE programme while in opposition and even in the foreign policy of Adolfo Suárez. Inevitably, Spain's underlying priorities were Europe and more broadly the Euro-Atlantic alliance. The bipolar realities of the pre-1989 world frustrated the ideal commonly entertained on the left of full participation in the European Community while seeking to introduce a neutralist defence policy. González and his colleagues were convinced of the need to accept NATO in large part by the linkage that was made between this decision and EC responses to Spain's application to join the Community.

The international system perspective is also crucial for an understanding of Spanish foreign policy initiatives in the early 1990s. As shown by Andrés Ortega, no sooner had Spain 'normalized' its external relations as a Western democracy than it was faced with a further need to adapt as a result of the end of the cold war. The prospect of a larger, more integrated European Union was one that appealed strongly to Spain, but only so long as the country was able to defend key national interests, including those in the Mediterranean area that risked being eclipsed by EU interest in central–Eastern Europe. As European integration deepened, it became even more crucial than in the past for Spain to place itself among the 'core' European countries in order to avoid the danger of 're-peripherization' in the event of the moves towards European convergence breaking down and a 'two track' Europe resulting.

In turn, the society of states perspective emphasizes the cohesiveness of western Europe and Spain's adherence to its norms. It is a perspective that helps explain the desire of Spaniards to dispense with the anachronistic structures of Francoism and the hopes that democratic Spain invested in the European Community as a society that would show solidarity with its less developed member states. During the early years of membership, Spain did very well out of the structural and later the cohesion funds. Doubts persisted, however, about whether Spain could converge sufficiently with the leading European economies to join the lead group of states as further steps in European integration were contemplated. If not, then one might expect Spanish support for a federal Europe to wane and for Madrid to 'multilateralize' its strategy within the EU more, rather than dwelling upon the cultivation of close ties with Union leaders, Madrid's strategy in the early years of membership having been to seek diplomatic proximity to the dominant German–French axis.

From the regions of Spain, perceptions of the European ideal and hopes invested in Europe differed markedly from the common attitude held in Madrid. This justifies the attention given in this volume to the external relations of Catalonia and other 'autonomous communities' that seek to cooperate with other regions within Europe through the EU. They also look to the European Union as an educational experience for the Spanish political class; as Caterina García shows, it is one that already has led to more toleration in Madrid of the Spanish regions' external relations, now seen as something that is normal in other parts of Europe.

The attraction of the interdependence perspective is that it is less state-centred and reflects the proliferation of the multifarious types of exchanges that have occurred since 1945: economic, political, social and cultural. This is why this volume has focused on external relations and not merely on foreign policy, for it is only by adopting the broader scope of the former that a comprehensive picture of democratic Spain's adjustment to its external environment can be obtained. Interdependence is a particularly strong theme in the economic chapters by Keith Salmon and Alfred Tovias, which present Spain as having had little option but to embrace European integration, while always seeking to extract compensation from the EC for the more negative consequences of this for the weaker member states' economies. The interdependence perspective is also clearly in evidence in the account of the external activities of the 'autonomous communities', depicted as often emanating from the functional requirements of different branches of regional government, whose activities naturally extend into the international arena, where they may be assisted periodically by political initiatives taken by regional presidents.

The domestic political perspective is also valuable so long as any assertions of its primacy are qualified by some recognition of interdependency and the placing of domestic politics in a broader international context. The NATO issue was one of very few foreign policy issues that divided the centre-left and centre-right parties before 1982, when ideology was certainly a differentiating factor. Subsequently, however, with the Socialists in government, their volte-face on this issue was based entirely on international considerations, and above all the need to overcome obstacles to Spanish accession to the European Community.

The historical evidence provided by Charles T. Powell is relevant here since it shows how the relation between domestic politics and external policy has evolved during the twentieth century as Spain has changed from one regime to another within the context of the international state system. The continuities to be found in the external policy of different Spanish regimes – for instance, in the policies of the restoration monarchy and the Second Republic towards the Moroccan protectorate – show the sometimes limited impact of regime change upon external relations. On the other hand, different political factions within Spain have always attempted to reinforce their domestic political positions by supporting external options: Spaniards took sides during the first world war, adopted attitudes towards the League of Nations, and later reacted to NATO and the EC in ways that indicated that Spain's position on these matters might also have implications for domestic politics.

The domestic perspective can never be absent from the consideration of Spain's external relations, for even when there is considerable consensus among the country's leading political parties, public opinion is often a constraint upon foreign policy options. In a country whose army has relied heavily on conscripts, there have frequently been mass demonstrations when the military has been mobilized for action overseas. Even in peacetime, external relations impinge very directly on domestic policy, as has been seen, for example, in the link between Spanish policy towards the Maghreb and public fears about increased immigration from the south. Moreover, in the European context of growing integration, 'foreign policy' has increasingly become domestic, especially since Maastricht, and the basic lines of Spanish economic policy are directly attributable to the imperatives of European convergence.

How successfully has Spain reshaped its external relations since the death of Franco? The country has certainly achieved its ambition to overcome the diplomatic isolation of past decades, and indeed of past centuries. Fast growth in the late 1980s brought with it the prospect even of enhanced external influence based on an increased investment of resources in the promotion of external relations, but this period was preceded and followed by more troubled years for the Spanish economy. It was more realistic then, for Spain as a middle-order country, to base its external strategy on 'prestige' rather than resources, as Esther Barbé puts it. Prestige has been derived from various sources: the relatively smooth nature of the Spanish transition to democracy and the effective decentralization of political power that followed, both of which have made Spain a model for other countries, for example in central and eastern Europe; the continuity and stability at the governmental level resulting from four successive PSOE electoral victories, all achieved under González; the good international image of the King, of Prime Minister González and of several of Spain's Eurocrats; apparent success in modernizing the country, with external support; and a remarkably energetic diplomatic effort, giving the country a high profile in most of the major international organizations, where Madrid's support has been given generally to the dominant coalitions, often bringing reciprocal support for Spain on the very few issues that are really of crucial national importance.

The evidence presented here suggests only moderate success in obtaining policy objectives in relation to Latin America and the Maghreb. Yet it is equally clear that influence in these regions would have been minimal if there had not been the political commitment within Spain to adopt conventional Western external relations and responsibilities. The country would certainly not have proved so attractive to foreign investment as it did during the 1980s. Although Spanish entry to the EC had certain disadvantages for Morocco and Latin America, Spain is still regarded by its traditional partners as a potentially valuable advocate for their interests within the European Union, although not the only one.

The benefits to Spain from the early years of EC membership included: external support for democratic consolidation; European aid for modernization, its effects most visible in Spain's much improved transportation infrastructure; the spur to greater economic efficiency and competitiveness; the opportunity afforded to Spain to strengthen the Community's Mediterranean policy; and the acquisition of a voice in the planning of the new Europe.

A mark of the successful reshaping of external relations was the fact that old controversies, such as that over NATO membership, once politically resolved, did not persist or recur. Over Europe, there was admittedly less public enthusiasm by the early 1990s because of the price being paid by ordinary Spaniards for the pursuit of European convergence, yet there remained an overwhelmingly strong consensus that the country had done the right thing by returning to the European society of states and peoples. This underlying commitment to Europe lent credibility to Spain's representatives within the EU, to the extent that in 1994 Felipe González was encouraged by the German and other European governments to stand for the presidency of the European Commission, to succeed Jacques Delors.

Spain's successes have been achieved in large measure by Europeanizing its foreign policy while still being able in the European context to retain a degree of national autonomy, which has been used in particular to revive traditional relations with Latin America and the Arab world. Whether Spain can continue to exert influence through the EU as it expands will depend partly on maintaining the existing international strategy of *presencia* and *prestigio*, and partly on the country's capacity to reinforce this effort through further economic progress within Europe.

Appendix: Decision-making in Spanish external affairs

The constitution of 1978 describes the institutions of the parliamentary monarchy. It establishes the division of powers between executive, legislature and judiciary. Article 1.2 declares that 'national sovereignty resides in the Spanish people, from whom emanate all the powers of the State'. Political parties, Article 6 states, 'contribute to the formation and manifestation of the popular will'. 'Political decisions of especial significance' may be submitted to 'consultative referendum' (Article 92). The unity of the Spanish nation is stressed, along with the right to autonomy of its component regions and nationalities. The latter's potential powers are spelt out (Article 148, Armero 1983: 80–8), but international relations are entrusted to the exclusive competence of the central organs of the state (Article 149.1.3). The autonomous communities have their own statutes, granting considerable internal powers, and including provisions with regard to external relations. They may not conclude international treaties. The delineation of the powers of the state and the autonomous governments in the constitution is controversial (Remiro Brotons 1984: 234–5).

The state has three pillars (Sabá 1986: 24–33): the King, the government and the General Cortes or Parliament.

- The head of state, in the words of Article 56.1, 'assumes the highest representation of the State in international relations, especially with the nations of the Hispanic community', and is 'to be informed of the affairs of State' (Article 62). The King holds weekly or fortnightly meetings with the Ministers of External Affairs and of Defence. He presides over the Council of Ministers, at the invitation of the prime minister (the president of the government). By his frequent visits abroad, the King projects the image of Spain 'as a figure who incarnates the sovereignty of the State' (Ministerio de Asuntos Exteriores 1978: 216–17).

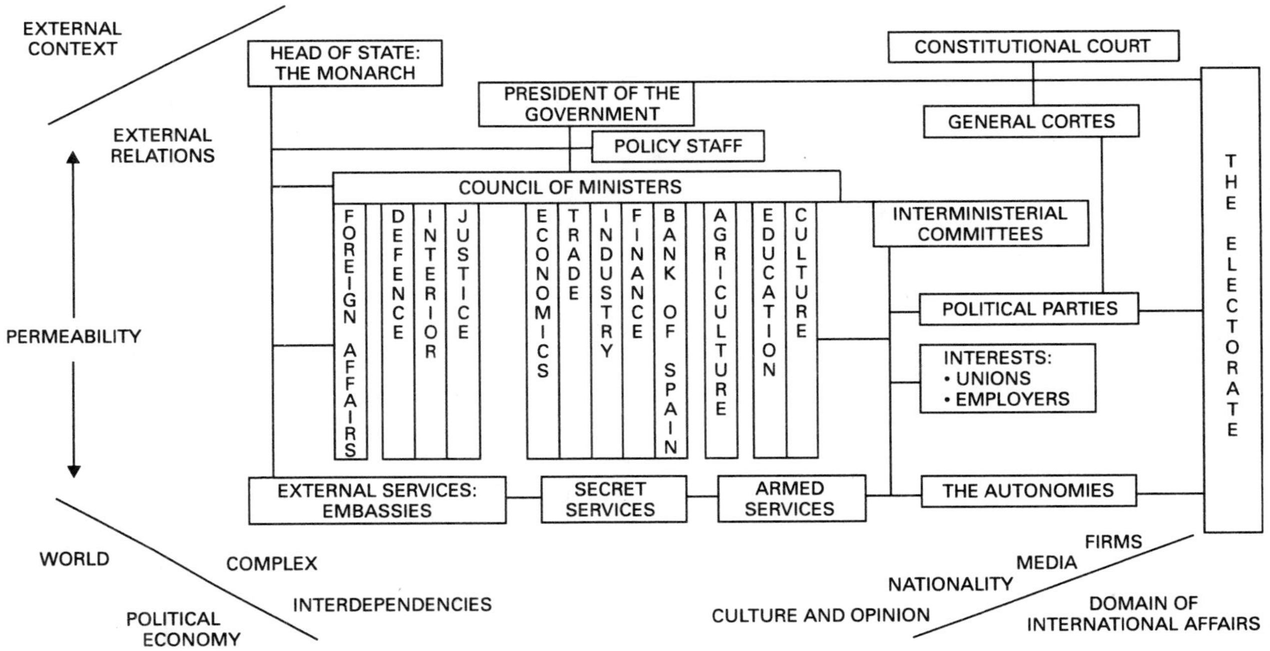

Figure 3 External relations: an organigram of decision-making
Source: Adapted from Niehus 1989, vol. 1, p. 452

- The prime minister is sworn in on the constitution, and voted into office by Parliament. The prime minister may be removed from office by a positive vote of no-confidence in the Congress. The government and especially its prime minister conducts foreign policy (Articles 97 and 98.2). Foreign policy is carried out by the Ministry of External Affairs, under mandate from the prime minister. The prime minister's control over external affairs is facilitated by his specialized policy staff. The Council of Ministers incorporates the ministers, who act as a collegial body, with collective responsibility for their acts. The government, though, does submit matters of external policy to discussion by the political parties. The decision to call a referendum is the preserve of the prime minister. The executive retains considerable discretionary powers over how or when to ratify treaties.
- The Cortes, composed of the Congress of Deputies and the Senate, is the legislative arm of the state (Article 66.1). The Cortes exerts a function of control over the executive (Article 66.2). In fact, its powers are restricted, notably in external affairs. The Cortes examines budgets and scrutinizes government actions. The Cortes participates in key decisions of the state, such as the declaration of war or peace (Article 63.3), or the ratification of treaties (Articles 93, 94). According to the internal regulations, the two houses may not modify treaties, but may request their non-ratification, postponement or reservation. Fifty senators or Congress representatives may appeal to the constitutional court to declare on the constitutionality *a posteriori* of the relevant accord or treaty.

Organized interests 'contribute to the defence and promotion of economic and social interests' (Article 7). 'Freedom of enterprise is recognized in the context of the market economy' (Article 38).

Bibliography

Aja, E. (1992) *Informe Pi i Sunyer sobre Comunidades Autónomas 1991*, Barcelona: Fundación Pi i Sunyer

Albi, E. (1992) *Europa y la competitividad de la economía española*, Barcelona: Ariel

Allen, D., Rummel, R. and Wessels, W. (eds) (1982) *European Political Cooperation*, London: Butterworth

Almarcha Barbado, A. (ed.) (1993) *Spain and EC Membership Evaluated*, London: Pinter

Alonso, A. (1985) *España en el Mercado Común: Del Acuerdo del 70 a la Comunidad de Doce*, Madrid: Espasa-Calpe

Alonso Zaldívar, C. (1992) 'El año en que acabó un mundo: La política exterior de España en 1991', *Anuario Internacional CIDOB 1991*, Barcelona: Centre d'Informació i Documentació Internacionals a Barcelona

—— and Castells, M. (1992) *Spain beyond Myths*, Madrid: Alianza

—— and Ortega, A. (1992) 'The Gulf crisis and European cooperation on security issues: Spanish reactions and the European framework', in N. Gnesotto and J. Roper (eds), *Western Europe and the Gulf*, Paris: Institute for Security Studies

Antonio Alonso, J. (1988) 'El sector exterior', in J. García Delgado (ed.), *España*, vol. 2 (Economía), Madrid: Espasa-Calpe

Archer, C. and Butler, F. (1992) *The European Community*, London: Pinter

Areilza, J. M. (1984) *Memorias exteriores: 1947–1964*, Barcelona: Planeta

Armero, J. M. (1978) *La política exterior de Franco*, Barcelona: Planeta

—— (1983) *Autonomía y política exterior*, Madrid: INCI

—— (1989) *Política exterior de España en democracia*, Madrid: Espasa-Calpe

Bajo, O., and Torres, A. (1992) 'La integración española en la CE y sus efectos sobre el sector exterior', *ICE* 708–9: 25–39

Banco Bilbao Vizcaya (1993a) 'The Spanish economy in 1991 and 1992', *Situación*, 21, international edn, Bilbao

Banco Bilbao Vizcaya (1993b) *Informe económico 1992*, Bilbao

Banco de España (1976) *Informe anual 1975*, Madrid

Banco de España (1993) *La balanza de pagos de España en 1991 y 1992*, Madrid

Barbé, E. (1992a) 'Spanien', in W. Weidenfeld and W. Wessels (eds), *Jahrbuch der Europäischen Integration 1991–92*, Bonn: Institut für Europäische Politik

—— (1992b) 'Hacia una política exterior y de seguridad común', *Anuario*

Internacional CIDOB 1991, Barcelona: Centre d'Informació i Documentació Internacionals a Barcelona
Barros, R. (1986) 'The left and democracy: some recent debates', *Telos* 68, Summer: 25–49
Bayó, F. (1994) 'La democracia en la política latinoamericana de España: El caso del Cono Sur', *Síntesis* (Madrid), 25
Ben-Ami S. (1980) *La revolución desde arriba: España 1936–1979*, Barcelona: Ropedras
Bledsoe, G. B. (1975) 'The quest for Permanencia: Spain's role in the League crisis of 1926', *Iberian Studies*, 4: 14–21
Boletín Económico del ICE (1993) 'La Ronda Uruguay del GATT: Un primer balance', no. 2396, 27 December: 3591–8
Boletín Informativo (1992), Banco Central Hispanoamericano, no. 482, January
Borrás, A. (1988) 'Intervenció en els tractats i convenis internacionals', and 'Relacions amb la CEE', in *Comentaris sobre l'Estatut d'Autonomia de Catalunya*, vol. 3, Barcelona: Institut d'Estudis Autonòmics
Bourgois, C. (1977) *El PC español, italiano y francés cara al poder*, Madrid: *Cambio 16*
Brinton, C. (1965) *The Anatomy of Revolution*, New York: Vintage Books
Bull, H. (1980) *The Anarchical Society: A Study of Order in World Politics*, London: Macmillan
Bulmer, S. and Wessels, W. (1987) *The European Council: Decision-Making in European Politics*, London: Macmillan
Cahen, A. (1989) *The Western European Union and NATO*, London: Brassey's
Calduch, R. (ed.) (1994) *La política exterior de España*, Madrid: Ediciones Ciencias Sociales
Calvo Hernando, P. (1976) *Juan Carlos, escucha*, Madrid: Ultramar
Calvo-Sotelo, L. (1981a) 'Discurso en la sesión de investidura. 18 de febrero de 1981', in *Actividades, textos y documentos de la política exterior española, 1981*, Madrid: Ministerio de Asuntos Exteriores
—— (1981b) 'Rueda de prensa del Presidente del Gobierno. 24 de abril', in *Actividades, textos y documentos de la política exterior española, 1981*, Madrid: Ministerio de Asuntos Exteriores
—— (1981c) 'Intervención ante el Pleno del Congreso de los Diputados del Presidente del Gobierno en solicitud de autorización para la adhesión de España a la OTAN. 28 de octubre de 1981', in *Actividades, textos y documentos de la política exterior española, 1981*, Madrid: Ministerio de Asuntos Exteriores
—— (1990) *Memoria viva de la transición*, Barcelona: Plaza & Janés
Carr, R., and Fusi, J. P. (1979) *Spain: Dictatorship to Democracy*, London: Allen & Unwin
Carrillo, S. (1974) *Hacia el post-franquismo*, Paris: Librairie du Globe
Círculo de Empresarios (1992) *Estabilidad macroeconómica y crecimiento en un contexto de apertura externa: la política económica española en los años 90*, Argentaria, December
CIS (1983) 'La opinión pública española ante la OTAN: 1975–1983', *Revista Española de Investigaciones Sociológicas*, 22: 187–262
CIS (1987) *Actitudes de los españoles ante la OTAN*, Madrid: Centro de Investigaciones Sociológicas
CIS (1990) Estudio no. 1882, *Inmigración y racismo*, Madrid: Centro de Investigaciones Sociológicas

CIS (1991) Estudio no. 1964, *Immigración y racismo*, Madrid: Centro de Investigaciones Sociológicas

Clark, R., and Haltzel, M. (eds.) (1987) *Spain in the 1980s: The Democratic Transition and a New International Role*, Cambridge, Mass.: Ballinger

Comín, F. (1988) 'Reforma tributaria y política fiscal', in J. García Delgado (ed.), *España*, vol. 2 (Economía), Madrid: Espasa-Calpe

Conférence Intergouvernementale sur l'Union Politique (1991) 'Le "communiqué conjoint" franco-allemand-espagnol', *Europe Documents (Agence Europe)*, no. 1737, 17 October

Conroy, M. (1987) 'Patterns of changing external trade in revolutionary Nicaragua: voluntary and involuntary trade diversification', in R. Spalding (ed.), *The Political Economy of Revolutionary Nicaragua*, London: Allen & Unwin

Cortada, J. (ed.) (1980) *Spain in the Twentieth-Century World: Essays on Spanish Diplomacy, 1898–1978*, London and Westport, Conn.: Aldwych Press

Criado, R. (1975) *Sáhara: Pasión y muerte de un sueño colonial*, Paris: Ruedo Ibérico

Crozier, B. (1967) *Franco: A Biographical History*, London: Eyre & Spottiswoode

Daboussi, R. (1991) 'Economic evolution, demographic trends, employment and migration movements', Mediterranean Information Exchange System on International Migration and Employment, *International Labour Office*, Geneva.

Daguzan, J. F. (1988) *L'Espagne:à la croisée des chemins*, Fondation pour les Études de Defense Nationale, Midi-Pyrenées

de Arenal, C. (1992) 'La posición exterior de España', in R. Cotarelo (ed.), *Transición política y consolidación democrática: España (1975–1986)*, Madrid: Centro de Investigaciones Sociológicas

—— and Aldecoa, F. (1986) *España y la OTAN: textos y documentos*, Madrid: Editorial Tecnos

de Ojeida, J. (1989) 'El modelo español de participación en la Alianza Atlántica', *Política Exterior*, 3 (9): 58–90

De Sebastián, L. (1991), 'Proceso de adaptación de la economía española al Mercado Interno', Barcelona, Papers ESADE, no. 59

Dehousse, R. (1991) *Une Politique étrangère pour l'Europe*, EUI, European Policy Unit, Working Paper no. 91/8, Florence: European University Institute

Del Campo, S. (1992) *Informe INCIPE 1992: La opinión pública española y la política exterior*, Madrid: Tecnos

Del Pino, D. (1985) 'España y el Sáhara', *Leviatán*, 21: 45–55

Delgado Gómez-Escalonilla, L. (1992) *Imperio de papel. Acción cultural y política exterior durante el primer franquismo*, Madrid: CSIC

Dezcallar, J. (1992) 'Las relaciones España–Magreb', *Anuario Internacional CIDOB 1991*, Barcelona: Centre d'Informació i Documentació Internacionals a Barcelona

Di Palma, G. (1990) *To Craft Democracies: An Essay on Democratic Transitions*, Berkeley, Calif.: University of California Press

Dicken, P. (1992) *Global Shift: The Internationalization of Economic Activity*, London: Paul Chapman

—— (1994) 'Global–local tensions: firms and states in the global space-economy', *Economic Geography*, 70, (2): 101–28

Diego Aguirre, J. R. (1991) *Guerra en el Sáhara*, Madrid: Istmo
Diez Moreno, F. (1992/93) 'España: la ratificación de Maastricht', *Política Exterior*, 6 (30): 89–103
Donges, J. *et al.* (1982) *The Second Enlargement of the European Community*, Tubingen: Mohr
Eaton, S. (1981) *The Forces of Freedom in Spain: 1974–1979. A Personal Memoir*, Stanford, Calif.: Hoover Institution Press
Economía Industrial (1993a) 'Competitividad industrial 1', no. 291, Madrid: Ministerio de Industria y Energía
Economía Industrial (1993b) 'Competitividad industrial 2', no. 292, Madrid: Ministerio de Industria y Energía
EFE (1989) 'Relaciones entre España y Túnez'
El País (1993) *Anuario El País 1993*, Madrid
—— (1994) *Anuario El País 1994*, Madrid
Espadas Burgos, M. (1987) *Franquismo y política exterior*, Madrid: RIALP
Espina, A. (1992) *Recursos humanos y política industrial*, Madrid: Fundación Fundesco
Eurobarometer (1990) 'The mood of the Community', *European Affairs*, 4/90, Winter: 15–20
Eurobarometer (1993), 39, Spring, Brussels: Avant-Première
Eurostat (1993a) *National Accounts Aggregates 1970–1991*, Series C2, Luxemburg
—— (1993b) *External Trade Statistical Yearbook Recapitulation 1958–1992*, Luxemburg
Fagot Aviel, J. (1992) 'The role of Spain in the pacification process of Central America', in J. Roy (ed.), *The Reconstruction of Central America: The Role of the European Community*, Coral Gables, Fla.: University of Miami
Fanjul, O. (1987) 'La economía mundial y el petróleo', *Anuario El País 1987*, 56–7
Fernández Ordóñez, F. (1987) 'Política exterior española 1987–1990', *Política Exterior*, 1 (1), Winter: 14–27
—— (1990a) *Diario de Sesiones del Congreso de los Diputados* (Comisión de Asuntos Exteriores), no. 169, 8 November
—— (1989, 1990b, 1991 and 1992) *Discursos y declaraciones del Ministro de Asuntos Exteriores*, Madrid: Oficina de Información Diplomática, Ministerio de Asuntos Exteriores
Financial Times (1994) 'FT500', *Financial Times* supplement, 20 January
Fishman, R. (1990) *Working-Class Organization and the Return to Democracy in Spain*, Ithaca, NY: Cornell University Press
Fleming, S. (1980) 'North Africa and the Middle East', in J. W. Cortada (ed.), *Spain in the Twentieth-century World*, London: Aldwych
Franco, G., Alonso, I., and Pindado, A. (1990) 'La exportación española a los países del Norte de Africa', *Información Comercial Española*, 26 November to 2 December: 43–67
Freres, C. (1992) 'Investing in Latin America', *The IberoAmerican Community*, Florida: Latin Finance Supplement, October: 10
—— and Grugel, J. (1995) 'Western European NGOs and political parties in the democratization and reconstruction of Central America', *Afers Internacionals* (Barcelona), forthcoming
—— Ruiz-Giménez, G. and Van Klaveren, A. (1992) 'Europa y América Latina: La búsqueda de nuevas formas de cooperación', *Síntesis*, 32–74

Frey, P. (1988) *Spanien und Europa: Die Spanischen Intellektuellen und die Spanische Integration*, Bonn: Europa Union

Fuentes, J. (1988) *El círculo de Helsinki*, Madrid: Ministerio de Asuntos Exteriores

García Segura, C. (1993) 'La presència de les entitats polítiques subestatals a les relacions internacionals. Segona part: Balanç d'una dècada de projecció exterior de Catalunya', Barcelona, unpublished

Ghebali, V. Y. (1991) 'Le rôle de la CE dans le processus de la CSCE', *Revue du Marché Commun*, 343, January: 8–13

Gilmour, D. (1985) *The Transformation of Spain: From Franco to Constitutional Monarchy*, London: Quartet

Godoy, J. (1986) *La Internacional Socialista en la Argentina*, vol. 1, Buenos Aires: Centro Editor de América Latina

Goldman, R., and Douglas, W. (1988) *Promoting Democracy. Opportunities and Issues*, New York: Praeger

González, F. (1981) 'Debate que siguió al discurso de investidura de Don Leopoldo Calvo Sotelo. 20 de febrero de 1981', in *Actividades, textos y documentos de la política exterior española, 1981*, Madrid: Ministerio de Asuntos Exteriores

—— (1984) 'Debate sobre el Estado de la Nación. 23 de octubre', in *Actividades, textos y documentos de la política exterior española, 1984*, Madrid: Ministerio de Asuntos Exteriores

—— (1986) 'Debate sobre política de paz y seguridad. 4/5 de febrero', in *Actividades, textos y documentos de la política exterior española, 1986*, Madrid: Ministerio de Asuntos Exteriores

—— (1987) 'Beitrag zur europäischen Integration' Bonn, *Europa Archiv*, 20: 569–76

—— (1988a) 'Declaración conjunta hispano–norteamericana', in *Actividades, textos y documentos de la política exterior española, 1988*, Madrid: Ministerio de Asuntos Exteriores

—— (1988b) 'Les Grandes Conférences Catholiques' (Brussels, 12 December 1988), in *Actividades, textos y documentos de la política exterior española, 1988*, Madrid: Ministerio de Asuntos Exteriores

—— (1989) 'Intervención de Don Felipe González en las Jornadas "América Latina y Europa en los Años 90", Madrid 5/6/1989', *Actividades, textos y documentos de la política exterior española, 1989*, Madrid: Ministerio de Asuntos Exteriores

—— (1991a) *Diario de Sesiones del Congreso de los Diputados*, no. 155, 17 December

—— (1991b) 'Spain must learn to compete on a national level' (interview), *European Affairs*, June/July: 64–7

—— (1992) 'Interview', *New Perspectives Quarterly*, Winter: 50–4

—— (1992/93) 'La Europa que quiere España', *Política Exterior*, 6 (3): 7–21

González Campos, J. (1990) 'La participación de las CCAA en la celebración y ejecución de los tratados internacionales', in *Relaciones internacionales y comunidades autónomas*, Barcelona: Institut d'Estudis Autonómics

Goulemot Maeso, M. (1986) *L'Espagne de la mort de Franco à l'Europe des Douze*, Paris: Minerve

Gourevitch, P. (1978) 'The second image revisited: the international sources of domestic politics', *International Organization*, 32 (4): 881–911

—— (1979) 'The reemergence of "peripheral nationalism": some comparative speculation on the spatial distribution of political leadership and economic growth', *Comparative Studies in Society and History*, 21 (3): 303–22

Granell, F. (1989) 'Aims and outcome of the first Spanish presidency of the Council of the European Communities', Centre for Mediterranean Studies, University of Bristol, unpublished paper

Grugel, J. (1991) 'Spanish foreign policy in the Caribbean', *European Review of Latin American and Caribbean Studies* 50, June: 135–154

—— (1993) 'External support for democratization in Latin America: European political parties and the Southern Cone', *Estudios Interdisciplinarios de América Latina y el Caribe* (Tel Aviv) 4 (2): 69–86

Hassner, P. (1971) 'The new Europe, from cold war to hot peace', *International Journal* (Toronto) 27 (1): 1–17

Hillgarth, J. N. (1976) *The Spanish Kingdoms 1250–1516*, Oxford: Clarendon .

Hills, G. (1967) *Franco: The Man and His Nation*, London: Hale

Hine, R. (1989) 'Customs union enlargement and adjustment: Spain's accession to the European Community', *Journal of Common Market Studies*, 28 (1): 1–28

Hoggart, K. (1991) 'The changing world of corporate control centres', *Geography*, April: 109–20

Holsti, K. J. (1988) *International Politics. A Framework for Analysis*, London: Prentice-Hall

Huntingdon, S. (1968) *Political Order in Changing Societies*, New Haven, Conn.: Yale University Press

ICI (1990) *Plan Estratégico de Cooperación (PEC) España–Chile*, Santiago de Chile: Instituto de Cooperación Iberoamericana

ILPES (1992) *The Link Iberoamerica–European Community: Development Plans, Policies and Strategies*, Conference of Ministers and Heads of Planning of Latin America and the Caribbean, 22–26 March 1992, Instituto Latinoamericano de Planificación Económica y Social

IMF (1993) *World Economic Outlook*, Washington: International Monetary Fund

IRELA (1987) *The Role of Spanish NGOs in Relations between Europe and Latin America*, Conference Report no. 1, Madrid: Instituto de Relaciones Europeo-Latinoamericanas

Jáureguí, G. (1986) *Las comunidades autónomas y las relaciones internacionales*, Oñati: Instituto Vasco de Administración Pública

Jover, J. M. (1986) 'La percepción española de los conflictos europeos: notas históricas para su entendimiento', *Revista de Occidente*, 57: 30–7

Jurdao Arrones, F. (1979) *España en venta*, Madrid: Ayuso

Kaiser, K. (1971) 'Das Internationale System der Gegenwart als Faktor zur Beeinträchtigung demokratischer Aussenpolitik', in *Probleme der Demokratie Heute. Sonderheft 2 der PVS*, Cologne: Opladen

Keohane, R., and Hoffmann, S. (eds) (1991) *The New European Community: Decision-making and Institutional Change*, Boulder, Colo.: Westview

Kirchner, E. J. (1992) *Decision-making in the European Community: The Council Presidency and European Integration*, Manchester: Manchester University Press

Kohler, B. (1982) *Political Forces in Spain, Greece and Portugal*, London: Butterworth

La Porte, M. T. (1992) *La política europea del régimen de Franco, 1957–1962* Pamplona: Eunsa

Larribau, J. F. (1993) 'La politique économique, contraintes et perspectives de l'integration européenne', *L'Espagne Aujourd'hui*, Paris: La Documentation Française

Levitt, K. (1970) *Silent Surrender*, Toronto: McClelland & Stewart

Linz, J. J. (1978) *The Breakdown of Democratic Regimes: Crisis, Breakdown and Reequilibration*, Baltimore: Johns Hopkins University Press

Llimona, J. (1992) 'La cooperació interregional: balanç i perspectives', in *Seminari sobre integració europea i participació regional: les regions després de Maastricht*, Barcelona: Institut d'Estudis Autonòmics

López de la Torre, S. (1987) 'España-OTAN: pasado, presente y futuro', *Política Exterior*, 1 (1): 115–32

López Rodó, L. (1977) *La larga marcha hacia la monarquía*, Barcelona: Naguer

Mangas, A. (1987) *Derecho comunitario europeo y derecho español*, Madrid: Tecnos

—— (1990) 'La aplicación del derecho comunitario por las comunidades autónomas', *Relaciones internacionales y comunidades autónomas*, Barcelona: Institut d'Estudis Autonòmics

Maravall, F. (ed.) (1987) *Economía y política industrial en España*, Madrid: Pirámide

Maravall, J. (1982) *The Transition to Democracy in Spain*, London: Croom Helm

Marín, M. (1986) 'La cooperación entre Iberoamérica y las Comunidades Europeas', in *Encuentro en la democracia: Europa-Iberoamérica*, Madrid: Instituto de Cooperación Iberoamericana

Marquina Barrio, A. (1986) *España en la política de seguridad occidental, 1939–1986*, Madrid: Ediciones Ejército

—— (1991) 'Spanish Foreign and Defense Policy since Democratization', in K. Maxwell (ed.) *Spanish Foreign and Defense Policy*, Boulder, Colo.: Westview

Martínez, M. A. (1984) 'Occidente y América Central', *Leviatán* (Madrid) 6, Spring: 12–21

Menéndez del Valle, E. (1993) 'Política exterior y transición democrática en España', in José Félix Tezanos (ed.) *La transición democrática española*, Madrid: Sistema

Merle, M. (1984) *La Politique etrangère*, Paris: Presses Universitaires de France

Mesa, R. (1988) *Democracia y política exterior en España*, Madrid: Eudema

Mesa, R. (1992) 'La normalización exterior de España', in R. Cotarelo (ed) *Transición política y consolidación democrática: España (1975–1986)*, Madrid: Centro de Investigaciones Sociológicas

Ministerio de Asuntos Exteriores (1978) 'Discursos y declaraciones del Ministro de Asuntos Exteriores, Don Marcelino Oreja Aguirre, Enero a Octubre 1978', Madrid, November

—— (1989) *Informe sobre la presidencia española de la Comunidad Europea*, Madrid, 1 July

—— (1991) 'La CSCM. Documento conjunto de España, Francia, Italia y Portugal', Madrid. January

Ministerio de Defensa (1986) *Memoria de la legislatura (1982–1986)*, Madrid

Ministerio de Economía y Hacienda (1977) *Estadística del comercio exterior de España*, Madrid
Minoría Catalana (1985) 'Moción a favor de la permanencia de España en la OTAN', in C. de Arenal and F. Aldecoa (eds) *España y la OTAN: Textos y documentos*, Madrid: Tecnos
Morales Lezcano, V. (1984) *España y el Norte de Africa: el Protectorado en Marruecos, 1912–1956*, Madrid: Universidad Nacional de Educación a Distancia
Morán, F. (1980) *Una política exterior para España*, Barcelona: Planeta
—— (1983) 'Declaraciones del Ministro de Asuntos Exteriores, Don Fernando Morán, a "El Socialista", in *Actividades, textos y documentos de la política exterior española, 1983*, Madrid: Ministerio de Asuntos Exteriores
—— (1984) 'La política exterior española', *Leviatán*, 16, Spring: 57–68
—— (1985a) 'El papel de Europa en América Central', *Cambio 16* (Madrid), 9 April
—— (1985b) 'Intervención ante la Comisión de Asuntos Exteriores del Senado del Ministro de Asuntos Exteriores Don Fernando Morán (BOGC – Senado – 5–3–85)', in *Actividades, textos y documentos de la política exterior española, 1985*, Madrid: Ministerio de Asuntos Exteriores
—— (1986) Speeches before the Foreign Affairs Committees of the Congress of Deputies and Senate, in *Actividades, textos y documentos de la política exterior española, 1985*, Madrid: Ministerio de Asuntos Exteriores
—— (1990) *España en su sitio*, Barcelona: Plaza y Janés
Moratinos, M. A. (1991) *Política exterior y de cooperación en el Magreb*, Madrid: Ministerio de Asuntos Exteriores
Musto, S. (1983) 'The European Community in search of a new Mediterranean Policy: a chance for a more symmetrical interdependence?', in C. Pinkele and A. Pollis (eds) *The Contemporary Mediterranean World*, New York: Praeger
Nadal, J., Carreras, A. and Sudria, C. (eds) (1987) *La economía española en el siglo XX: Una perspectiva histórica*, Barcelona: Ariel
Navarro, A. (1993) *La Comunidad Europea, el Magreb y España*, Madrid: INCIPE
Niehus, G. F. (1989) *Aussenpolitik im Wandel*, 2 vols, Frankfurt: Vervuet Verlag
Nieto Solís, J. (1993) 'Trade and development policies during the process of EC integration', in A. Amparo Barbado (ed.), *Spain and EC Membership Evaluated*, London: Pinter
Nutall, S. (1986) 'European Political Cooperation: annual surveys', *Yearbook of European Law*, Oxford: Clarendon
—— (1992) *European Political Cooperation*, Oxford: Clarendon
Nye, J., and Keohane, R. (1977) *Power and Interdependence: World Politics in Transition*, Boston: Little Brown
O'Donnell, G., and Schmitter, P. (1986) *Transitions from Authoritarian Rule: Tentative Conclusions about Uncertain Democracies*, Baltimore: Johns Hopkins University Press
OECD (1993) *Economic Surveys: Spain 1992–1993*, Paris
OID (1985) 'Discurso del Presidente del Gobierno', 12 June, Madrid: Oficina de Información Diplomática
Opello, W. C. (1991) 'Portugal: A case study of international determinants of

regime transition', in G. Pridham (ed.) *Encouraging Democracy: The International Context of Regime Transition in Southern Europe*, London: Leicester University Press

Ortega, A. (1986) *El purgatorio de la OTAN*, Madrid: Ediciones El País

—— (1991) 'Spain and the European security puzzle', *European Affairs*, June/July: 68–71

—— (1992) 'A Spanish and south European perspective, in *Peace and Common Security in Europe*, Stockholm: Olof Palme International Center

—— (1994) *La Razón de Europa*, Madrid: El País/Aguilar

Ortega, E. (1993) 'La inversión extranjera en el sector servicios', *ICE*, 719, July: 67–76

Palomares Lerma, G. (1994) 'La política exterior española: de la dictadura a la guerra civil', in R. Calduch (ed.) *La política exterior de España*, Madrid: Ediciones Ciencias Sociales

Papeles de Economía Española (1993), no. 56, 'La competitividad de la industria española' Madrid: Fundación Fondo para la Investigación Económica y Social, Confederación Española de Cajas de Ahorros

Payne, S. G. (1987) *The Franco Regime, 1936–39*, Madison: University of Wisconsin Press

Pereira, J. C. (1983) *Introducción al estudio de la política exterior de España*, Madrid: Akal

Pérez-Díaz, V. (1993) *The Return of Civil Society: The Emergence of Democratic Spain*, Cambridge, Mass.: Harvard University Press

Pérez González, M., and Pueyo Losa, J. (1982) 'Las comunidades autónomas ante el orden internacional', in Pérez González and Pueyo Losa (eds), *Constitución, comunidades autónomas y derecho Internacional*, Santiago de Compostela: AEPDI-Xunta de Galicia

Pérez-Llorca, J. P. (1981) 'Intervención del ministro de Asuntos Exteriores ante la Comisión de Asuntos Exteriores del Congreso en solicitud de dictamen favorable para la adhesión de España a la OTAN. 6 de octubre de 1981', in *Actividades, textos y documentos de la política exterior española, 1981*, Madrid: Ministerio de Asuntos Exteriores

Perpiñá Robert, F. (1989) 'La Cooperación Política Europea', *Política Exterior* 3 (9): 40–54

Pike, F. B. (1971) *'Hispanismo', 1898–1936: Spanish Conservatives and Liberals and their Relations with Spanish America*, Notre Dame: University of Notre Dame Press

Piñol, J. (1982) 'España y Lationoamérica: el período de Suárez 1976–1980', *Afers Internacionals*, 0: 27–38

Plummer, M. (1991) 'Efficiency effects of the accession of Spain and Portugal to the EC', *Journal of Common Market Studies* 29 (3): 317–25

Poch, R. (1993) 'El análisis de González y Gorbachov sobre la Europa y la URSS de hace 3 años', *La Vanguardia* (Barcelona), 2 December

Pollack, B. (1987) *The Paradox of Spanish Foreign Policy*, London: Pinter

Portales, C. (1991) 'External factors and the authoritarian regime', in P. Drake and I. Jakrie (eds) *The Struggle for Democracy in Chile, 1982–1990*, Lincoln: University of Nebraska

Porter, M. (1990) *The Competitive Advantage of Nations*, London: Macmillan

Portero, F. (1989) *Franco aislado, 1945–50*, Madrid: Aguilar

Preston, P. (1986) *The Triumph of Democracy in Spain*, London: Methuen

—— (1993) *Franco: A Biography*, London: Harper Collins

Pridham, G. (ed.) (1991) *Encouraging Democracy: The International Context of Regime Transition in Southern Europe*, Leicester: Leicester University Press

PSOE (1981) 'Resoluciones del XXIX Congreso sobre política internacional celebrado del 21 al 24 de octubre', in C. de Arenal and F. Aldecoa (eds) *España y la OTAN: Textos y documentos*, Madrid: Tecnos

—— (1982) 'Programa electoral. Política exterior de España', in C. de Arenal and F. Aldecoa (eds) *España y la OTAN: Textos y documentos*, Madrid: Tecnos

—— (1984) 'Resoluciones del XXX Congreso sobre política internacional celebrado del 13 al 16 de diciembre', in C. de Arenal and F. Aldecoa (eds) *España y la OTAN: Textos y documentos*, Madrid: Tecnos

—— (1985) 'Propuesta para una política de paz y seguridad. 21 de diciembre de 1985. Comisión Ejecutiva Federal', in C. de Arenal and F. Aldecoa (eds) *España y la OTAN: Textos y documentos*, Madrid: Tecnos

Quintana Navarro, F. (1993) *España en Europa, 1931–36*, Madrid: Nerea

Regelsberger, E. (1989) 'Spain and the European Political Cooperation – no enfant terrible', *The International Spectator* 24 (2): 118–24

Rein, R. (1993) 'Outpaced by the West: Israel's Spanish policy, 1953–1956', *Mediterranean Historical Review*, 8 (2): 74–104

Remiro Brotons, A. (1984) *La acción exterior del Estado*, Madrid: Tecnos

—— (1987) 'Armas nucleares y territorio español', *Política Exterior*, 1(3): 112–34

—— (1988) 'La cooperación europea en asuntos de seguridad: una perspectiva española', *Política Exterior* 2 (8):110–24

Rodrigo, F. (1992) 'The end of the reluctant partner: Spain and Western security in the 1990s', in R. Aliboni (ed.) *Southern European Security in the 1990s*, London: Pinter

Rupérez, J. (1986) *España en la OTAN. Relato parcial*, Barcelona: Plaza & Janés

Rustow, D. (1970) 'Transitions to democracy: towards a dynamic model', *Comparative Politics*, 22 (3): 337–63

Sabá, K. (1986) 'The Spanish foreign policy decision making', *The International Spectator*, 26 (4): 24–33

Salmon, K. (1991) *The Modern Spanish Economy*, London: Pinter

Schoutheete, Ph. de (1986) *La coopération politique européene*, Brussels: Labor (first edn 1980)

Schoutz, L. (1987) *National Security and United States Policy toward Latin America* Princeton, NJ: Princeton University Press

Segura, J. (1988) 'Intervención pública y política de bienestar: el papel del Estado', in J. García Delgado (ed.), *España*, vol. 2 (Economía), Madrid: Espasa-Calpe

—— (1992) *La industria española y la competitividad*, Madrid: Espasa-Calpe

Semprún, J. (1993) *Federico Sanchez vous Salue Bien*, Paris: Grasset

Serra, N. (1991) Speech at the closing of the CIDOB seminar on 'The change of economic system in Poland, Hungary and Czechoslovakia, and the problems of the transition in the USSR', 16 November, Barcelona: Centre d'Informació i Documentació Internacionals a Barcelona

Shepherd, D., Silberston, A. and Strange, R. (1985) *British Manufacturing Investment Overseas*, London: Methuen

Skocpol, T. (1979) *States and Social Revolutions: A Comparative Analysis of France, Russia and China*, Cambridge: Cambridge University Press
Story, J. (1991) 'Spain in the European diplomatic system', *Diplomacy and Statecraft*, 2 (1): 54–78
—— (1993) 'Europe: from one containment to another', in J. Story (ed.), *The New Europe: Politics, Government and Economy Since 1945*, Oxford: Blackwell
Strange, S. (1988) *States and Markets*, London: Pinter
Sueiro, S. (1992) *España en el Mediterráneo. Primo de Rivera y la 'Cuestión Marroquí'*, Madrid: Universidad Nacional de Educación a Distancia
Swinbank, A., and Ritson, C. (1988) 'The Common Agricultural Policy, customs unions and the Mediterranean basin', *Journal of Common Market Studies* 28 (2): 97–112
Tamames, R. (1986) *Guía del Mercado Común europeo. España en la Europa de los Doce*, Madrid: Alianza
—— (1991) *Estructura económica de España*, 20th edn, Madrid: Alianza
The Economist (1992) 'After the fiesta: a survey of Spain', 25 April
Tilly, C. (1975) 'Revolutions and collective violence', in F. Greenstein and N. Polsby (eds), *Handbook of Political Science 3: Macropolitical Theory*, New York: Addison Wesley
—— (1993) *European Revolutions: 1492–1992*, Oxford: Blackwell
Tovias, A. (1988) (guest ed.) 'The enlarged European Community and the Mediterranean', special issue of *The Jerusalem Journal of International Relations*, 10 (3)
—— (1990) *Foreign Economic Relations of the European Community: The Impact of Spain and Portugal*, Boulder, Colo.: Lynne Rienner
Tsoukalis, L. (1993) *The New European Economy*, Oxford: Oxford University Press
Tusell, J. (1984) *Franco y los católicos*, Madrid: Alianza
United Nations (1993) *World Investment Report 1993: Transnational Corporations and Integrated International Production*, New York: UN
Van Praag, N. (1982) 'Political cooperation and southern Europe: case studies in crisis management', in D. Allen, R. Rummel and W. Wessels (eds), *European Political Cooperation*, London: Butterworth
Vázquez Montalbán, A. (1974) *La penetración americana en España*, Madrid: Edicusa
Vickers, J., and Wright, V. (1988) 'The politics of industrial privatisation in western Europe: an overview', *West European Politics* 11 (4): 1–30
Vilanova, P. (1994) 'El sistema político y la política exterior: el ciclo formal', unpublished paper, Barcelona
Villar, F. (1992) *El proceso de autodeterminación del Sáhara*, Valencia: Torres
Viñals, J. *et al.* (1979) *Política comercial exterior de España, 1931–1975*, 2 vols, Madrid: Banco Exterior de España
Viñals, J., Viñas, A., Viñuela, J. (1990) 'Spain and the "EC cum 1992" shock', in C. Bliss and J. Braga de Macedo (eds), *Unity with Diversity in the European Economy: The Community's Southern Frontier*, Cambridge: Cambridge University Press
Viñas, A. (1980) 'La administración de la política económica exterior en España, 1936–1979', *Cuadernos Económicos* (Información Comercial Española), 13: 157–272

—— (1981) *Los pactos secretos de Franco con Estados Unidos: bases, ayuda económica, recortes de soberanía*, Barcelona: Grijalbo
—— (1984) *Guerra, dinero, dictadura*, Barcelona: Grijalbo
—— (1986) 'Spain and NATO: internal debate and external challenges', in J. Chipman (ed.), *NATO's Southern Allies: Internal and External Challenges*, London: Routledge
Wallace, H. (1985) 'The presidency of the Council of Ministers', in C. O. Nuallaim (ed.), *The presidency of the European Council of Ministers*, London: Croom Helm
Waltz, K. (1979) *Theory of International Politics*, Reading: Addison-Wesley
Whitaker, A. (1961) *Spain and the Defense of the West: Ally and Liability*, New York: Praeger
Whitehead, L. (1991) 'Democracy by convergence and southern Europe: a comparative politics perspective', in G. Pridham (ed.), *Encouraging Democracy: The International Context of Regime Transition in Southern Europe*, Leicester: Leicester University Press
World Economic Forum (1993) *The World Competitiveness Report*, Lausanne: IMD
Yannopoulos, G. N. (1988) *Customs Unions and Trade Conflicts*, London: Routledge
—— (ed.) (1989) *European Integration and the Iberian Economies*, London: Macmillan
Yáñez, J. A., and Viñas, A. (1992) 'Diez años de política exterior del gobierno socialista (1982–1992)', in A. Guerra and J. F. Tezanos (eds), *La década del cambio*, Madrid: Sistema

Index